10.09
scn

Shechner,

Joyce in Nighttown; a psychoanalytic inquiry into
Ulysses.

Date Due JUL 2000

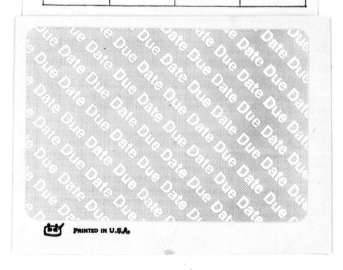

Joyce in Nighttown

MARK SHECHNER

Joyce in Nighttown

A PSYCHOANALYTIC INQUIRY
INTO *ULYSSES*

University of California Press

Berkeley • Los Angeles • London

74-1295

University of California Press
Berkeley and Los Angeles, California

University of California Press, Ltd.
London, England

ISBN: 0–520–02398–6
Library of Congress Catalog Card Number: 72–95308

Printed in the United States of America

For Anne

Contents

Acknowledgments

I hope that debts which go deep and are unpayable may nevertheless be acknowledged in brief. First of all I must mention Frederick Crews, who is a model to all his students of lucid *and* radical *and* humane intelligence. From him I have learned, I think, how to tell the truth. I hope that knowledge is visible in this book. My grateful thanks, too, to others who have read and criticized the manuscript of this book, as a whole or in part. Thomas Flanagan, Thomas Connolly, and Alan Dundes proved themselves to be fair and discerning readers of the work in an earlier, cruder version, and this refinement of it owes much to their suggestions. My understanding of psychoanalysis and my faith in it were much enhanced by members of the San Francisco Psychoanalytic Institute, especially Drs. Victor Caleff and Ed Weinshel, whose own desire to explore literature through psychoanalysis brought us together for a fruitful year of interdisciplinary study. Since I have been in Buffalo, my colleagues in the State University of New York Group for Applied Psychoanalysis, most especially Norman Holland, Robert Rogers, and Murray Schwartz, have taken over the task of providing a context for my work, and I am grateful to them for the environment of psychoanalytic thought they have fostered here. I am indebted, too, to Sheldon Brivic, who first saw many of my supposed insights. His own book on Joyce will, I trust, soon be in print.

Mr. Carl Gay, librarian of the poetry room in the SUNY Lockwood Library and keeper of the Joyce collection, has been gracious and helpful in making manuscripts available to me for this task and others, and I thank him for his innumerable aids and courtesies. Also, Mr. Donald Eddy of the Cornell Library was most kind in allowing me to see Joyce manuscript materials under his care, including the letters to Nora. I am grateful also to my research assistant, Jeanne McKnight Nalbone, her husband, Patrick, and Laurence Yep, whose aid has been indispensable at several stages in the preparation of this book.

My thanks to Anne Munro-Kerr of the Society of Authors and to the trustees of the James Joyce Estate for permission to quote from James Joyce's letters, from the epiphany "She Comes at Night," the poem "Ruminants," and the narrative essay "A Portrait of the Artist." My thanks to Random House, Inc. and the Bodley Head, Ltd., for permission to quote liberally from *Ulysses,* and to The Viking Press, Inc. and Faber and Faber, Ltd., for permission to quote from *The Collected Letters of James Joyce.*

The Mabelle McCleod Lewis Memorial Fund of Stanford, California, made the early stages of this work possible by affording me a year to write. A subsequent summer fellowship from the SUNY Research Foundation allowed me time to slim my overstuffed PH.D thesis down into something resembling a book. Both are thanked for their generosity. Neither grant would have been sufficient had my wife, Anne Shechner, not been willing to underwrite my work with her own. She made this book possible—as wife first and as financier, proofreader, and critic. It is to her that the book is dedicated.

Abbreviations

and a Note on Editions Used

References to *Ulysses* are to both the 1934 and 1961 Random House editions, the former being given first. Thus, the reference (186/188) refers the reader to page 186 of the 1934 edition and page 188 of the reset edition of 1961.

For the sake of convenience, references to other books quoted frequently are abbreviated in the text as follows.

WORKS BY JAMES JOYCE

CM   *Chamber Music*. The text used is that in James Joyce, *Collected Poems* (New York: Viking, 1957).

CW   *The Critical Writings of James Joyce*, eds., Ellsworth Mason and Richard Ellmann (New York: Viking, 1959).

D   *Dubliners*, ed., Robert Scholes (New York: Viking, 1967).

E   *Exiles* (New York: Viking, 1951).

FW   *Finnegans Wake* (New York: Viking, 1939).

GJ   *Giacomo Joyce* (New York: Viking, 1968).

Letters   *Letters of James Joyce*, vol. 1, ed., Stuart
Gilbert; vols. 2 and 3, ed., Richard Ellmann (New
York: Viking, 1966).
PA   *A Portrait of the Artist as a Young Man*
(New York: Viking, 1964).
SH   *Stephen Hero* (New York: New Directions,
1963).

WORKS ABOUT JOYCE

Budgen   *James Joyce and the Making of Ulysses*,
Frank Budgen (Bloomington: Indiana University
Press, 1960).
CDD   *The Complete Dublin Diary of Stanislaus
Joyce*, ed., George Harris Healey (Ithaca: Cornell
University Press, 1971).
JJ   *James Joyce*, Richard Ellmann (New York:
Oxford, 1959).
MKB   *My Brother's Keeper*, Stanislaus Joyce
(New York: McGraw-Hill, 1964).

WORKS BY SIGMUND FREUD

SE   *The Standard Edition of the Complete Psychological Works of Sigmund Freud*, ed. James
Strachey, Anna Freud, Alix Strachey, and Alan
Tyson, 24 vols. (London: The Hogarth Press and
the Institute of Psycho-Analysis, 1953–1966).

Introduction

> So that gesture, not music, not odours,
> would be a universal language, the gift
> of tongues rendering visible not the lay
> sense but the first entelechy, the struc-
> tural rhythm.　　—STEPHEN DEDALUS

As EVERY heir knows, succession has its advantages. This book inherits the obvious bounty that accrues to a third-generation endeavor. Thanks to many others who have previously worked to join psychoanalysis to literary study, this essay on *Ulysses* can attend to its explanations without the cramped apologies for method and the heavy, metallic introductions to theory that form the customary armor of a modern criticism. Those who came before have explained and justified the use of psycho-analytic interpretation in literary study far better than I ever could, and anything I might add to their eloquence would be superfluous.[1] Moreover, in the presence of such a dizzying proliferation of criticisms and metacriticisms as we now have, students are coming to view all apologetics with a cold, pragmatic eye. They want a criticism that explains the text first and congratulates itself later. Psychoanalysis, like any criticism, is justified by its re-

1. The best available introduction to the backgrounds of psychoanalytic criticism is Frederick C. Crews's bibliographical essay for the Modern Language Association: "Literature and Psychology," in *Relations of Literary Study: Essays on Interdisciplinary Contributions*, ed., James Thorpe (New York: Modern Language Association, 1967), pp. 73–88.

1

sults, by whether "it can make fuller sense of literary texts than could the most impressive instances of a rival criticism."[2] This book claims only that for itself: to make better sense of *Ulysses* and its author, James Joyce.

It may not be possible to talk in the abstract about the task of psychoanalytic criticism, since psychoanalytic criticism per se does not exist. Psychoanalysis is a way of knowing that does not itself choose what is to be studied. We make more sense when we talk about psychoanalytic *criticisms*, since the analytic method can inspect literature from virtually any angle and has potentially as many uses as we have designs upon a text. We can pass easily beyond the three ways of psychoanalytic criticism described by Norman Holland[3] to describe or invent an abundance of ways. Beside the now-commonplace analyses of characters or of authors or of reader response, we can imagine a number of literary psychohistories given to the study of movements, genres, schools, or disputes. We could invent a psychoanalysis of themes, as Maud Bodkin once tried to do, or of media, of imagery or of the absence of imagery. We could imagine without difficulty hybrid studies by Freud out of Marx of the economic or class origins of a poem, novel, *oeuvre*, genre, national literature, or language. And, as is already standard practice among working analysts, we can use psychoanalysis to discover in a Shakespearean character a symptom we have just encountered in a patient. Psychoanalysis can point a moral or adorn a tale as well as the next criticism.

2. Crews, "Anaesthetic Criticism," in *Psychoanalysis and Literary Process*, ed., Frederick C. Crews (Cambridge, Mass.: Winthrop, 1970), p. 15.

3. Norman Holland, "Shakespearean Tragedy and the Three Ways of Psychoanalytic Criticism," in his *Psychoanalysis and Shakespeare* (New York: McGraw-Hill, 1966).

Clearly, the purview of psychoanalysis is sweeping, and nothing we can call literary lies outside the radius of its prehensile grasp. Of the criticisms that currently urge their vanities upon us only psychoanalysis can seriously claim the potential of becoming a general criticism. If literary study is a subcategory of anthropology, as I believe it is, and if our proper study is man, then we need a criticism that can locate art, creativity, plot, style, character, and reader response inside the continuum of normal human behavior without prearranged, defensive fictions about what is to be discovered. That calls for a grammar of motives and a transformational theory that can get us from motives to art. For better or for worse, psychoanalysis is the only body of theories we possess that has such equipment.

This is an essay on art as gesture. Its assumptions about creativity as action follow the remarkably Freudian lesson delivered by Stephen Dedalus in the "Scylla and Charybdis" chapter of *Ulysses*. Against the insistence of AE and his satellites that "art has to reveal . . . formless spiritual essences" (183/185), Stephen proclaims art to be action—specifically, action in that most "Freudian" of arenas, the family. As Stephen understands it, Shakespeare wrote *Hamlet* in order to act the part of a murdered king in a play of his own creation and to undo, in a symbolic action, what had been done to him in fact. "The play begins," he declares. "A player comes on under the shadow, made up in the castoff mail of a court buck, a wellset man with a bass voice. It is the ghost, the king, a king and no king, and the player is Shakespeare who has studied *Hamlet* all the years of his life which were not vanity in order to play the part of the spectre" (186/188). Stephen is the weaver, weaving the wind. It is a ghost-

story he tells them. They list, and in the porches of their
ears he pours. "He speaks the words to Burbage, the
young player who stands before him beyond the rack of
cerecloth, calling him by a name: *Hamlet I am thy
father's spirit* bidding him list." The mystery unfolds,
the playwright is performing in his own play, *le livre du
lui-même*, before a son who is no son. "To a son he
speaks, the son of his soul, the prince, young Hamlet and
to the son of his body, Hamnet Shakespeare, who has died
in Stratford that his namesake may live for ever." His
auditors are confounded. There is no easy logic here;
it is a lesson in dialectic, the useful art Socrates learned
from Xanthippe. Stephen knows how to bring thoughts
into the world. "Is it possible that that player Shakespeare, a ghost by absence, and in the vesture of buried
Denmark, a ghost by death, speaking his own words to
his own son's name (had Hamnet Shakespeare lived he
would have been prince Hamlet's twin) is it possible, I
want to know, or probable that he did not draw or fore-
see the logical conclusion of those premises: you are the
dispossessed son: I am the murdered father: your mother
is the guilty queen, Ann Shakespeare, born Hathaway?"
And in the porches of their ears . . . .

   They'll have none of it. It flies in the face of tradition.
It is heretical. An outrage on art, on beauty, on the in-
effable Platonic realities. The nightmare of history has
no place in debates about literature. "Art has to reveal
to us ideas, formless spiritual essences," Russell oracles
out of his shadow. Stephen is driven to persist in his
folly. Art is action, behavior. The dramatist gestures, "He
acts and is acted on" (210/212). "He walks. One life is
all. One body. Do. But do. Afar, in a reek of lust and

squalor, hands are laid on whiteness" (199/202). On a wife, a guilty queen. A brother's hands.

ʼ ʼ ʼ

It is an extraordinary story. A young man has been injured and betrayed. He flees into exile and recreates, in dramatic form, the crime against himself. In that play he acts a part written for a ghost of himself in order to counsel vengeance to the image of a son who is, in fact, a ghost. Psychoanalysis, as an instrument of literary analysis, does not often propose quite so dialectical a vision of art. But it is not unique in this; few criticisms are prepared to thread their ways through the devious byways of a lifelong family romance. The obstacles to doing so are self-evident. The study of a complex gesture, when undertaken from afar and through the veil of artistic form, yields complicated and indeterminate conclusions. And the closer we scrutinize an act, the less we understand it. That is the Socratic law of diminishing returns. The more we know, the less. Under the clinical scrutiny of psychoanalysis, the simplest gesture unfolds as an array of unsteady compromises among levels of intent. Arrogance may be the external form of ambivalence or of terror; pacifism may disclose repressed violence; worship may proclaim lust. Moreover, all gestures are transitive; they address objects. And objects are ambiguous; the psychological interpenetration of inner and outer is such that simple objects, under analytic scrutiny, resemble musical chords, containing harmonics of implication. Parts of *Ulysses*, we know, are Joyce's gestures toward Oliver Gogarty, the "stately, plump Buck Mulli-

gan" who greets us with his sacramental shaving gear at
the beginning of the book. "Telemachus" is the lancet of
Joyce's art and Mulligan the object of murderous apotropaic lancing. Yet a wispy cloud of unknowing surrounds
even the simplest gestures toward the gayclad Mulligan.
We still do not know how properly to define him and
assign him his part in the Ulyssean psychodrama. Is he
merely a foolish and treacherous acquaintance? Is there
a place for him in the gallery of domestic villains pre-
scribed by Freudian theory? Is he a "brother figure"? A
"father figure"? Is John Stanislaus Joyce, a ghost by absence from his son's life, implicated in this attack on
Gogarty? Is some impersonal superego or "father imago"? Is brother Stanislaus implicated? What of Gogarty's other Irish selves: Vincent Cosgrave, J. F. Byrne, or
Tom Kettle? Where do we assign Mulligan his proper
domain—in *Ulysses,* in Dublin, or in the mind of James
Joyce? And the gesture itself—is it wholly militant? Is
there no admiration in it? Does it betray a sexual motive:
a tinge of jealousy, of homosexual attraction, of homosexual panic?

In Gogarty's case these are not overwhelming questions. We have an intuitive sense of his place in the book
that does not wait upon the solution of formal questions.
But other persons in Joyce's life who turn up in *Ulysses*
raise darker questions. What are we to make of the image
of Nora in Molly Bloom, of John Joyce in Simon Dedalus,
of the dead mother, May Murray Joyce, in the ghost of
May Dedalus? And how does the book approach that
multitude of persons who are not in it but for whom
Joyce surely wrote it: brother Stanislaus, son Giorgio,
publisher Grant Richards, George Roberts of Maunsel
and Company (Robber and Mumsell, he calls them in

Finnegans Wake), and all the virginal prototypes of
Gerty MacDowell? And what, most of all, of Joyce himself, who, under the dual aspect of Stephen and Bloom,
wrote himself into the book of himself, in which he
speaks to himself, over coffee and cocoa, as sonless father
to fatherless son? *Ulysses* is, above all, a reflexive gesture, a repertoire of self-regarding dances and charades,
an inventory of dramatic poses which Joyce struck endlessly by and for himself.

✔ ✔ ✔

As Philip Rieff has pointed out, psychoanalytic interpretation is a hermeneutics of reconciliation.[4] It proposes
to bring the manifest details of the dream, fantasy, or
story into sensible alignment with a latent content which
conforms to certain standard and redundant paradigms
of psychic possibility. Redundancy is the key element
in such an interpretive scheme. *Ulysses* is the most cha-
meleonlike of books. It hails the protean man, Bloom,
the Everyman, the hero with a thousand gimmicks. And
it does so amid an array of stylistic changes that leap
exuberantly from "young narrative," "personal cate-
chism," "male monologue," through "narcissism," "in-
cubism," "dialectic," and the whole bag of linguistic
tricks that make up the style of *Ulysses*. Yet the purpose of this criticism, like any truly radical criticism, is
to make sense of this variation by discovering in it a principle of replication, a level of meaning upon which it is
intelligible as the elaboration of a few, repetitive theorems.

4. Philip Rieff, "The Tactics of Interpretation," in his *Freud:
The Mind of the Moralist* (Garden City: Doubleday, Anchor, 1961),
pp. 113–162.

Psychoanalysis is a radical criticism only insofar as it it does deindividualize the text. It differs from other such criticisms, not in its insistence upon reductionism and the discovery of simple roots, but in looking for those roots in deep-psychic processes, be they of an author, a character, an audience, an age, or a culture. In some deep-psychic arena that is not exactly coextensive with our terms *id, unconscious,* or *the repressed,* the contents of the human mind are few, simple, and boring. But it is from that primitive level of psychic redundancy that complex intellectual and imaginative materials draw their emotional power. If this study is successful, the characteristic terms of Joyce's psychic redundancy should come clearly into focus, and otherwise disparate aspects of style, imagery, theme, characters, and ideas in his work should make sense as functions or transformations of the same, ultimately tiresome, conflicts. In fact, Joyce's creation of a protean hero itself makes fine sense as an attempt to deny the sameness of his own psychic life, and his experiments in style may be intelligible as efforts to work upon his language and his art the changes he could not work upon himself.

And yet—and this is the dilemma of an interpretive scheme that seeks to be a general criticism—psychoanalysis is theoretically less well-equipped than it should be to appreciate surfaces, nuances, and idiosyncracies. And that theoretical problem is redoubled for the critic, for his contact with artists is normally limited to that ground of involvement chosen by the artists themselves—the text. The old cavil against psychoanalytic criticism that it must fail because it can't get the artist on the couch is a bit naïve, but it is not wholly unjust. An artistic gesture, like any other, is specific and concrete. It is con-

tained in a web of circumstances from which it accumu-
lates meaning—intrapsychic circumstances that are partly
hidden from critical view and interpersonal ones which
may be wholly obscured. Joyce himself, in a rare flourish
of lean, unlovely English in *Finnegans Wake*, complained
that "to concentrate solely on the literal sense or even
the psychological content of any document to the sore
neglect of the enveloping facts themselves circumstantiating it is . . . hurtful to sound sense" (*FW*, 109). Where
we lack, as we so often do, knowledge of specific circumstantiating facts and the details of the author's creative
response to them, we tend to focus on the most primitive
and impersonal psychic materials: the oedipal fantasies
underlying the dramatic situation in a literary work and
the intrapsychic conflicts that are darkly outlined in
them. Thus, we have a criticism whose habitual province
is a realm of general truisms: that art is a dream, a fantasy, a symptomatic expression of a finite assortment of
predictable dilemmas. These truths are vital, but they deliver us, to our discomfort, to the impersonal in art: *the*
mother, *the* father, the stereotyped variations on the
themes of incest and parricide, and those predictable,
anxious flights from castration down the back alleys of
infantile sexuality.

It may be that Stephen Dedalus on Shakespeare is our
ideal model for psychoanalytic criticism. Stephen has no
formal theory of the unconscious, but he knows something about jealousy, castration, repressed anger, betrayal, retribution, and, most important, about how the
family ramifies itself into every thought, act, gesture,
and creation of the obsessed artist. As a critic and as a
would-be artist, he understands the continuity of life
and art. His surmises about Shakespeare's mysterious

life are treacherous but necessary. His theory of *Hamlet* is impossible without the "enveloping facts themselves circumstantiating it," and where they are not immediately available he unselfconsciously invents them. *We* know that Hamnet Shakespeare, had he lived, would not have been Hamlet's twin. Not by some fourteen years. And while Stephen may at times be intimidated and confused by the complexity of his own invention, he is not deterred by its apparent circularity. To infer details about Shakespeare's life from his plays, only to reinterpret his plays in light of a theory of his life is not tautological. It is the very essence of dialectical analysis which aims at the achievement of a portrait of the artist and his art as a unified interrelated whole. Stephen answers for himself Yeats's question about the dancer and the dance. He cannot tell the artist from the art.

Joyce, we know, regarded his art as a kind of public action; a mirror held up to Ireland. He wrote *Ulysses* in part as a public gesture toward the Irish people, both specific and generic. And yet, we may suspect that the deepest meanings and values it held for him had little to do with its real social effects, which, from his distant prospect on the Continent, he could scarcely judge. However strongly Joyce may have wished *Ulysses* to have an effect on others, it was written at least as much for the one audience whose attention he could count on—himself. Joyce, like Shakespeare, was "the hornmad Iago ceaselessly willing that the moor in him shall suffer" (210/212). He acted and was acted on. He was "all in all" (210/212). Our own attention, as we read *Ulysses*, is arrested by the author brooding upon himself as the center of an epical event, acting and being acted upon. We may see the book both as a social gesture and as the product and record of seven years of self-regarding activity. Stephen's description, in "Scylla and Charybdis," of life as a dramatic series of solipsistic self-encounters is a definition too of the life we discover in *Ulysses*. "Every life is many days, day after day. We walk through ourselves, meeting robbers, ghosts, giants, old men, young men, wives, widows, brothers-in-love. But always meeting ourselves" (210/213). What follows is a study of Joyce's own self-encounters and a theory of *Ulysses*, both as the record of those encounters and as an instrument for handling them. Art, as Stephen has shown us, is a strategy for meeting the faces that we meet within ourselves, day after day, and it is a lesson Joyce knew by heart.

TELEMACHIA

1. The Passion of Stephen Dedalus

> Art is born of the coitus between the
> masculine element and the feminine ele-
> ment of which we are all composed, in
> finer balance in the artist than in other
> men. The result is a sort of incest, a
> union of one's self with one's self, a par-
> thenogenesis. That is what makes mar-
> riage so dangerous for artists, for whom
> it represents a pleonasm, a monster's at-
> tempt to approach the norm.
>
> —JEAN COCTEAU

> You find my words dark. Darkness is in
> our souls, do you not think?
>
> —STEPHEN DEDALUS

In *Ulysses* Joyce is popularly thought to have written a
"Freudian" novel, meaning presumably that he concerned
himself with such "Freudian" themes as neurosis, the
dream, the unconscious, and employed such appropriately Viennese techniques as free association, linguistic dis-
tortion, and the interior monologue to illuminate those
themes. Lionel Trilling, for one, has pronounced Joyce
the most thorough of Freudian writers. "James Joyce,"
he has observed, "with his interest in the numerous
states of receding consciousness, with his use of words
as things and of words which point to more than one
thing, with his pervading sense of the interrelation and
interpenetration of all things, and, not least important,
his treatment of familial themes, has perhaps most thor-

oughly and consciously exploited Freud's ideas."[1] This
view of *Ulysses* has settled into commonplace, and the
book itself, with its imposing interior monologues and its
ecumenical lineup of fantasies, obsessions, perversities,
dreams, parapraxes, and other disclosures of the dynamic
unconscious, parades its Freudian biases. Yet, in the face
of this apparent evidence, there is Joyce's own silence
about his knowledge and use of psychoanalysis, a silence
broken only by occasional bursts of derision.[2] Joyce's
public stance toward psychoanalysis was never friendly;
it oscillated between indifference and downright hostility.

Of course, the rampant analytic gestures of *Ulysses*
could imitate psychoanalysis without being properly
Freudian. Psychoanalysis, as Freud readily acknowledged,
did not spring into the world fully grown from the master's forehead. It had its precursors in Western thought,
notably Romanticism, in which Joyce was thoroughly
steeped, and many of the insights it now claims as its
own were achieved independently of it. Bishop Berkeley,
Wordsworth, Coleridge, Nietzsche, de Nerval, and Dostoevsky among others, are the fathers of psychic realism, the idea that significant reality inheres neither in
sensible phenomena nor in a transcendent realm beyond
a trembling veil, but in the human mind. Wordsworth's
Hartleyan hero, the man of sensibility, and Dostoevsky's
obsessive-compulsive underground man, are two faces of
the same psychological man. Moreover, Joyce knew well

1. Lionel Trilling, "Freud and Literature," in his *The Liberal
Imagination* (Garden City: Doubleday, Anchor, 1957), pp. 37–38.

2. See Frederick Hoffman's "Infroyce," in his *Freudianism and
the Literary Mind* (Baton Rouge: Louisiana State University
Press, 1945). It is reprinted in *James Joyce: Two Decades of Literary Criticism*, ed., Seon Givens (New York: Vanguard, 1948), pp.
390–435.

the work of the Marquis de Sade and Leopold von Sacher-Masoch, whose names have passed into our language as eponyms for categories of psychosexual behavior.

But aside from what he might have gotten from Romanticism and the *fin de siècle* worship of the perverse, Joyce's native insight into the patterns of human thought and behavior was extraordinarily acute. Throughout his creative life he indulged in forms of analysis that were remarkably Freudian in their methods and results. His epiphany is a version of Freud's parapraxis, the thoughtless gesture that lays bare the hidden motive, though Joyce's theory, revealed in *Stephen Hero*, surely antedates any possible acquaintance he could have had with Freud's work.[3] "By an epiphany he meant a sudden spiritual manifestation, whether in the vulgarity of speech or of gesture or in a memorable phase of the mind itself" (*SH*, 211). In the epiphanic moment, Stephen tells Cranly, the "soul" of an object, "its whatness, leaps to us from the vestment of its appearance" (*SH*, 213). Joyce's own collection of epiphanies, the unbound pages on which he kept a record of such revelations between 1900 and 1904, explores two very Freudian types of *quidditas*: that which is revealed in dreams and that which emerges from the psychopathology of everyday life. Both are sudden spiritual manifestations. The dream epiphanies postdate the publication of Freud's *The Interpretation of*

3. The surviving epiphanies are published in Richard Kain and Robert Scholes, *The Workshop of Daedalus* (Evanston: Northwestern University Press, 1965), pp. 3–51. Freud's *The Psychopathology of Everyday Life*, which is also a study of the everyday epiphany, was published in periodical form in Berlin in 1901, and there is little chance that Joyce knew anything about it until some time during his sojourn in Trieste.

Dreams by four years at most and must be considered
Joyce's original attempts to research the same realm of
unconscious motivation that Freud was just beginning to
explore in Vienna. Years later, in *Finnegans Wake*, Joyce
bragged, I "can psoakoonaloose myself any time I want"
(*FW*, 522), and in large measure his books are the records
of his analytic transactions with his own unconscious.
Systematic self-analysis was a habit of mind that had
everything to do with a Catholic upbringing and a Jesuit
education that fostered self-observation and confession
as modes of piety and subjected all pious gestures to
rigorous scholastic scrutiny.

But, having come this far, we must acknowledge the
obvious. We must assume that by 1914, when he began
Ulysses, Joyce knew something of Freud's work, that
he was aware of the possibilities that psychoanalysis
had opened up for fiction and that he looked to it, at the
very least, as scientific validation of his own artistic
practices. Psychoanalysis was as much a part of the intellectual ambience in Trieste as it was in Zürich. In
Trieste Joyce could have absorbed what he needed from
Italo Svevo and in Zürich from Ottocaro Weiss, whose
brother, Edouardo Weiss, was a pioneer in Italian psychoanalysis. Svevo's own claim that Joyce knew nothing of
psychoanalysis when he left Trieste in 1915 must be held
in doubt.[4] After all, Svevo did know his Freud, and Joyce
knew Svevo. Joyce had a way with secondhand knowledge. In Joyce, Freud and Aquinas walk arm in arm. In
his notes for *Exiles*, for example, we find Joyce prac-
ticing free association for the dual purpose of analyzing
himself and of generating images for the play. And yet
this creative free association, like other evidence of

4. Italo Svevo, *James Joyce* (San Francisco: City Lights, n.d.).

Freudian biases, must be considered part and parcel of Joyce's lifelong practice of self-scrutiny and would seem to be a Viennese overlay on the old Jesuitical habit of detailed inquiry into the minutiae of the soul.

Ulysses is both a psychoanalytic study of character and a documentary of Joyce's self-analysis. The descent into the psyches of Leopold Bloom and Stephen Dedalus is a thinly disguised exercise in self-analysis and self-revelation on Joyce's part. Two chapters in particular are attempts by Joyce to psoakoonaloose himself and lay bare the roots of his creativity. In "Scylla and Charybdis" this analysis takes the form of Stephen's parable of Shakespeare, while in "Circe" Joyce discloses the contours of his own most obsessive fantasies in the fantasy lives of Stephen and Bloom.

"Scylla and Charybdis" is a curious theoretical interruption of the factual stream of Bloom's day in the Odyssey section of the book. It intersects the text with unexpected urgency and dominates the surrounding chapters, "Lestrygonians" and "Wandering Rocks," by its greater affective presence. Its role in the development of the narrative line of *Ulysses* is anomalous. *Ulysses*, by and large, grows by accretion; each chapter both fills out the plot (insofar as the book can be said to have a plot) and extends the allusive range of those interlocking motifs through which meaning is made in the novel. "Scylla and Charybdis" partakes well enough of the first task but only nominally of the second. It does not so much extend the range of existing motifs as inject into *Ulysses* a new and dynamic body of motifs which radiate through the text in both directions. It is a belated overture which states a number of themes to which preceding variations tend and succeeding ones refer. In short, the

chapter bears an extraordinary burden of meaning in the
book and seems to have borne great significance for
Joyce as well. A great many of the quasi-mythic categories of experience by which Joyce interpreted his own
life are compressed into "Scylla": seduction, betrayal,
cuckoldry, fratricide, revenge, incertitude, exile, sundering, and reconciliation. "Scylla and Charybdis" is Joyce's
biography of himself as a mythic hero, an allegory of his
own wounding and exile.

The theory that Stephen develops before a hostile audience in the National Library in Dublin may first have
been outlined by Joyce in a series of lectures he gave in
Trieste in 1912 and 1913.[5] We know little about the contents of the lectures, or even their number, which is
variously accounted at one, two, three, ten, or twelve,
depending on one's source. Joyce's working notes have
apparently been lost, and any attempt to reconstruct them
is necessarily treacherous. In addition to notes on Shakespeare and Elizabethan drama recently acquired by the
Cornell University library,[6] there are, in the Lockwood

5. See *JJ*, pp. 355–356. See also Richard M. Kain, "James Joyce's
Shakespeare Chronology," *Massachusetts Review* 5 (Winter 1964):
342–355. In *JJ* Ellmann set the date for the first lecture at Novem-
ber 5, 1913, but revised it backward by a year and a day, to
November 4, 1912, in his introduction to *Giacomo Joyce*. The
Cornell University Joyce collection contains a portion of a ticket
to a series of ten lectures by Joyce (in English) on "Amletto di G.
Shakespeare" to begin November 4. Robert Scholes has placed the
year at 1912. See Scholes, *The Cornell Joyce Collection* (Ithaca:
Cornell University Press, 1961), Item 1384.

6. These notebooks are recent acquisitions of Cornell and are
not listed in the Scholes catalogue. One of them is on Shakespeare
and the other on Elizabethan drama. Both contain what can only
be described as a student's lecture notes—all dates and "facts."
They tell us nothing about how Joyce used these facts in his
lectures or interpreted them for *Ulysses*.

Library at Buffalo some notes on Shakespeare that Joyce
had culled from various current biographies, most especially Sidney Lee's biography, George Brandes' biographical and critical study, and Frank Harris's essays in
the *Saturday Review*.[7] Presumably these notes were used
both in the preparation of the lectures and in the writing
of Stephen's discourse. But they are not of much help to us
in reconstructing the lectures; they are minimal notes,
brief and factual. Otherwise we have but one reference
to the lectures by Joyce himself, an ironic self-observation
in the *Giacomo Joyce* manuscript. The remark is the
original of one of Stephen's' observations about artistic
narcissim: "I expound Shakespeare to docile Trieste:
Hamlet, quoth I, who is most courteous to gentle and
simple is rude only to Polonius. Perhaps, an embittered
idealist, he can see in the parents of his beloved only
grotesque attempts on the part of nature to produce her
image . . . . Marked you that?" (*GJ*, 10).

It cannot be far wrong to suppose that Joyce's portrait
of Shakespeare was based on private allusions to his own
condition. Exile must have been a central theme, along
with paternity, cuckoldry, fratricide, and the power of
the artist to transcend the limits and threats of his real
environment by recreating it as art. Like Stephen Dedalus
in "Scylla and Charybdis," Joyce must have subtly
transplanted his Shakespeare from history into myth by

7. Sidney Lee, *A Life of William Shakespeare* (New York:
Macmillan, 1898); George Brandes, *William Shakespeare: A Criti-
cal Study* (New York: Macmillan, 1899); Harris's essays were
published in 1909 in his *The Man Shakespeare and His Tragic
Life-Story* (New York: M. Kennerly, 1909). The best accounts of
Joyce's use of these materials are the Kain article (note 5) and
William Schutte, *Joyce and Shakespeare: A Study in the Meaning
of Ulysses* (New Haven: Yale University Press, 1957).

accommodating the historical reality of the poet's life to self-idealizing fantasies about his own. Shakespeare, then, is only the pretext of "Scylla"; James Joyce is the text.

✓ ✓ ✓

Like Christ, with whom he sometimes identifies, Stephen speaks in parables. His theory of Shakespeare is such a parable—gnomic, understated, emblematic, and guardedly confessional. It is a tale of two Shakespeares: one a middle-class actor and playwright whose plays bear the imprint of family intrigue, and the other a metaphysical deity who is transcendent, autonomous, fatherly, and yet bisexual.

Stephen begins with the family theme. Against the objections of AE and the others of the Celtic Twilight *cénacle* for whom art is the revelation of "formless spiritual essences," Stephen insists on the domestic drama that is rehearsed, not merely in *Hamlet*, but in all of Shakespeare's plays. *Hamlet*, like *Ulysses*, is domestic art; it projects the family onto myth and into history. Though the Freudian view of literature insists that all literature is based on fantasies that recall the family, the Stephen-Joyce view differs in one significant respect. The Freudian focus of attention is on a core of infantile fantasies in which the author, as psychic child, identifies with one or more central characters in his work and projects parental roles onto the other persons in the story. The Shakespearean family, as Stephen defines it, is not strictly the oedipal family; its defining myths are not only those that radiate from the infantile perspective on the classical oedipal triangle. The hero envisioned by Stephen is a husband at war with a wife and a brother armed against brotherhood.

The other Shakespeare in Stephen's parable is the artist-God who is raised by his art to the condition of universal fatherhood, being and feeling himself to be "the father of all his race, the father of his own grandfather, the father of his unborn grandson . . ." (205/208). Bisexual, and therefore complete, he brings forth his creations without the mediation of a second party. His art is a kind of selfbegetting and is defined by Stephen in terms of psychodrama: "He found in the world without as actual what was in his world within as possible (210/213). His creations are avatars of himself, embodiments of his own fantastic possibilities.

Without so naming it, Stephen has constructed a dialectic of creativity that transforms Shakespeare *immanent* (in and of the family) into Shakespeare *transcendent* (a family unto himself). But though these Shakespeares are antithetical figures, they are similarly derived from the same constellation of terrors in Stephen's mind and are natural counterparts in the fantasy life of an oppressed and bewildered young artist. Thus, the ease with which Stephen converts the one into the other is a function of the normal dialectical logic of human fantasy.

SHAKESPEARE IMMANENT

The parable of the two Shakespeares is like the Christian myth of the two Adams. It begins with a fall, "the original sin that darkened his understanding, weakened his will and left in him a strong inclination to evil" (209/212). The seductress is Ann Hathaway, "sweet and twenty-six," who beguiles the eighteen-year-old Shakespeare.

Overborne in a ryefield by a woman older than himself, he is psychologically castrated, unmanned; "Belief in himself has been untimely killed" (194/196). He weds her in haste, for Ann is pregnant, and endures three years of unsatisfactory domesticity, during which three children are born—Susannah and the twins, Hamnet and Judith.

Hamnet, the poet's only son, dies early; he does not live to see his twelfth birthday. Shortly after the birth of the twins, Shakespeare leaves Stratford for London and exile, becoming a "ghost by absence." Though attractive to women, he has neither confidence nor success as a lover. His affairs, indifferently hetero– and homosexual, are uniformly disastrous, and "assumed dongiovannism will not save him" (194/196). Back in Stratford, Ann takes up with one or both of Shakespeare's younger brothers, Richard and Edmund, whose names are significantly those of the most malignant of Shakespearean usurpers and fratricides. There follows a long period of alienation and creativity, which encompasses the writing of the great tragedies. In 1608 a granddaughter is born, Elizabeth Hall, and a symbolic and psychological reconciliation of Shakespeare and Ann is effected through her. The spirit of reconciliation yields the sweet peace at the end of the last romances.

Hamlet, Stephen argues, was written in 1601, in the months following the death of John Shakespeare, the playwright's father. And while Stephen doesn't say so directly, his emphasis on the proximity of the two events implies that John Shakespeare's death had creative consequences for his son, freeing him or driving him to write his greatest play. *Hamlet* is the family theme once again, and in deadly earnest. Gertrude is the unfaithful

Ann; Claudius is the usurping brother; the murdered king is Shakespeare himself (and Shakespeare, living out the fantasy, plays the part of the ghost); and the hesitant prince is the dead son, Hamnet. The dream of revenge that Shakespeare has harbored for years in exile is embodied in a dramatic event in which the role of the avenger is devised upon the dead son, Hamnet. "To a son he speaks, the son of his soul, the prince, young Hamlet and to the son of his body, Hamnet Shakespeare, who has died in Stratford that his namesake may live for ever" (186/188).

Stephen's Shakespeare, impotent to act out his fratricidal fantasies, embodies them in a tragic drama where he can play at being himself and take his revenge without fear of bad consequences—guilt, retribution, or failure. In reconstructing these circumstances, Stephen is alluding to his own condition. But this fantasy of Stephen's, as revealed in his historical reconstruction, is, like art in Plato's view, twice removed from reality. Shakespeare, in his impotence, settles for the public display of a violent fantasy in which symbolic reprisals are taken for real injuries. Stephen, it seems, aspires, not to the condition of real doing but to the Shakespearean condition of symbolic doing. His conscious identification is not with the man of action but with the master of symbolic creation. Thus, virtue, for the creative genius who is immobilized by anxiety, does not lie in the forceful encounter with life but in the skillful evasion of it, and the passions that might find expression in action are, for him, dedicated to the artfulness of the evasion. But Stephen's knifepoint metaphor for argument—the dagger definition—and his fascination for the carnage in *Hamlet* make it apparent that unconscious fantasies of violence underlie his conscious aspiration toward art. "—A deathsman of the soul Robert Greene called him, Stephen said. Not for nothing was he a butcher's son wielding the sledded poleaxe and spitting in his palm. Nine lives are taken off for his father's one."[8] (185/187). In Stephen's mind, Shakespeare the lord of language is identified with Shakespeare the avenger. Stephen's conscious identification is with the former. His recital is witty, virtuoso, and fantastical. But the constant interjection of daggers and poleaxes into the rarified stream of his consciousness betrays the murderous ground in which his thoughts have taken root.

Though Stephen is not Joyce in any simple way, there is little doubt that his attraction toward the violence in Shakespeare is a reflection of Joyce's. We may recognize in Joyce a Bloomian equanimity, a humanity and comic genius that Stephen lacks, but unless we perceive these qualities of Joyce's in their dialectical relation to the Stephen in him—the angry, paranoic, and murderous temperament—we neither perceive them rightly nor value them sufficiently. Joyce's sense of injury and outrage is fundamental to *Ulysses,* and all other attitudes develop in relation to it. Bloom's gentleness, his pacifism in a violent world, and his equanimity in the face of cuckoldry are formal attitudes that have been defensively arrayed against powerful paranoia and aggression. Bloom, in this respect, is a human edition of the transcendent Shakespeare. He overcomes oppression through stoicism and self-control, while Stephen, like the immanent Shake-

8. The confusion of Hamlet with Shakespeare here is characteristic. Despite his formal theory that identifies Shakespeare with King Hamlet, Stephen intuitively sees Shakespeare in the younger Hamlet as well. Later on he acknowledges that Shakespeare is all in all.

speare, is hopelessly enmeshed in a web of treacherous circumstances and immobilizing passions.

For both Stephen and Joyce this tour de force of literary criticism and historical reconstruction is both creative identification and covert self-revelation. Creative identification in the sense that they bring something of themselves into existence, much as children do quite naturally, by their identification with a father figure—in this case, Shakespeare. Each sees Shakespeare as a type of himself, a forerunner, an apostolic father, a "grotesque [attempt] of nature to foretell . . . himself" (193/196). And in making this identification Joyce and Stephen both confess their sense of castration while insisting on its creative consequences, or, in terms made famous by Edmund Wilson, on the dependence of the bow upon the wound. This castration is the seminal event in Shakespeare's creative life. "The tusk of the boar has wounded him there where love lies ableeding" (194/196). It is the aboriginal wound which, paradoxically, is the source of his artistic potency. But if Stephen's focus on Shakespearean castration is an allusion to his own condition, it is not an obvious one. How has Stephen been castrated? What meaning can Shakespeare's seduction and cuckolding have for a young man who has yet to experience either? And what "goad of the flesh" drives him to enact his passion in the library?

AGENBITE OF INWIT

In Stephen's mind, the death of his mother and the sexual undoing of Shakespeare are significantly related. The deathbed scene hovers darkly about the threshold of his consciousness throughout the day and informs his soliloquy in the library, for aspects of the Shakespearean story resonate with his maternal obsession. As his mother lay dying, Stephen had sung for her Aleel's song from Yeats's *The Countess Cathleen*: "And no more turn aside and brood/ Upon love's bitter mystery/ For Fergus rules the brazen cars . . . ." She had cried, "For those words, Stephen: love's bitter mystery" (11/9). And yet, proud in his newly acquired free thought, he had refused to kneel and pray for her. That, he imagines, was his original sin, the act of disobedience that has rendered him psychologically impotent. He is ensnared in a paralyzing net of self-accusation far more constricting than those of nationality, language, or religion. His mother's image in his psyche controls him through the evocation of guilt and the manipulation of his anxieties.

Stephen is in a state of protracted mourning. His manner is marked by the classic symptoms of grief: profound dejection, lack of interest in the world, incapacity to love, and incapacity to act.[9] His mother had died the previous August,[10] some ten months before, but his mourning has outlived the immediate task of psychological accommodation to loss. Stephen has not been able to repress successfully or in any way come to terms with the death of his mother. He has internalized and preserved her image and established it within himself as the voice of his own superego. His mourning is most Hamlet like inasmuch as it seems to be a permanent disposition, a constitutional melancholy disguised as fresh grief. In addition to the

9. See Sigmund Freud, "Mourning and Melancholia," *SE*, vol. 14.

10. The exact date of May Dedalus's death is not revealed in the book, but Joyce's mother, May Murray Joyce, died August 13, 1903. I think it safe to transfer the date of the real death onto the fictive one.

characteristic signs of sorrow, Stephen displays the classic melancholic symptoms of self-debasement and delusional expectation of punishment, feelings that do not normally accompany simple grief.[11]

The burden of Stephen's self-reproach is one insistent theme, his betrayal of his mother by refusing to pray at her deathbed. In recompense, he rehearses throughout the day the prayer for the dying, as though it were the *Confiteor*. But this guilt is deceptive; it has attached itself to the deathbed scene and yet appears to reach beyond it. And, as we recall from *Portrait*, Stephen has known guilt and melancholy before. It seems likely that while Stephen associates his guilt with his refusal to pray, the deathbed fantasy really functions for him as a screen memory. For, though Stephen is haunted by a real event, it may be that the immobilizing affects that accompany the fantasy have been displaced onto it from other, more permanent sources. If this is in fact classic Freudian melancholia, we should be looking for a good deal of defensive misdirection in Stephen's self-accusations. For in melancholia the content of the self-accusation may be a charge against the other, the lost lover, that has been turned by guilt and narcissism against the self.

Some of the hidden sources of Stephen's melancholy fleetingly suggest themselves in "Proteus": "Wombed in sin darkness I was too, made not begotten. By them, the man with my voice and my eyes and a ghostwoman with ashes on her breath. They clasped and sundered, did the coupler's will" (39/38). Stephen's real fall from grace, it seems, was effected at the moment of his conception, his guilt assured before his birth. His conception was sinful because it involved his mother's betrayal of his unborn

11. "Mourning and Melancholia."

self. "Is that then," he wonders, "the divine substance
wherein Father and Son are consubstantial?" Stephen's
burden is nothing less than the burden of parental sexuality and his plight that of the oedipal son who has lost
his faith in the virgin mother, loved only and most
chastely by himself, because knowledge of his own conception renders such faith impossible. This parental
coupling is obsessive in Stephen's' imagination, and he
sees it everywhere. In a fantasy of his mother's death he
imagines the moment of expiration to have been a ghostly
kiss by the fearsome *dio boia,* the hangman God: "Bridebed, childbed, bed of death, ghostcandled. *Omnis caro ad
te veniet.* He comes, pale vampire, through storm his eyes,
his bat sails bloodying the sea, mouth to her mouth's kiss"
(48/47–48). Later in the day he commemorates this fantasy in verse on a portion of the letter given him by Deasy:

> *On swift sail flaming*
> *From storm and south*
> *He comes, pale vampire,*
> *Mouth to my mouth.*
> 　　　　　(131/132)

This vision of death as a sexual attack is threateningly
problematical for Stephen. For one thing, it contains
homosexual implications. Stephen's original vision of
death coming to his mother as a batlike kiss, "mouth to
her mouth's kiss," has been altered in the writing to
"mouth to *my* mouth." The victim-lover of the poem is
the speaker—no, the singer—of it. And how do we read
that? Can Stephen be identifying with his mother at the
moment of her strange *Liebestod*? Could this be his
fantasy of his own submission to the incubus of death,
the fearsome vampire? Or does this poem, like the primal-
scene fantasy from which it derives, show us Stephen

peering in at the ambiguous kiss of death? Is it proper to assign Stephen a point of view at all? Might it be that Stephen's identifications are diffused throughout this imagined event and that he is at once a witness to the murderous kiss *and* the deadly incubus *and* the victim of murderous oral rape? This is not a problem to be solved here, but perhaps this very puzzle is a version of Stephen's overwhelming obsession—love's bitter mystery.

Toward the mother who had betrayed him, Stephen appears to have harbored a murderous hostility, albeit a hostility well-repressed in the service of filial piety. But his anger and her death unhappily coincide for him, and his guilt is the visible sign of his unconscious conviction that he has killed her. To the purveyor of guilt, the unconscious superego, the wish is equivalent to the act. For us, the unsentimental glare of psychoanalysis strips away the aura of principle and the sanctity of stubborn self-assertion from Stephen's refusal to pray. From this perspective, it seems quite sinister, a covertly matricidal act. Stephen appears to have worked a cruel exchange with his mother at her deathbed, betrayal for betrayal. Mulligan's allusion to Stephen's having killed his mother is unbearable to Stephen because he fears it to be true. With characteristic incisiveness, Mulligan mocks Stephen's refusal to wear a pair of grey trousers: "Etiquette is etiquette. He kills his mother but he can't wear grey trousers" (8/6).

Rather than alleviate Stephen's guilt by liberating him from the oedipal situation, May Dedalus's death has redoubled it. Stephen is beset by obsessive images of parental retribution. Like Bloom, he is a type of the selftormenting Shakespeare. His unremitting superego is the

vengeful mother ceaselessly willing that the son in him
shall suffer. Later in the day, at Bella Cohen's brothel,
the deathless, internalized mother accuses him. "I was
once the beautiful May Goulding. I am dead" (565/580).
Stephen recoils and cries out in fierce denial, "They said
I killed you, mother . . . Cancer did it, not I." Her reply
is the deadliest of all maternal accusations. She had loved
him and borne him in her womb, and *he* had been the
one to violate the sanctity of *amor matris*. "Who saved
you the night you jumped into the train at Dalkey with
Paddy Lee? Who had pity for you when you were sad
among the strangers . . . Years and years I loved you, O
my son, my firstborn, when you lay in my womb."

   That reproach is prelude to a terrifying symbolic castration which moves Stephen to rebellion and precipitates
his climactic shattering of the chandelier:

THE MOTHER

(*Her face drawing near and near and nearer, sending out an
ashen breath.*) Beware! (*She raises her blackened, withered
right arm slowly towards Stephen's breast with outstretched
fingers.*) Beware! God's hand! (*A green crab with malignant
red eyes sticks deep its grinning claws in Stephen's heart.*)
                                                   (566–567/582)

   The green crab is cancer, the killer of his mother, which
now confronts Stephen as the devouring mother herself.
This crablike mother, bearing God's hand, is no doubt the
combined force of the parental army to which Stephen
needs to submit and yet must struggle with for his freedom. He makes a quixotic gesture of phallic defiance,
smashing the chandelier with his ashplant and freeing
himself momentarily from the mind-forged manacles of
melancholia. With his Siegfried cry of *"Nothung"* "*He
lifts his ashplant high with both hands and smashes the*

*chandelier. Time's livid final flame leaps and, in the fol-
lowing darkness, ruin of all space, shattered glass and
toppling masonry''* (567–568/583).

⚹ ⚹ ⚹

The seduction of Shakespeare by Ann Hathaway is not
the only bitter mystery to be read in the poet's work.
"Two deeds are rank in that ghost's mind: a broken vow
and the dullbrained yokel on whom her favor has de-
clined, deceased husband's brother" (200/202). The
most vicious of Shakespearean malignities—Claudius,
Iago, Edmund, and crookback Richard—are types of the
poet's brothers, "two noble kinsmen nuncle Richie and
nuncle Edmund" (208/211). And Stephen finds these
nuncles everywhere in Shakespeare. "The theme of the
false or the usurping or the adulterous brother or all
three in one is to Shakespeare what the poor is not, always with him" (209/212).

The theme was always with Joyce, as well. At the end
of *Portrait*, Stephen feels he is about to be betrayed by
Cranly, and *Exiles*, of course, is about the attempted
cuckolding of Richard Rowan by Robert Hand. In *Finnegans Wake*, the theme of the false or usurping or
adulterous brother seems to have taken over Joyce's
imagination. Brotherhood, defined as treachery, appears
everywhere in the interpenetrating, internecine struggles
of Shem and Shaun, Abel and Cain, Esau and Jacob,
Isaac and Ishmael, Saint Kevin and Saint Patrick, the
Ondt and the Gracehoper, Othello and Iago, *etcetera, ad
infinitum.*[12] And in *Ulysses*, where the motif is less of a

12. See Adaline Glasheen, "Who Is Who When Everybody Is
Somebody Else," in her *A Second Census of Finnegans Wake*
(Evanston: Northwestern University Press, 1963), lx–lxvi.

survey course in the history of fraternal strife, it is present in Mulligan's usurpations and mockery of Stephen
and the cuckolding of Bloom by Boylan, the dandy Claudius. The motif is also recapitulated in minor key in
Bloom's fascination with the Childs' murder case, the
littoral warfare of Tommy and Jacky Caffrey, and, of
course, its many Shakespearean permutations.

This treacherous brother in Joyce's work tends to
crystallize into the image of the false Judas or Tim Healey. Stanislaus observed, "My brother was always of
opinion that a dramatist could understand only one or
two of life's tragedies, and that he always presented different aspects of the few he understood. One of the
tragedies that obsessed my brother's imagination, beginning from the time when he first understood the Mass as
drama, was the tragedy of dedication and betrayal. In
later life, the story of Parnell became for him another aspect of that tragedy."[13] Time and again, Joyce reworked
the theme, with Parnell as hero, or himself, in verse, in
novels, and in occasional lectures and periodical articles.

To what extent real brotherhood is the basis for the
obsessive *idea* of brotherhood, for both Stephen and
Joyce, is problematical. After *Stephen Hero,* where he
appears as Maurice, brother Stanislaus all but disappears
from brother James's work and is granted one meager
allusion in *Ulysses.* "A brother is as easily forgotten as
an umbrella," Stephen muses in "Scylla" and then wonders, "where is your brother? Apothecaries' hall. My
whetstone. Him, then Cranly, Mulligan: now these"
(208/211). The allusion to Stanislaus (Maurice?) in the
context of these dangerous friends intimates that friendship, for Stephen, is a version of brotherhood and that

13. Stanislaus Joyce, *MBK*, p. 168.

his attitudes toward the former are conditioned by his experience of the latter. As Ellmann has pointed out, in the Joycean universe "your friend is someone who wants to possess you mentally and your wife physically, and longs to prove himself your disciple by betraying you."[14] For Joyce, as for Stephen, every friendship is prelude to a crime. As Ellmann has shown well, Joyce's sense of himself as hero-betrayed was prophetic, and he went to extraordinary lengths to court the treachery of his friends in order to fulfill that prophecy.

It is likely that Stanislaus stands behind this ubiquitous false brother. He was the most intimate and therefore most dangerous of Joyce's siblings. At James's request, Stanislaus came to live with his brother's family in Trieste in 1905 and established himself there as the household superego. His sober and rigorous presence ably represented Irish puritanism among the exiled Joyces for nine difficult years. But, though his roles in his brother's house were various and complicated during the Trieste years, there is no evidence that Stanislaus was a rival for Nora's love, however brother James may have teased himself with that possibility.[15]

Though the real adult Stanislaus was at best a benign irritant to his brother, the same cannot be said of the infant Stanislaus, usurper and rival *par excellence*. If

14. Richard Ellmann, "A Portrait of the Artist *as Friend*," in *Joyce's Portrait: Criticisms and Critiques*, ed., Thomas E. Connolly, (New York: Meredith, 1962), p. 96.

15. The real emotional configurations of the Trieste ménage are a mystery. Hélène Cixous suggests that "It may be that Stannie was tempted to take Jim's place more completely while the latter was away; for Cain's diary does not tell us to what extent he came to confuse himself with his brother" (*The Exile of James Joyce* [New York: David Lewis, 1972], p. 129).

fraternal usurpation is an obsessive theme in Joyce's work, it was no less the habitual condition of a childhood in which the almost yearly birth of a brother or sister set a formidable barrier between his mother and himself. As opposed to classical oedipal paradigms which Freud discovered in the patriarchal, Germanic family, the patterns of childhood devotion and jealousy in Joyce's life and fantasies were more typical of the fecund and matriarchal Irish household.[16] In such a household, the libidinals bonds between husband and wife are tenuous and a child's primary rival for the mother's love is not the father but a sibling. Love is at a premium in such a family, and brotherhood is a zero-sum game which one wins only when one's brother loses.[17] The problem of the father in *Ulysses* is that he is missing. His office is a legal fiction and he himself a ghost by absence, obsessive because he cannot be located. Even in *Portrait*, where Simon Dedalus is at his most robust, Heron, Cranly, Davin, and Lynch are the more potent of Stephen's rivals. Yet the question of why these "friends'" should be the objects of a fratricidal impulse which the real brothers escape in *Portrait* and *Ulysses* is a subtle one that

16. Unfortunately, we have no thoroughgoing study of the typical patterns of love and rivalry in the Irish family and culture. One study that does work on the periphery of this subject is Marvin K. Opler's comparison of Irish and Italian schizophrenics, "Schizophrenia and Culture," *Scientific American* 197 (August 1957): 103–112. A statement of the problem of defining the oedipus complex in appropriately universal terms is Anne Parsons, "Is the Oedipus Complex Universal?" *The Psychoanalytic Study of Society*, ed., Warner Muensterberger (New York: International Universities Press, 1964) 3:278–328. An excellent analysis of the dynamics of matriarchy in general is Philip Slater, *The Glory of Hera: Greek Mythology and the Greek Family* (Boston: Beacon Press, 1968).

17. Slater, *Hera*, p. 37.

has in part to do with real betrayals, one of which is recounted in chapter 2.

It has to do, too, with the complicated experience of brotherhood, which encompasses not only infantile rivalry, but boyhood friendship, adolescent intimacy, and adult financial dependency. Yet it *is* Stanislaus after all who was foredoomed to play Shaun to his brother's Shem, Jacob to his Esau, and Cain to his Abel, this last a role he ironically acknowledged in the title of his biography of James, *My Brother's Keeper*. It was in fact brothers Stanislaus, Charles, and George, as well as the never-ending sisters, who usurped the place of the eldest in the mother's bed, much as Shakespeare's do in Ann Hathaway's. Joyce's constant need to be *almost* betrayed makes abundant sense as a need to reenact an annual childhood threat in order to triumph over it. Including James's birth in February 1882, May Joyce gave birth to at least ten children from 1882 to 1893.[18] Usurpation, for Joyce, was the very definition of brotherhood, and it is small wonder that he insisted upon it as a condition of friendship as well.

The recurring form of this psychic struggle, as it asserted itself time and again in Joyce's imagination, was to be betrayed, to struggle against his enemies, to triumph, to err and fall, to arise and triumph once again.

18. In a letter to Nora while they were still courting (if that is a word one can use for their early relationship) Joyce placed the family size at seventeen, and one assumes he included his parents in that figure (*Letters* 2:48). In his diary Stanislaus two-ups his brother, claiming that his mother had had seventeen children (*CDD*, p. 10). Ellmann, however, counts only four boys, six girls, and three misbirths, for a total of thirteen. However that may be, such a household must have seemed like seventeen. As Ellmann notes, "John Joyce filled his house with children and with debts" (*JJ*, p. 20).

Like so many of Joyce's other obsessions, this unending courtship of treachery was a form of repetition compulsion, and the purpose of his repeated fantasies of fall and restoration and his subtle stratagems for introducing incertitude into his marriage was to recapitulate the childhood situation on his own terms—to be active in a situation that he had once borne passively and thereby to learn to manage the old threat of the usurping brother.[19] His art, like Stephen's unremitting intellect, is organized around this struggle against the brother.

Stephen believes that Mulligan "fears the lancet of my art as I fear that of his. The cold steelpen" (8/7). His engagement with AE and the others in the library is an intellectual commando raid. He delivers his arguments with murderous erudition: "Unsheathe your dagger definitions," he urges himself. Elsewhere, preparing his theorems with the guile of a Claudius, he muses, "They list. And in the porches of their ears I pour" (194/196). In such a world, where love begets injury and brotherhood begets betrayal, human contact cannot comfort; it can only threaten. Stephen's choices, then, are two: to submit or to dominate, to render up his manhood or to master his Dublin cruelly and completely.

SHAKESPEARE TRANSCENDENT

It is out of such a dilemma that the figure of Shakespeare the creator-God is born. Stephen supposes that Shake-

19. See Freud on this function of repetition-compulsion in *Beyond the Pleasure Principle*, *SE*, vol. 18. The validity of Freud's observation about the function of repetition-compulsion in the mastery of trauma is fortunately not dependent upon his larger thesis in that book, the presence of a biological death instinct in all organic life.

speare was such a man as himself: betrayed, unmanned, isolated, and proud. His response to this dilemma, Stephen imagines, was to fly by the nets of brotherly treachery and sexual incapacity through the power of art. Oppressed by family circumstances, he became a family unto himself.

Invoking the African heresiarch Sabellius, who believed the three persons of the Trinity to be merely modes of the same being,[20] Stephen constructs a theory of creativity on the triune mysteries of paternity, apostolic succession, and Sabellian modalism. Paternity, he avers, may be a legal fiction: "in the sense of conscious begetting, [it] is unknown to man" (204/207). True paternity is "a mystical estate, an apostolic succession, from only begetter to only begotten." Human conception and birth are spoiled by shame and guilt. The oedipal crime is implicit in every male birth: "The son unborn mars beauty: born, he brings pain, divides affection, increases care. He is a male: his growth is his father's decline, his youth his father's envy, his friend his father's enemy" (205/207–208).

On the metaphysical base of Sabellian thought, paradoxical to the logical mind and heretical to the orthodox, Stephen elaborates his theory. The burden of the Sabellian heresy, as Stephen notes twice, is that "the father was Himself His own Son" (22/21, 205/208). Hamlet *père* and Hamlet *fils*, then, are one and the same, and Shakespeare must be consubstantial with both. Thus, Stephen is ready to agree when John Eglinton interjects

20. The best study of these Trinitarian subtleties and Stephen's use of them is William T. Noon, S.J., *Joyce and Aquinas* (New Haven: Yale University Press, 1957). The book is exceedingly knowledgeable but flawed by Father Noon's dislike of Stephen and of heresy in general.

that Shakespeare is all in all, both ghost and prince. And Stephen is ready to adorn that theme with examples: "In *Cymbeline*, in *Othello* he is bawd and cuckold. He acts and is acted on. Lover of an ideal or a perversion, like José he kills the real Carmen. His unremitting intellect is the hornmad Iago ceaselessly willing that the moor in him shall suffer" (210/212).

Such an artist creates by giving body to fantasy versions of himself. He puts reality to work in the service of fantasy and finds "in the world without as actual what was in his world within as possible" (210/213).

Maeterlinck says: *If Socrates leave his house today he will find the sage seated on his doorsteps. If Judas go forth tonight it is to Judas his steps will tend.* Every life is many days, day after day. We walk through ourselves, meeting robbers, ghosts, giants, old men, young men, wives, widows, brothers-in-love. But always meeting ourselves. The playwright who wrote the folio of this world and wrote it badly (He gave us light first and the sun two days later), the lord of things as they are whom the most Roman of Catholics call *dio boia*, hangman god, is doubtless all in all in all of us, ostler and butcher, and would be bawd and cuckold too but that in the economy of heaven, foretold by Hamlet, there are no more marriages, glorified man, an androgynous angel, being a wife unto himself.
                                                                    (210/213)

The dialectic of artistic transcendence is completed by the internalization of art and the hermaphrodization of the artist. The sexual victim becomes the creative hero. His flaws become virtues, his wounds, capacities. Shakespeare's sexual incapacity, which had manifested itself in joyless promiscuity or homosexuality, is transformed into divine androgyneity. Isolation through loss and betrayal becomes Godlike autonomy. The threatening brothers are one's own possible selves, and a treacherous reality that threatened confinement and castration is internalized and subordinated to a fantasy life over which the artist exercises total dominion.

The particular mode of artistic transcendence imagined by Stephen is an oral strategy: Shakespeare overcame the world by internalizing it. This oral strategy, a kind of megalomania, is not uncommon among artists generally and may in fact be necessary to the creative process. By means of this strategy, an artistic ego that is threatened by a reality it cannot manage may undertake to master it through introjection, thus systematically taking possession of bits and pieces of the external world and reforming them into mental images which are also counters in its own psychic equilibrium.[21] Of course, this strategy is available to everyone, but the artist may carry it further by reembodying these images in verbal, plastic, or dramatic form in order to work upon the world with images of itself. Stephen's project at the end of *Portrait*, to forge within the smithy of his soul the uncreated conscience of his race, is, in effect, a proposal to recreate his race, nation, and language as his possessions. In "Eumaeus" Stephen announces to Bloom, "You suspect . . . that I may be important because I belong to the *faubourg Saint-Patrice* called Ireland for short. But I suspect . . . that Ireland must be important because it belongs to me" (629/645). And that may express Joyce's primary task in *Ulysses*: the absorption and containment within himself of a fickle reality which may be controlled in the manner of a bodily function. In fact, Stephen in *Stephen Hero* formulates the visionary function of the artist in barely disguised alimentary terms. "The poet is the intense centre

21. See Ernst Kris, *Psychoanalytic Explorations in Art* (New York: Schocken, 1964), pp. 51–52.

of the life of his age to which he stands in a relation than which none can be more vital. He alone is capable of absorbing in himself the life that surrounds him and of flinging it abroad amid planetary music" (*SH*, 80). This exalted gesture of flinging abroad a well-digested life amid planetary music recalls the rather more prosy image of artistic creation in the description of Shem in *Finnegans Wake*, who "winged away on a wildgoup's chase across the kathartic ocean and made synthetic ink and sensitive paper for his own end out of his wit's waste" (*FW*, 185).

But alimentary analogies for the end product of creative digestion aside, the oral strategy for the management of reality puts a number of psychic tactics at the disposal of the fantast or the artist. One is the reconstruction of relationships for the purpose of bringing them into conformity with wishes. Thus, the conception of true fatherhood as an apostolic succession "from only begetter to only begotten" is a strategic one because it hints at the unstated proposition that underlies the discourse on Shakespeare. Namely, that Stephen is the apostolic successor to Shakespeare and only apparently the son of Simon Dedalus, to whom he is connected only by "an instant of blind rut." In this light, the general shape of Stephen's argument is recognizable as a variation on one of the oldest of literary themes and commonest of childhood fantasies, the family romance.

STEPHEN'S FAMILY ROMANCE

As Freud described it, the family romance is the fantasy of being the child of nobility who has been stolen or lost or abandoned in infancy and raised by foster parents under degraded circumstances. The fantasy has many phases and takes many forms. Freud himself spoke of two phases of the family romance—a naïve pre-oedipal phase in which the child doubts the authenticity of both parents, and a sexual stage in which the child accepts the mother but denies the father, whom he regards as *semper incertus.*

The similarity of certain of Stephen's remarks to Freud's description of the sexual phase of the family romance is striking. Freud attributed the change in the family romance to the child's discovery of parental sexuality: "When presently the child comes to know of the various kinds of sexual relations between fathers and mothers and realizes that *'pater semper incertus est,'* while the mother is *'certissima,'* the family romance undergoes a peculiar curtailment: it contents itself with exalting the child's father, but no longer casts any doubts on his maternal origin, which is regarded as something unalterable."[22]

Stephen's peroration on the insubstantiality of fatherhood is suggestively similar, and it is conceivable that Joyce read Freud on the family romance before or during his work on *Ulysses.*[23] *"Amor matris,* subjective and objective genitive, may be the only true thing in life. Paternity may be a legal fiction. Who is the father of any son that any son should love him or he any son?" (205/ 207).

There are actually two versions of the family romance

22. Freud, "Family Romances," *SE,* vol. 9. See also *Moses and Monotheism, SE* 23:11–15.

23. If Joyce did read Freud on the family romance, he most likely came to him through Otto Rank. Rank's *Der Mythos von der Geburt des Helden* (Leipzig and Vienna: F. Deuticke, 1909) contained Freud's notes on the family romance in full.

in Stephen's fantasy, though they are ambiguously co-mixed. The simpler version involves Stephen's wish to be the spiritual son of Shakespeare. This fantasy is an extension of a situation implicit in *Portrait*—Stephen's turning away from Simon Dedalus and projecting a paternal role onto the fabulous artificer, Daedalus. Daedalus is still invoked by Stephen in *Ulysses*, but he is clearly a secondary figure. Shakespeare is the apostolic father on whom Stephen has projected his hopes of personal election. The idea of Shakespeare as the father as opposed to Daedalus has the advantages of complexity as well as the peculiar attractiveness of the former's tawdry life. Stephen's family romance in either case may be a youthful fantasy, but the identification with a cuckolded Shakespeare rather than a sexually innocent Daedalus reveals a young man who has been down and out in Paris. The cuckold father figure is attractive to him also because as father, the unmanned Shakespeare has already been wounded in accordance with the parricidal wishes of the son who aspires to succeed him.

But the mysteries of apostolic succession and the arguments from Sabellian analogies give Stephen's scenario a subtler configuration than that of the classic family romance. They suggest that Stephen fancies himself not merely a spiritual son of Shakespeare but the true apostolic successor, who is in all ways consubstantial with him who came before. As the son, he *is* the father or, in Sabellian terms, a mode of the same being. Thus, it is possible for Stephen to fancy himself both Hamlet *père* and Hamlet *fils*, ghost and prince, all in all. And the figure of the wounded Shakespeare who is of one substance with his creations expresses Stephen's own wish for himself—to be betrayed.

Stephen's dream of apostolic succession is a radically isolationist version of the family romance, which preserves the impulse toward self-ennoblement while doing away with parents entirely. Stephen's Shakespeare is ennobled by generational autonomy. Instead of the hero as secret prince, Stephen gives us the hero as self-made man. For if father and son be one and the same and if generation requires no third party, no mother, then there are no relationships. The son, his own father, is always only himself and alone, "an androgynous angel, being a wife unto himself." The family romance differs from the song of myself only in degrees of narcissism.

The autonomous creator-God is free from the authority of the father, the treachery of the brothers, and the seductions of the mother, for he has triumphed over childhood and sexuality. As bisexual creator of his own family, he is not only free from sexuality and guilt, but, as creator of his own parents, is free of infantile helplessness and filial dependence. He is infallible.

Turning from Shakespeare to Joyce for a moment, we can see how the latter used his books to turn the tables on John Stanislaus Joyce by recreating him as Simon Dedalus, "A medical student, an oarsman, a tenor," and so on. This deflation of the father in art follows an old magical formula, not unlike primitive image magic, in which one gains control over an object by making an image of it. Manipulation of images, which is the business of the artist, does very nicely when a direct attack upon the real thing is either impossible, dangerous, or taboo.

There seems to be at least one weakness in the logic of Stephen's dialectics. For, while it is the false or usurping or adulterous brother who betrays and threatens Shake-

speare the man, it is an otherwise shadowy father who is
overcome and made unnecessary by Shakespeare the artist. Yet this illogic is more apparent than real, since, in a
larger perspective, it is the family itself that threatens
and the family that is overcome. The treachery of a
brother, the infidelity of a wife, and the death of both
father and son are *all* overcome by the internalization of
the family, whereby Shakespeare becomes a family unto
himself. Omnipotence solves all problems. However, for
the purposes of making sense of Stephen's lecture, the
apparent disjunction in Stephen's logic does suggest that
Joyce's metaphors for psychic transcendence were borrowed and do not fit the specifications of real fantasy.
And since the masculine threat in Joyce's imagination
primarily took the form of a brother or an appropriately
fraternal "friend," Freudian or Trinitarian metaphors
which measure the distance between sons and fathers
can represent these fraternal conflicts only by indirection. The attack upon the father can answer the threat of
the brother inasmuch as both father and brother are incest rivals and each can represent the other in fantasy,
and because the fatherless "self-made" man has, by definition, no brothers. But it makes more sense in Joyce's case
to recognize the brother as the genuine object of anger
and jealousy and to see Stephen Dedalus's formulas for
overcoming the father in "Scylla and Charybdis" as imperfect overlays of theory, in part Freudian theory, upon
the materials of fantasy. Not that the brother is missing
from Stephen's theory of artistic transcendence, for it is
the fraternal crime, after all, that Shakespeare symbolically repays by killing off Claudius, Iago, Edmund, Richard, and the rest. But it is the father specifically whom
Stephen imagines Shakespeare to have overcome through

the act of writing plays, that act through which Shake-speare became the God of his own universe, the father of his own father, father of his race, and wife unto himself.

The creator-God who is wife unto himself is an important figure in *Ulysses*, for he is a composite God in whom a number of major tendencies in Joyce's psychosexual fantasy life are condensed. For one thing, he is a symbol of sexual ambivalence, and Joyce's anxiety about the true nature of his sexual role is the primary condition of the theme of Shakespearean androgyneity. As the fantasy content of "Circe" and Joyce's letters to Nora demonstrate, real sexuality was always problematical for Joyce and his ambivalence unrelenting. He invested much of his erotic effort in the invention of exclusive and tortuous conditions for sexual pleasure, being apparently unmoved by pleasures that were available without constraint or condition. This ambivalence was reinforced by a general ambivalence toward all relationships, most especially those involving dependency. In the rebelliousness of Stephen, Joyce depicted his own rebellion against dependency and restraint, while in Bloom, the alien who wishes to be no more than an Irishman among Irishmen, he embodied the countertendency, his dread of isolation. We should not think, as too many critics have in the past, that this opposition makes Bloom a moral hero and Stephen a villain. It is rather a case of Joyce exploring his own possibilities by resolving his ambivalence toward relationships into contrasting alter egos. Just as we can neither understand nor appreciate Bloom's humor and equanimity until we see them in dialectical relation to Stephen's resentment and aggression, so Stephen's radical denial of the family makes its best sense as a solution to the problems posed by Bloomian dependency. It should be apparent that the drives toward autonomy and dependency coexisted for Joyce in a condition of dynamic equilibrium. All of Bloom's efforts toward sexual autonomy are held in balance by his emotional dependence upon Molly, while, on the other hand, Stephen's radical self-isolation must end, as we know, in lifelong nostalgia. It is in the very logic of filial ambivalence that Joyce, who kept his distance from home and family throughout his creative life, made them ever so much more the subject and substance of his books the longer he remained in exile.

Autonomy, or transcendence of family relations, then, is an ambiguous ideal that stands, in all its complexity, at the heart of *Portrait* and *Ulysses*. The creative autonomy of Shakespeare, the intellectual autonomy of Stephen, and the sexual autonomy of Bloom are all variations on a single theme. Bloom's preference for masturbatory love-at-a-distance to real sexual relations is a comic imitation of Shakespeare's conquest of reality, for both are strategies of transcendence by withdrawal and introjection. Both abandon reality in favor of fantasy; both value the psychic representations of the real world over reality itself. The idea that one can find release from guilt and threat through narcissism or the total internalization of reality and sexuality pervades the book and organizes the psychic lives of both Stephen and Bloom—making them both versions of the creator-God. Bloom's fantasy life is his creative activity, his masturbation his version of divine androgyneity. At the conclusion of Stephen's discourse on art as Godlike self-begetting, Mulligan interrupts to announce his latest "play for the mummers," *Everyman His Own Wife or A Honeymoon in the Hand* (214/216). Thus, at the end of "Scylla and

Charybdis" the elaborate metaphysic of Stephen's parable is reduced to a simple joke: to copulate is human, to masturbate divine. But that joke is one of the meanings of *Ulysses*.

ODYSSEY

2. Interlude:
A Correspondence of Joyces

> . . . and his mad crazy letters my Pre-
> cious one everything connected with your
> glorious Body everything underlined that
> comes from it is a thing of beauty and of
> joy for ever something he got out of some
> nonsensical book that he had me always
> at myself 4 or 5 times a day sometimes
> and I said I hadn't are you sure O yes
> I said I am quite sure in a way that shut
> him up. . . .   —MOLLY BLOOM

As STEPHEN embarks upon his biographical reading of
Hamlet in the library, AE interrupts to protest his "prying into the family life of a great man" (187/189). "Peep-
ing and prying into greenroom gossip of the day, the
poet's drinking the poet's debts. We have *King Lear*:
and it is immortal." Stephen's answer is slow in coming
and indirect—in the imagination of the artist the opposition of art and life is not exclusive but dialectical. Thus
Stephen can tell John Eglinton, "A man of genius makes
no mistakes. His errors are volitional and are the portals
of discovery" (188/190). Stephen agrees with Freud that
there are no accidents, that every error reveals an intention. He adds, with Joyce, that nothing the artist experiences or does is wasted.

This reading of Joyce's letters to Nora is a study of
the intricate symbiosis of art and life that underlies *Ulysses*. Joyce's domestic and creative lives fed upon each

other; he adopted books as foster parents and regarded
the books he wrote as his all-but-living children. His
character and his affairs with the world were partly
shaped by the writers with whom he identified in his
youth—Aquinas, Dumas, Dante, Ibsen, Mallarmé,
Shakespeare—and he saw his own life always as material for the book of himself. Like Stephen's Shakespeare, his errors and sufferings were portals of artistic
discovery; "All events brought grist to his mill" (202/
204). And, finally, his books were real gestures toward
the real world; he wrote with the intention of acting
upon those around him, as well as upon his enemies at
home, as Gogarty well understood.[1]

Ulysses, like most novels that are based on the private
lives of artists, solicits our prying. Certainly, autobiographical art in general invites us to follow Stephen's
practice in the library, to seek both the author in his
work and the work in the author. It may be, in fact, that
what we honorifically call the critical temper is really a
kind of nosiness on our part and criticism a sort of for-
malized gossip. For the artist who has written the book
of himself has in the reader a secret sharer, an anonymous
confessor to whom he unburdens himself in devious
ways. And as the reader partakes of the confession, making it his own, he wants to get to know this secret brother, if only out of the need for self-discovery. But this

1. When they met for the last time, in 1909, Joyce warned Gogarty of his intentions, saying, "I must write as I have felt." To
which the latter replied, "I don't care a damn what you say of me
so long as it is literature." (Letter to Stanislaus, August 4, 1909,
Letters 2:231.) But Gogarty then spent most of his life disputing
the status of *Ulysses* as literature. See Gogarty, "They Think They
Know Joyce," *Saturday Review of Literature* 33 (March 18, 1950),
8 ff.

author-reader conspiracy is commonly more a matter of shared affect than shared understanding. The communion is valued even when both reader and author misunderstand what is being shared. Especially in literature, where self-revelation is also a show-and-tell performance, the element of show may overwhelm and disguise what is being told, even from the author. As Nietzsche said, "What someone *is*, begins to be revealed when his talent abates, when he stops showing what he can *do*. Talent . . . is a form of cosmetics."[2] That *Ulysses* is an act of continuous confession is, I hope, self-evident. But what is confessed is so hedged by wit and qualified by style (talent) that few of those who have written about the book have been able to agree on what it is. Fortunately, we have other ways into Joyce's mind, most notably a remarkable collection of sexual fantasies contained in a series of letters to Nora, written in 1909, while Joyce was in Dublin and Nora in Trieste. Like his books, the letters are blatantly confessional, and the erotic fantasy materials they contain are most obviously relevant to *Ulysses*.

Yet, when we turn to Joyce's letters for clues to the books, we encounter an elaborate literary coyness. For even at its simplest, confession is an art in which truth is revealed through those forms of denial we call the techniques of fiction. "The most secret diary," said François Mauriac, "is a literary composition, an arrangement, a fiction."[3] And Joyce's letters, not unexpectedly, are

2. Friedrich Nietzsche, *Beyond Good and Evil*, tr., Marianne Cowan (Chicago: Gateway, 1955), #130.

3. François Mauriac, *La Vie de Racine* (Paris, 1928), p. 4, translated by Maurice Z. Shroder in *Icarus: The Image of the Artist in French Romanticism* (Cambridge: Harvard University Press, 1961), p. 54.

most artistic when most confessional. The 1909 letters to
Nora are virtuoso performances. The sudden alternations
of mood and mask are dazzling. Now he is her lover and
now her child, now her lord and master and again a
guilty supplicant for her love. Seduced himself by the
masterly performance of these letters, Joyce used them
years later as notebooks for his major works.[4] These letters stand midway between the ore of fantasy and the
artifice of the Joycean novel. They are the half-finished
rhetoric of a passionate and guilt-ridden man, being at
once the freest of associations and the most labored of
elaborations. And, while it can be no more than a conjecture, it seems likely that Joyce intended these letters
to survive and be read, out of both the exhibitionistic
joy of telling all and an aggressive delight in parading
his intimacy with Nora before the treacherous fathers
and brothers in Ireland. As Herbert Howarth has pointed
out, Kitty O'Shea's published reminiscences of her life
with Parnell made a great impression on Joyce, and we
may imagine that Joyce, who unfortunately lacked a
mistress who could or would immortalize his private life,
contrived to be his own Kitty O'Shea, preserving his letters in the hope that they might someday come to light,
as it were, by accident.[5]

4. The evidence for this is inferential. There are other ways to
explain the recurrence of the imagery of the letters in later work,
the simplest being that both were written by the same man. But
for Joyce the experiences of 1909 were portals of discovery, and
he undoubtedly used whatever he had at hand, letters included,
in rewriting these discoveries for publication. See David Hayman,
"On Reading Ellmann's Edition: Notes on Joyce's Letters," *James
Joyce Quarterly* 4 (Winter 1967):56–61, for some notes on Joyce's
use of these letters in several of his books, most especially *Finnegans Wake*.

5. Herbert Howarth, *The Irish Writers: Literature and National-*

James and Nora Joyce did not wed legally until 1931.
Yet their special, troubled intimacy can only be described
as marriage. To Nora, James Joyce was always Jim, not
Mr. Joyce, as he was to everyone else, nor just Joyce, the
critic's shorthand for an author's name. In this study,
too, they will be Jim and Nora, as they were to each
other. *Jim*, in addition to being a term of intimacy, is also
the name of someone who was in age, twenty-seven, and
in manner, still a young man. Henceforth in this chapter
I shall use the impersonal *Joyce* only for the Godlike
artist Jim became when he had his singing robes about
him.

✓ ✓ ✓

"A nation exacts penance from those who dared to leave
her payable on their return," Jim reminded himself in
1914 while working on *Exiles.*[6] The play itself is a dramatization of the story of the prodigal son, as revised by
James Joyce. In the biblical story the father took the side
of the prodigal, but, as Jim came to believe, "This is
probably not the way of the world—certainly not in Ireland." As he told his friend Svevo, "It is dangerous to

---

ism, 1880–1940 (New York: Hill and Wang, 1958), pp. 245–288.
See also Katherine O'Shea, *Charles Stewart Parnell. His Love-
Story and Political Life*, 2 vols. (London: Cassell, 1914). About the
letters themselves, it should be pointed out that Jim's letters to
Nora remained in Trieste with Stanislaus when Jim and Nora left
for Zürich in 1915. After Stanislaus's death his wife sold his
"Joyce papers" to Cornell University, where they now reside. It is
significant that while most of Jim's letters to Nora have been
carefully preserved, only one of hers, a short one, has survived.
See the introduction to Robert E. Scholes, *The Cornell Joyce Collection: A Catalogue* (Ithaca: Cornell University Press, 1961).
    6. From his notes to the play (New York: Viking, 1961) p. 114.

leave one's country, but still more dangerous to go back
to it, for then your fellow-countrymen, if they can, will
drive a knife into your heart."[7] And he had reason to
know. In July 1909, after almost five years in Europe,
Jim returned to Ireland accompanied by his son Giorgio,
for the dual purpose of resolving the deadlock over the
publication of *Dubliners* and seeking a professorship at
the newly reorganized National University.[8] His return
was an occasion for the resumption of the old jealousies
and hostilities that had driven him from Ireland to begin
with, or so he believed. Whether Jim's genius and arrogance had made it so or whether there is a meanness in
the Irish character that sets men at odds with each other,
Dublin was enemy territory. The niggling refusal of
George Roberts of Maunsel and Company to publish
Dubliners was the betrayal that had brought him home,
and once there Jim could hardly have hoped to escape
others.

Appropriately enough, close upon Jim's return to his
father's house in an Ireland he later characterized as "the
old sow that eats her farrow," a one-time crony, Vincent
Cosgrave (the Lynch of *Portrait*), undermined Jim's precarious psychic equilibrium with a bit of man-to-man
confidence. Before their elopement, Cosgrave confided,
Nora often lied to Jim about having to work on certain
nights in order to take regular walks along the quays
with himself. The universe Jim had so painfully constructed for himself and Nora from the chaotic fragments
of his childhood suddenly disintegrated. Within an hour

7. Italo Svevo, *James Joyce* (San Francisco: City Lights), p. 4.
8. Most of the details herein about the circumstances surrounding the two 1909 trips to Ireland are gathered from either the letters, which are in volume 2 of Ellmann's edition, or from Ellmann's *JJ*, Chapters 17 and 19.

of this revelation he wrote to her, accusing her of having betrayed him, demanding that she reveal everything that had gone on, and imploring her to "have pity for my poor wretched love" (August 6, 1909, *Letters* 2:231–232).[9] In the midst of his anguish and self-pity ("I am crying for my poor unhappy love"), he took the opportunity to play the voyeur. Cosgrave's revelation had given him an unexpected chance to pry: "You stood with him: He put his arm round you and you lifted your face and kissed him. What else did you do together?" That sleepless night he computed the time that had elapsed between their first love-making in Zürich and the birth of Giorgio. It was nine months and sixteen days. He wrote the following morning, "Is Giorgio my son?" (August 7, pp. 232–233). He recalled with a victim's alertness to clues, "I remember that there was very little blood that night . . ."[10] It was all up for Nora and himself. He had been met and defeated in Ireland, where brotherhood was synonymous with treachery and where a shadowy conspiracy of Dublin enemies still lay in wait for him: "I have been a fool. I thought that all the time you gave yourself only to me and you were dividing your body between me and another. In Dublin here the rumour here is circulated that I have taken the leavings of others. Perhaps they laugh when they see me parading '*my*' son in the streets."

9. The texts of all letters in this chapter are from *The Letters of James Joyce*, vol. 2, ed. Richard Ellmann (see Abbreviations). Subsequent references in text will include only dates and page numbers.

10. The ellipsis after *night* is Ellmann's editorial work. There follows a series of inquiries about the details of her past sexual experiences with Cosgrave and others. Unfortunately, Ellmann could not get permission to print a goodly portion of these letters. Scholars, however, may examine them at Cornell University.

Yet, in the excitement of having discovered himself a
cuckold, his sense of loss was equaled by a passion for
the details of the betrayal: "Tell me. When you were in
that field near the Dodder (on the nights when I was *not*
there) with that other (a 'friend' of mine) were you lying
down when you kissed? Did you place your hand on him
as you did on me in the dark and did you say to him as
as you did to me 'What is it, dear?' "

Though Jim's terror and dismay were quite real, his
characteristically melodramatic sense of himself betrayed
a touch of buffoonery. Having fancied himself the literary Parnell of his people, he suddenly found himself,
not only Parnell betrayed, but Captain O'Shea as well.
And recalling perhaps Keats and the *poètes poitrinaires*
of French Romanticism, he discovered that he was a ter-
minal consumptive: "O, Nora, is there any hope yet of
my happiness? Or is my life to be broken? They say here
that I am in consumption. If I could forget my books and
my children and forget that the girl I loved was false
to me and remember her only as I saw her with the eyes
of my boyish love I would go out of life content. How
old and miserable I feel!"

The next day, in a state of great agitation, Jim told
the story to J. F. Byrne, the Cranly of *Portrait*, who insisted that Cosgrave's story was "a blasted lie" and part
of a plot by Cosgrave and Gogarty to break up Jim's marriage. Predisposed as he was to discover treachery in
these two Dubliners, Jim accepted Byrne's account of the
plot and promptly fell victim to remorse for having
doubted Nora's fidelity and having been so cruelly petu-
lant with her. Yet, he strangely kept silent for twelve days
before begging her forgiveness. His letter of August 19
was penitent and conciliatory. "My darling," he wrote, "I

am terribly upset that you haven't written. Are you ill?
. . . What a worthless fellow I am! But after this I will be
worthy of your love, dearest" (pp. 235–236). His apology
was expressed in terms of infantile adoration as well as
such adolescent posturing as we associate with Richard
Rowan in *Exiles*. "Take me again into your arms. Make
me worthy of you. I will conquer yet and then you will be
at my side." This was also the first of the amatory letters
which, as the correspondence progressed, grew more candid and elemental. But he was already on the true path of
love's progress and only twelve days later concluded a
letter, "There is a place I would like to kiss you now,
a *strange* place, Nora. *Not* on the lips, Nora. Do you know
where?" (August 31, pp. 241–242).

Jim quickly introduced into the correspondence a psychosexual dialectic that was central to his erotic life and
which became increasingly dominant as the correspondence developed—the conflict between the idealized images of a Catholic youth and a new ideal of true beauty,
Nora, that transcended the virginal charm of those images. He wrote on August 21:

You were not in a sense the girl for whom I had dreamed and
written the verses you find now so enchanting. She was perhaps (as I saw her in my imagination) a girl fashioned into a
curious grave beauty by the culture of generations before her,
the woman for whom I wrote poems like 'Gentle lady' or
'Thou leanest to the shell of night'. But then I saw that the
beauty of your soul outshone that of my verses. There was
something in you higher than anything I had put into them.
(pp. 236–237) [11]

11. While Jim was gone, Nora was at last reading his *Chamber
Music* poems. He noted archly in the same letter, "It took you five
years to find them out."

There was a private irony in this praise that Nora could hardly have caught. The lady in "Thou leanest to the shell of night" may have been a "curious grave beauty," but she was also among the first of James Joyce's urinary heroines, and as subsequent letters make clear, Nora too partook of the urethral potency her husband projected onto the objects of his affection.[12]

In a previous study of these letters, Mary T. Reynolds has shown that Jim's carefully wrought praise of Nora's higher spirituality was a way of patronizing his peasant wife and mollifying her anger.[13] It was also a standard preliminary gesture in a courtship ritual he was forever acting out with her. For example, his lapidary similitude of himself to an opal, whose colors had been imprinted by her ethereal charms, was a sort of foreplay, or setup for a sexual coup: "Do you know what a pearl is and what an opal is? My soul when you came sauntering to me first through those sweet summer evenings was beautiful but with the pale passionless beauty of a pearl. Your love has passed through me and now I feel my mind something like an opal, that is, full of strange uncertain hues and colours, of warm lights and quick shadows and of broken music" (August 21, pp. 236–237). The punchline had a broken music of a different sort: "Do you remember the day I asked you indifferently 'Where will I meet you this evening?' and you said without thinking 'Where will you meet me, is it? You'll meet me in bed, I suppose'."

Jim was reminding her, as he did often, that the first

12. For a confirmation of my reading of this poem, see William York Tindall's edition of *Chamber Music* (New York: Columbia University Press, 1954). See also Chapter 5 here.

13. Mary T. Reynolds, "Joyce and Nora: The Indispensable Countersign," *Sewanee Review* 72 (Winter 1964):37–38 *et passim*.

sexual overtures in their relationship had been hers and
that any he might now make were only in accord with her
own erotic desires. But this antiphony of Romantic "enchantment of the heart" and straightforward sexuality
was not just tactical. It was the condition of Jim's erotic
life in 1909 and represented, in terms of his work, the unstable coexistence of Stephen Dedalus and Leopold Bloom
already in him, some four and one-half years before the
completion of *Portrait* and the beginning of *Ulysses*.

Once the floodgates of Eros had been opened, his letters became increasingly direct and bodily. On the twen-
ty-second he wrote to her: "I think always of you. When
I go to bed at night it is a kind of torture for me. I will
not write on this page what fills my mind, the very madness of desire. I see you in a hundred poses, grotesque,
shameful, virginal, languorous. Give yourself to me,
dearest, all, all when we meet. All that is holy, hidden
from others, you must give to me freely. I wish to be lord
of your body and soul" (p. 239).

Jim's Catholic education was now proving a boon to
his erotic imagination. The Church that had repressed his
sexuality in his youth now provided the language of his
desublimation and the appropriate sacred objects upon
which to practice it in fantasy. Ultimate erotic experiences, such as those he was imagining as he wrote these
letters, involve the breaking of taboos and the profanation
of what is holy and hidden. He endowed Nora with attributes of the forbidden mother, whose avatar in the
Church is the Blessed Virgin. In the same letter he recalled to her "the three adjectives I have used in *The Dead*
in speaking of your body. They are these: 'musical and
strange and perfumed'." While these are not customary
attributes of the Blessed Virgin Mary, they were qualities

the young Joyce had for some time associated with an erotically charged type of her, a figure whom I call the virgin-temptress.[14] The sexual consummation Jim was setting up for his return would be a ritual event, an anti-mass in which the body of Nora would yield up, not just its own secrets, but those of the most inviolable Virgin as well. To that end he begged her to array herself for the feast of love. "Adorn yourself for me, dearest. Be beautiful and happy and loving and provoking, full of memories, full of cravings, when we meet."

These demands on Nora, like many yet to come (such as the exhortation to drink plenty of cocoa in order to develop her breasts), were the promptings of a would-be Pygmalion. Jim was not wholly pleased with the woman he had married and set out to remake her in accordance with his own sense of the feminine ideal, ill-defined as it was. He would be to her not only son and husband, but father and creator-God as well. He noted approvingly that William Blake had married an uneducated woman, Catherine Boucher, and suggested in a lecture in Trieste that Blake had perhaps wanted "the soul of his beloved

14. See Joyce's two essays on James Clarence Mangan in *CW*, especially pp. 78 and 182–183. In the latter he describes this figure in Mangan's poetry: "This figure which he adores recalls the spiritual yearnings and the imaginary loves of the Middle Ages, and Mangan has placed his lady in a world full of melody, of lights and perfumes, a world that grows fatally to frame every face that the eyes of a poet have gazed on with love. There is only one chivalrous idea, only one male devotion, that lights up the faces of Vittoria Colonna, Laura, and Beatrice, just as the bitter disillusion and the self-disdain that end the chapter are one and the same." See also Chapter 4 of this study and Harry Stone, "'Araby' and the Writings of James Joyce," in *James Joyce, Dubliners: Text, Criticism, and Notes*, eds., Robert Scholes and A. Walton Litz (New York: Viking, 1969), pp. 344–367.

to be entirely a slow and painful creation of his own."[15] In *Exiles*, Robert Hand acknowledges to Richard Rowan, "She [Bertha Rowan] is yours, your work," and, "You have made her all that she is" (*E*, 62, 67).

The sources of Jim's dissatisfaction with Nora and his consequent attempts to refashion her were many. As Mary Reynolds has pointed out in her study of these letters, Nora presented obstacles to her husband's happiness that were all but insuperable. She had no sympathy whatever with the aesthetic side of his nature and steadfastly refused to read his books; she made no concessions to his intellectual superiority and refused to flatter his sense of his uniqueness among men; she was rude with him, both in public and in private, and, like Molly Bloom, kept a dirty house.

These were real and serious problems. But during these years of Jim's sexual renaissance an even more urgent problem lay in his sense of his own sexual inadequacy, which he tended to blame on the insufficiency of Nora's feminine image.[16] He found her "little body" sometimes

15. The lecture on Blake was given in March 1912 at the Università Popolare Triestina. The manuscript, saved by Stanislaus, is incomplete, but what we have of it is reprinted in *CW*, pp. 214–222. The entire passage is worth quoting: "Like many other men of great genius, Blake was not attracted to cultured and refined women. Either he preferred to drawing-room graces and an easy and broad culture . . . the simple woman, of hazy and sensual mentality, or, in his unlimited egoism, he wanted the soul of his beloved to be entirely a slow and painful creation of his own, freeing and purifying daily under his very eyes, the demon (as he says) hidden in the cloud."

16. This anxiety about his capacity to satisfy her is more or less acknowledged in the letters of December 3 and December 16, but unfortunately in passages which Ellmann was unable to publish. But this anxiety may be easily inferred from what is in print.

unexciting (September 7, p. 249) and urged her variously
to adorn herself for him (August 22, p. 239) and to wear
black underwear on his return "to provoke my desire of
you" (September 7, pp. 248–250). He complained of her
"little girl's breasts" (September 7) and importuned her
to drink cocoa in order to develop them. He thought her
plain and lacking in style and chastened her angrily,
"You have no right to be ugly and slovenly at your age
and I hope now you will pay me the compliment of looking well" (September 7, pp. 251–252; not the same letter
quoted above). During his second trip to Dublin that
same year Jim undertook to outfit Nora in his own version of feminine *haute couture*. He promised to send her
"a splendid set of sable furs, cap, stole and muff" (October 25, pp. 254–255), which he later changed to "a grey
squirrel cap with violets at the side and a long broad flat
stole of grey squirrel and a beige granny muff of the same
on a steel chain, both lined with violet satin" (November
1, pp. 258–259). He sent her gloves of reindeer skin,
which, he told her, "should be warm, nearly as warm as
certain districts of your body, Butterfly." Needless to
say, this was not the proper attire for the curious grave
beauty of *Chamber Music*. After five years of marriage,
the aristocratic ingénue of Jim's adolescent imagination
had at last given way to a new image of the ideal woman,
Venus in furs.

This Venus, as in Sacher-Masoch's novel, is the proper
sexual complement to the masochist. Her black undergar-
ments, heroic breasts, and opulent furs (complete with
"granny muff") are psychological clichés, being fetishes
or imitation penises, which render their possessor a more
enchanting object of love as well as a more convincing

figure of authority.[17] The fetish in Jim's case brought together the erotic and aggressive currents of his instinctual life and was the symbol in which love and power were nicely reconciled. It appears, then, that Jim's insistence that Nora develop her breasts and be "a full happy loving woman" (September 7, pp. 248–250) was paradoxically a vehicle for the antithetical unconscious wish that she grow a penis. But, then, Jim's image of womanhood itself was paradoxical, being an ambiguous array of male and female qualities. The fetish itself is a paradox by definition, since it both is and is not the female penis.[18] The black underclothes, for example, can satisfy two principles of mental functioning at once: the reality principle, by not denying what is consciously known, that they conceal nothing unusual, and the fantasy-oriented pleasure principle, by hinting provocatively at a surprise yet to be revealed.[19] (As Bloom reflects in "Nausikaa," "Say a woman loses a charm with every pin she takes out" 362/368.) And black is a favorite color of those who love "drawers" because it is both semiopaque and psychologically assertive. Breasts, too, by virtue of their general convexity and the assertive protrusiveness of their nipples, may be bearers of phallic

17. Of course such fetishistic charms play a part in the sexual arousal of all men. Only those for whom this phallic accessory has become the sole erotic object, and the woman who bears it an unfortunate auxiliary presence are properly fetishists. In later years Jim's fetishism did reach this stage, but in 1909 it was still undeveloped. See Chapter 5.

18. See Sigmund Freud, "Fetishism," *SE*, vol. 21. See also Otto Fenichel, *The Psychoanalytic Theory of Neurosis* (New York: Norton, 1945), pp. 131, 145, 341–344.

19. See Sigmund Freud, "Formulations on the Two Principles of Mental Functioning," *SE*, vol. 12.

significance to the unconscious. And, finally, velvet and fur, as Freud pointed out in his paper on fetishism, are imitations of the pubic hair which may or may not harbor a woman's penis.[20]

The fetish has a multitude of important psychosexual ramifications. In rendering a woman sexually desirable by redesigning her in the image of a man, the fetish may be the covert expression of a latent (or even manifest) homosexuality. Such a latent homosexuality in fact played a vital role in Jim's sexual and fantasy life. While it did not betray itself much beyond simple fetishism in the letters, it did develop in extraordinarily complex ways in *Portrait, Exiles,* and *Ulysses.*[21]

20. The standard Freudian interpretation of the fetish is that it is a defense against castration anxiety. The childhood discovery that women lack a penis is commonly understood by the male child as a sign of female castration and arouses in him anxiety about the fate of his own genitals. Not uncommonly, this anxiety is aroused during the oedipal crisis. At a time when the child perceives itself in a struggle with the father for the mother's love, he may imagine castration to be the father's way of dealing with persistent rivals and disobedient wives. In the course of "normal" sexual development, the child's oedipal wishes are successfully repressed, his castration anxiety is conquered by the many reassurances the real world provides, and women's bodies and genitals become proper and provoking sexual objects. But where this developmental process is incomplete or disturbed the anxiety may remain and become a barrier to normal sexual activity. The fetish, by being an illusory female penis, may reduce this anxiety that renders some men impotent at the sight or thought of female genitals. Needless to say, only in psychosis, where mental functioning is wholly divorced from reality, is such an illusion really possible. But the simulacrum of the female phallus, or the subtle hint of a possible phallic presence, is often sufficiently reassuring to liberate otherwise anxiety-inhibited sexuality. See Sigmund Freud, "The Dissolution of the Oedipus Complex," *SE*, vol. 19.

21. The most thorough account thus far of homosexuality in Joyce's work is Sheldon Brivic, "James Joyce: From Stephen to

The fetish, then, betrays a powerful ambivalence in the choice of a sexual object, and the woman who is in fantasy the object of such ambivalent and anxious longing may be an androgynous figure. A common version of this bisexual woman is a figure we will meet time and again in our reading of Jim's books—the phallic mother.[22] The phallic mother in Jim's imagination was a parental figure whose offices were ambiguously maternal and paternal. She was protective and punitive; she could love, and she could chastise. She was sometimes armed with a long, thin instrument of discipline,[23] though ordinarily her phallic accessory was a "charm" and was either a part of her body or an item of adornment. As she appears in *Ulysses,* she is a fitting counterpart to the book's bisexual males—the creator-God Stephen imagines Shakespeare to have been and the epicene figure Bloom imagines himself to be in "Circe." Circe herself, Bella/o Cohen, is the phallic mother *par excellence,* though all of Joyce's women partake of his bisexuality in one way or another.

The object, then, of outfitting Nora in furs was three-fold. Jim intended, for one thing, to propitiate her through the presentation of phallic gifts. As such, his gesture was a symbolic proferral of potency and constituted a graceful show of submission. A second, closely related aim,

---

Bloom," in *Psychoanalysis and Literary Process,* ed., Frederick Crews (Cambridge: Winthrop, 1970).

22. For a note on the ubiquity of the phallic mother as a fantasy object in certain psychosexual dispositions, see Robert C. Bak, "The Phallic Woman: The Ubiquitous Fantasy in Perversions," *The Psychoanalytic Study of the Child,* vol. 23 (New York: International Universities Press, 1968), pp. 15–36.

23. See the letter from Jim to Nora, September 2, 1909, *Letters* 2:242–243.

of course, was to recreate Nora as a sexually provoking, subtly masculine figure. And, finally, through these gifts Jim could fancy himself the fabulous artificer of his wife, Daedalus as couturier, the God of creation, above his handiwork, paring *her* fingernails.

A byproduct of Jim's passion for outfitting Nora was considerable expertise in the matter of women's clothing, as he demonstrated impressively in the "Nausikaa" episode of *Ulysses*. Indeed, he might have bragged with Carlyle's sartorial philosopher Teufelsdröckh, "As Montesquieu wrote a *Spirit of Laws*, so could I write a *Spirit of Clothes*." Nor was his concept of feminine fashion out of line with conventions of style that obtained in his time and remain, somewhat muted, in our own. What, after all, identifies the lady of fashion but her array of fetishes—earrings, furs, pendants, long hair either hanging over the shoulders or piled conically upon the head, and high, hard, and pointed breasts, made possible by the magic of the merry-widow corset?[24] For surely the ritual adornment of feminine high fashion is the sublimation into clothing of the desire for self-exhibition, though this exhibition of one's "possessions" (all of which are currently fashionable and appropriately expensive) is the exhibition of what one hasn't got—the penis.

✓ ✓ ✓

A sentimental journey is a return to the place of one's childhood, and, regardless of whether that childhood has been delightful or terrifying, the place is magical, for it

24. As a happy consequence of the women's liberation movement, such body-molding equipment is currently passé. It will be back.

is associated with one's first and most passionate love affair, the affair with the mother. A sentimental journey is a return to the repressed, a calculated expedition to the buried past by an ego that is willing to undergo the titanic sense of love and loss that is evoked by the landscape of childhood. For all but the most armored of characters, home means tears, and for the exile who returns in the face of threats and prohibitions this regression may provoke great and self-destructive emotions. The sentimental journey is a psychic *reculer pour mieux sauter*; a search for renewal or rebirth or, most accurately, renourishment through recollected love.

Jim's return to Dublin in 1909 might have been such a sentimental journey had it not been spoiled in advance by the knowledge of what lay waiting for him: the meanness of the city, the chaos and squalor of his father's household, the treachery of his former friends, and the ghost of the mother at whose deathbed he would not pray. The Cosgrave affair confirmed his apprehensions; there would be no renewal in Dublin, no rebirth or renourishment, only treachery and oppression. But Jim was not without alternative paths of regression. He turned a visit to Nora's family in Galway into a pilgrimage to *her* childhood. He stayed with Nora's mother and had her sing for him "The Lass of Aughrim," a song he had first heard from Nora and one he associated, as in "The Dead," with her secret life before and apart from him (August 26, pp. 240–241). He asked for childhood photos of her and was disappointed to find that her family had none. He visited the house on Augustine Street where she had lived with her grandmother and planned, as he wrote her, to return to it in the guise of a prospective buyer "in order to see the room you slept in." This trip to Galway was so fruitful that Jim proposed to make it again with Nora. "Who knows, darling," he wrote, "but next year you and I may come here. You will take me from place to place and the image of your girlhood will purify again my life."

This plan to visit her childhood bedroom, followed by the vision of self-purification through the image of her girlhood, was the symbolic culmination of his return home. For if the return to Ireland was a return to the land of his childhood, the journey to Nora's bedroom in Galway was no less than a symbolic return to the very center and source of things, the womb, in order to be reborn. But Jim's fantasy of purification through Nora's girlhood implied, not only his sense of himself as Nora's child, but his identification with her. It implied the wish, not only to be born _through_ his wife, but to be reborn _as_ her as well.[25] And, radical though it may seem, this conclusion is consistent with the general fantasy structure of the letters. In fact, this fantasy was only one of many reconciliation fantasies which proposed to end the separation between them by making them one spirit and one flesh or, in Stephen's language, consubstantial.[26] In a typical scenario of reconciliation, Jim fantasized Nora's womb to be the agent of union:

25. Evidence in this letter that he wished to be born _as_ Nora is admittedly tenuous. However, such a reading of the letter is well in keeping with Joyce's transsexual and bisexual fantasies, as well as with the restitution project of preserving his lost mother through introjection of her image and identification with it. See Chapter 6.

26. No doubt, Jim's sense of their spiritual consubstantiality was delightfully confirmed by his discovery that her grandmother's house was on _Augustine_ Street, with its auspicious echo of his own middle name.

Guide me, my saint, my angel. Lead me forward. *Everything* that is noble and exalted and deep and true and moving in what I write comes, I believe, from you. O take me into your soul of souls and then I will become indeed the poet of my race. I feel this, Nora, as I write it. My body soon will penetrate into yours, O that my soul could too! O that I could nestle in your womb like a child born of your flesh and blood, be fed by your blood, sleep in the warm secret gloom of your body! (September 5, pp. 247–248)

In the Galway fantasy Nora's childhood bedroom was the womb to which Jim would return in order to be reborn without sin or guilt. In this letter Nora's body itself was that promised land where he longed not only to return but to remain as an embryonic appendage of her flesh. He would be her child *and* be in all ways consubstantial with her. How better, after all, to secure her constant presence than to be literally flesh of her flesh, and how better to keep watch over her virtue (or be delightfully on hand when it gave way) than from within?

Nora's otherness was always problematic for Jim, and all the more so when compounded by the alien temper of her mind and their half-a-continent separation in 1909. His many fantasies of permanent reconciliation were primarily autoerotic and tended toward the forms of Dedalian narcissism. In his more active moods he entertained Pygmalion fantasies in which he proposed to bring an end to Nora's otherness by recreating her as his work, a product of his own artifice. One symptom of this tendency in their epistolary relationship was Jim's apparent desire to write both ends of the correspondence. He coached her incessantly on what she must write and how she must provoke him, as though it were his intention to dictate letters to himself through Nora and be, in effect, both halves of one androgynous angel. These attempts to recreate Nora as his work or to dictate the letters she must write him were active efforts to resolve the problem of separation and otherness, while the "take me into your soul of souls" aria proposed a passive solution to the same problem. This scheme for dissolving the self into the other (the maternal matrix) also recalls Stephen, for it is the passive version of Stephen's aggressive fantasy of transcending reality by incorporating it. Where Stephen would forge the conscience of his race in the smithy of *his soul*, Jim, in this letter, would become the poet of his race by an infusion of Nora's peasant wisdom in the cradle of *her* "soul."

But, beyond these few observations, Jim's letters to Nora do not yield definitive conclusions about his psychic strategies for managing the anxiety aroused by the "other." That the threat was there is beyond question. The dominant theme of all his thought and work was his distrust of a hostile reality. Jim regarded all relationships with suspicion. He saw treachery implicit in friendship and betrayal implicit in love. His attempts to deal internally with these threats often manifested themselves in characteristically oral fantasies, though of a puzzling variety of active and passive forms. Perhaps it was that in the face of a hostile masculine reality Jim's anxieties gave rise to fantasies of active incorporative mastery, while in the face of uncertain love he entertained the wish to submit and be absorbed. And, then again, it may be also that these alternatives, to swallow or be swallowed, were ultimately interchangeable. What is important for the reader of *Ulysses* is the multitude of ways this defensive orality ramifies itself through the book, from Stephen's theories of Shakespeare's art to Bloom's erotic life and millenarian fantasies to the cosmic-visual love feast of "Nausikaa." For Bloom eating is an act of love and love a matter of eating, while for Stephen eating is the assertion of power, just as his fear of being eaten is a source of terror. We may see the dialectic of Joycean orality in microcosm by placing side by side Stephen's bat poem and one of Bloom's reflections on the deliciousness of love. Stephen: "He comes, pale vampire/ Mouth to my mouth" (131/132). Bloom: "Lovers: yum yum" (370/377).

✦ ✦ ✦

Throughout the correspondence we find a good deal of hostility lurking beneath the real expressions and the obligatory forms of love and lust. One of its gentler expressions is in the condescension implicit in the overblown rhetoric of adoration. When Jim's language of idealized passion missed its proper tone, it betrayed his frustration over being unable to move a recalcitrant object. His worship was in part a manner of impatient coaxing, and he often addressed Nora as though she were a child. But Nora was not malleable; she would not easily be removed or remade. Perhaps his final judgment of her stubbornness is expressed in an allusion to Shaw's *Pygmalion* in *Finnegans Wake*: "You cannot make a limousine lady out of a hillman minx" (*FW*, 376), though a limousine lady, to be sure, was not exactly what Jim was after.

Jim's hostility surfaced toward the end of his first trip. While Jim was in Dublin, his secret adolescent love, Mary Sheehy, married his old school chum, Tom Kettle, and Jim discussed with Kettle the possibility of their vis-

iting Trieste on their honeymoon. In anticipation of a
visit that was never made, Jim wrote to Nora, "We will
try to entertain them the best way we can and I am sure
that my warm-hearted girl will be glad to give pleasure
to two people who are at the entrance of their life together. Will you not, dearest?" (September 5, pp. 247–
248) He instructed her to put the house in order and to
see that her dresses were right. Two days later, September
7, in two very anxious letters, he chided her again on her
appearance (pp. 248–252). He complained of her "little
girl's breasts" and called her disparagingly a "little curious Galway girl." "Have you any nice clothes now?" he
asked. "Is your hair a good colour or is it full of cinders?"
And, in a blunt attack already noted here, he whined,
"You have no right to be ugly and slovenly at your age
and I hope you will pay me the compliment of looking
well."

On the eve of their being reunited, then, his anxieties
were greatest and his hostility impossible to disguise.
And, while it isn't precisely clear why these anxieties
surfaced just when they did, a number of possibilities
suggest themselves. For one thing, Jim was returning to
exile and poverty in Trieste. Though he felt that he had
been driven from Ireland in 1904, it nevertheless had
remained his spiritual homeland and he was undoubtedly
loath to leave.[27] Secondly, the marriage of Mary Sheehy
to Tom Kettle must have been a major disappointment
to him. Mary Sheehy, whom he immortalized in his work
variously as Mangan's sister, Emma Clery (the shadowy
E. C. of *Portrait*), Beatrice Justice, and even Gerty Mac-
Dowell, was the girl "fashioned into a curious grave

27. See Richard Ellmann, "James Joyce, Irish European," *Tri-
Quarterly* 8 (Winter 1967):199–204.

beauty by the culture of generations before her." He carried on an imaginary affair with her for years after his elopement with Nora, an affair that can be traced in his work from *Stephen Hero* through *Exiles*, where it finally expires as a serious infatuation. *Exiles*, indeed, hints tantalizingly at a secret exchange of letters between them, though it is doubtful that such an exchange actually took place. The Emma Clery we encounter in *Stephen Hero* is not the girl for epistolary flirtations with married men. But seeing her may have been one of Jim's prime reasons for the trip to Dublin, and the disappointment of losing her to one of the ubiquitous brothers may have been one more source of bitterness for him.

Defeated in flirtation, if not exactly in love, Jim had only the prospect of returning to his curious Galway girl with the cinders in her hair. And on the eve of his long-awaited sexual rendezvous with Nora, the impossibility of realizing the erotic fantasies of the past months may have been on his mind. He had made his case for Eros all too well from a distance and now would be called upon to produce. And there were, in addition to his mysterious incapacities, the obvious limitations placed upon free sexuality by the crowd of six people that would now be living in their small Triestine flat.[28]

But the limitations set upon sexuality by his incapacities, by a residuum of feelings for another woman, and by the oppressive physical and financial circumstances in which he lived were not things that Jim could easily acknowledge. For in all cases he was the culprit. So, responsibility for the dissatisfaction he anticipated upon

28. Jim was returning to Trieste with sister Eva. This *ménage à six* would now include Jim, Nora, Stanislaus, Eva, Giorgio, and Lucia, a hearty Irish household.

returning was displaced onto Nora. And even that hostility was hedged by anxiety, for Jim, however he might have resented Nora, could not do without her. Thus, in his last letter he upbraided her for her shabby clothes, her hair, her slovenly appearance, and then, as in the past, attempted to atone with a perfunctory expression of passion, though this time his protestations were ambivalently passionate and angry: "I am excited all day. Love is a cursed nuisance especially when coupled with lust also. It is terribly provoking to think that you are lying waiting for me at this moment at the other end of Europe while I am here. I am *not* in a *nice* mood just now."

The womb to which he longed to return while safely away from it had undergone a Circean transformation into a crowded household, a demanding wife, an angry brother, and another hopeless round of battles against poverty. The warm, secret gloom of Nora's flesh promised more gloom than warm secrets. At the end, this last correspondence of his trip broke down in a jumble of scattered purposes and objectless anxieties:

Have some appearance of money when I go back. Will you make me a nice cup of black coffee in a nice small cup? Ask that sniveling girl Globocnik how to do it. Make a good salad, will you? Another thing don't bring onions or garlic into the house. You will think I am going to have a child. It is not that but I don't know what to do I am so upset and excited.

My dear, dear, dear little Nora goodbye now for tonight. I wrote you every night. Now I am not *too* bad: and I am bringing you my gift. O, Lord, how excited I am!

Then, with his business apparently in order, Jim set out for Trieste on September 9 with Giorgio and Eva in tow. The post at the National University had not materialized, but there was an agreement with Maunsel and Company for *Dubliners* to appear the following spring. As Jim wrote naïvely to Stanislaus just before his return, "I will make £ 500 out of *Dubliners* if they sell 12,000 copies" (September 7, pp. 250–251).

✦ ✦ ✦

Jim returned with a unique gift for Nora, a necklace bearing an ivory tablet on which was inscribed the motto, "Love is unhappy/ When Love is away." Upon seeing it, Stanislaus reportedly remarked, "So is love's brother." But love was unhappy at home as well. Life in Trieste was confining, and current prospects offered little hope of alleviating the poverty in which the Joyces were living. Thus Jim, by now a prototype of the commercial traveler Leopold Bloom, embarked on a return trip to Dublin on October 18. We'll never have a complete account of his motives for leaving so close upon his return. Ellmann's authoritative voice is laconic on the matter. We know that business was on Jim's mind; he hoped to make money by setting up Ireland's first commercial cinema, the Volta Theatre. In typical Bloomian fashion, the venture quickly proved a failure. But, as on the previous visit to Dublin, business occupied only his days, and sexual fantasies once again invaded his nights. He and Nora quickly resumed their erotic dialogue, a correspondence that ran this time for more than two months, from October 20 to December 26.

Unlike the first letters, these were precipitated by no convenient betrayal. There were issues enough between the Joyces, and Jim's first long letter, on October 25, broke into them *in medias res*. Just before his departure Nora had reproached him, calling him an imbecile for having returned home late one night (October 25, pp. 254–255). She subsequently wrote a letter in which she had called his love into question and threatened, it seems, to leave him and return with the children to Ireland. Jim responded to this challenge with all the weapons in his arsenal of dramatic poses: reproaches, protestations of love, avowals of dependence, and promises of presents to come. "Do you think now of the words on your ivory necklet?" he asked reproachfully. And he warned her not to fret, for "if you do you will ruin my chances of doing anything." It was in this letter, too, that Jim promised Nora the "splendid set of sable furs," those archetypal Joycean gifts that were both peace offerings and preludes to masochism. Jim concluded this letter with a series of shallow confidences and gentle reprimands. He reproached her in a tone of controlled condescension that was designed to both chide and appease. "You dear strange little girl! . . . I shall never be tired of you, dearest, if you will only be a *little* more polite." Then, the usual fine sentiments about *his* art and *her* spiritual nobility which by now were obligatory clichés: "My dear true good little Nora do not write again doubtfully of me. You are my only love. You have me completely in your power. I *know* and *feel* that if I am to write anything fine or noble in the future I shall do so only by listening at the doors of your heart."

Plainly, the conflicts and frustrations that marked the first group of letters were still with him. Indeed, they now asserted themselves with greater authority than before. The economic and emotional constraints of life in Trieste were more tyrannical than ever, and old conflicts renewed themselves on a higher level of intensity.

Jim's struggles with Nora were always struggles with himself as well. Her "treachery" was a product of his own connivance and was born of his constant need for an oedipal enemy—a threatening father or a crafty, dangerous brother. Moreover, as in his books, this oedipal drama in Jim's letters was bound up with social and political beliefs. On October 27 he wrote that he was heartily sick of Ireland and happy that Giorgio would grow up a foreigner speaking another tongue. The current source of his disgust and anger was the clergy, the "adulterous priests" of the Irish Catholic church: "I loathe Ireland and the Irish. They themselves stare at me in the street though I was born among them. Perhaps they read my hatred of them in my eyes. I see nothing on every side of me but the image of the adulterous priest and his servants and of sly deceitful women" (October 27, pp. 255–257).

In Jim's salacious imagination lechery was endemic to the Irish priesthood; he imagined that the church "fathers" were conspiring continually to appropriate sex for themselves alone. The figures of the lecherous priest and the priest who is attractive to women appear everywhere in his work. In *Stephen Hero* and *Portrait* Emma Clery carries on a shadowy liaison with Father Moran, while in *Ulysses* Gerty MacDowell has a secret crush on Father Conroy, and Molly recalls with pleasure the voyeuristic interest her confessor, Father Corrigan, took in her activities. And even Bloom reflects on the clergy in "Nausikaa." "The tree of the forbidden priest. O father, will you? Let me be the first to" (368/375). The identity of the "sly deceitful women" of Jim's complaint is obscure. He may have had specifically in

mind the curious, grave beauties of his youth, though
no doubt this complaint against female deceit was also
a warning to Nora, whose loyalty had not yet been sufficiently tested. But, of course, he saw deceit as being in
the very nature of a woman's love. Where Nora was concerned, Jim's oedipal anxieties were manifested in their
simplest and most naked form, for the imperatives of his
psychosexual fantasy life called for Nora to play the part
of the unfaithful mother who is carrying on a secret affair with another man. In this letter of the twenty-seventh,
Jim charged Nora with having conspired against him with
the fathers of the Church:

A few days before I left Trieste I was walking with you in the
Via Stadion. . . . A priest passed us and I said to you 'Do you
not find a kind of repulsion or disgust at the sight of one of
those men?' You answered a little shortly and drily 'No, I
don't'. You see, I remember all these small things. Your reply
hurt me and silenced me. It and other similar things you have
said to me linger a long time in my mind. Are you with me,
Nora, or are you secretly against me?

Where he lacked a real Cosgrave to provoke his anxiety
and spur his sexual imagination, Jim simply invented
one. Indeed, he invented many. Suspicion was a necessary precondition to his sexual arousal. As he has Richard Rowan admit to Robert Hand in *Exiles*: ". . . in the
very core of my ignoble heart I longed to be betrayed by
you and by her—in the dark, in the night—secretly,
meanly, craftily. By you, my best friend, and by her. I
longed for that passionately and ignobly, to be dishon-
ored for ever in love and in lust . . ." (*E*, 70). In light
of this confession by a Joycean alter ego and the corrob-
orating evidence of the Prezioso affair,[29] Jim's admoni-

29. See Ellmann, *JJ*, pp. 327–328.

tion to Nora not to betray him assumes the appearance of a sly suggestion that she might consider it.

Jim included in this letter the now-familiar pleas and complaints. In a hostile world, amid an ignorant, treacherous, and priest-ridden people, she was his solace. Yet she continually disappointed him; she neither hated the priesthood sufficiently nor loved *Madame Butterfly* enough. "I am a jealous, lonely, dissatisfied, proud man," he complained. "Why are you not more patient with me and kinder with me?" He felt abandoned; he could not live without her; they must go through life side by side; she must let him love her in his own way. He added, as something of a postscript, that she must continue to drink her cocoa and that he was sending her some Donegal tweeds for a dress and was inquiring about a set of "some very nice furs."

But, while a troubled Eros reigned in Dublin, a tyrannical necessity held power in Trieste. Nora and Stanislaus were trying to maintain a crowded household on the meagerest of resources and were beset by creditors.[30] The landlord threatened eviction, and Stanislaus had to wire Jim for money to meet the peremptory crisis. And Jim had little, for he was grandly loaning money about in Dublin or buying gifts for Nora or spending it in support of John Joyce's household while the latter was in the hospital. Nora, for her part, had had her fill of crises, of poverty, of her husband's absences, of his mad commercial schemes and odd sexual demands. She wrote angrily, as she apparently had before, that she was preparing to leave him. His response, on November 18, was appropriately abject and, when viewed from the right perspective, highly comical. Like so much of his behavior

30. See Ellmann, *JJ*, pp. 315 ff.

toward her, the letter was tactically masochistic; Jim intended to arrive at a position of strength through the show of weakness. The letter bore no salutation:

> I dare not address you tonight by any familiar name.
>
> All day, since I read your letter this morning, I have felt like a mongrel dog that has received a lash across the eyes. I have been awake now for two whole days and I wandered about the streets like some filthy cur whose mistress had cut him with her whip and hunted him from her door.
>
> You write like a queen. As long as I live I shall always remember the quiet dignity of that letter, its sadness and scorn, and the utter humiliation it caused me.
>
> I have lost your esteem. I have worn down your love. Leave me then. Take away your children from me to save them from the curse of my presence. Let me sink back again into the mire I came from. Forget me and my empty words. Go back to your own life and let me go alone to my ruin. It is wrong for you to live with a vile beast like me or to allow your children to be touched by my hands. (November 18, pp. 265–266)

Jim was learning that the best way to manage domestic crises was not through reason but through art. His characteristic strategy with Nora was to attack, to atone, then to turn the apology into a reproach. This letter was simply the atonement phase of a larger cycle of emotional manipulation.[31]

The game Jim and Nora played in these letters was based on the mutual manipulation of guilt. Jim had learned well one lesson of childhood, that in the marketplace of family love, weakness is strength. To be sure, the filial and masochistic attitudes on which his plea

31. Mary Reynolds, after reading these letters in manuscript at Cornell, has pointed out, "These passages are written in Joyce's most passionless handwriting, small and neat, carefully centered on the page" ("Joyce and Nora," p. 54).

rested were ingenuous; James Joyce as guilty child, as whipped dog, as "cursed presence" and vile beast, are Byronic overstatements of the real stuff of his inner life. But his willingness to exploit this inner life for manipulative ends makes these letters a great deal like his books. The open display of his guilt, of his dependence, of his masochism, properly elaborated with the language of Romantic self-loathing, was designed to defuse Nora's anger. "Leave me," he implored her. "It is a degradation and a shame for you to live with a low wretch like me. Act bravely and leave me. You have given me the finest things in this world but you were only casting pearls before swine." Finally, parlaying his guilt into a gesture of grand nonsense, he canonized her in language that could only provoke her amusement. "If you leave me I shall live for ever with your memory, holier than God to me. I shall pray to your name."

This comic scenario turned out to be unnecessary. On the heels of Nora's angry letter came two letters of apology. Nora seems to have anticipated her husband's gesture of self-reproach and tried to beat him to it. She, too, understood the power of self-abasement. "She asks me," Jim answered her in a peculiar third-person address, "to try to forget the ignorant Galway girl that came across my life and says I am too kind to her" (November 19, pp. 266–267). He returned the gesture, shame for shame. "Foolish good-hearted girl! Does she not see what a worthless treacherous fool I am? Her love for me perhaps blinds her to it." He confessed that he had just made another of his pilgrimages to her past, this time to Finn's Hotel, where she had lived and worked as a chambermaid upon coming to Dublin. Like the first sentimental journey to Galway, this visit was a time for tears. He imagined Nora in her maidenly innocence and wept:

Why do I cry? I cry because it is so sad to think of her moving about that room, eating little, simply dressed, simple-mannered and watchful, and carrying always with her in her secret heart the little flame which burns up the souls and bodies of men.

Though I cannot prove it, that little flame in her secret heart sounds to me suspiciously like a euphemism for the clitoris that Jim made a great to do over in the unpublished passages and letters. But, more significantly, this paean in praise of Nora's dead youth turned into a funeral oration. He spoke to her of herself in the third person and past tense. "I cry too with pity for her that she should have chosen such poor ignoble love as mine: and with pity for myself that I was not worthy to be loved by her." Yet Nora was not dead, nor, in fact, had she left him. Jim was memorializing, in his most passionless handwriting, a nonexistent situation.[32]

There is no way of knowing if Jim understood what he was up to in this letter, but it would appear that he was rehearsing with Nora another loss and source of filial guilt, the loss of his mother six years earlier. The guilt and nostalgia and air of melancholy strangeness were feelings evoked by a cold night in his father's wifeless household. And, though these feelings were easily transferred onto Nora, Jim was really being haunted by his mother:

32. In *Exiles* Richard Rowan does quite the same thing when he confesses to Robert Hand that he has "killed" Bertha: "Listen. She is dead. She lies on my bed. I look at her body which I betrayed—grossly and many times. And loved, too, and wept over. And I know that her body was always my loyal slave. To me, to me only she gave . . ." (*E* 68).

A strange land, a strange house, strange eyes and the shadow of a strange, strange girl standing silently by the fire, or gazing out of the window across the misty College park. What a mysterious beauty clothes every place where she has lived!

Twice while I was writing these sentences tonight the sobs gathered quickly in my throat and broke from my lips.

I have loved in her the image of the beauty of the world, the mystery and beauty of life itself, the beauty and doom of the race of whom I am a child, the images of spiritual purity and pity which I believed in as a boy.

Her soul! Her name! Her eyes! They seem to me like strange beautiful blue wild-flowers growing in some tangled, rain-drenched hedge. And I have felt her soul tremble beside mine, and have spoken her name softly to the night, and have wept to see the beauty of the world passing like a dream behind her eyes.

Jim's Faustian lament for this Gretchen whom he had sacrificed to his intemperate passion was a rehearsal of his guilt over his mother's death, and in that lies the secret of the third-person address. A third person was in fact being evoked, for Nora was May Murray Joyce reborn. But reborn not only to comfort and guide her son but to chastise his naughtiness and avenge the great wrongs he had done her.[33] That Jim's anxieties over his own faithlessness toward his mother before her death remained with him for years is clear enough in the fantasy life he gives to Stephen in *Ulysses*. And in *Exiles* the dialectic of filial betrayal and maternal revenge through the agency of another woman is a well-developed theme. Both Bertha Rowan and Beatrice Justice attack Richard Rowan for having betrayed his mother (see *Exiles*, pp. 23, 52). Bertha, Beatrice, and Molly Bloom

33. Some of the consequences of this for *Ulysses* are discussed in Chapter 5. See also Chapter 6, for an extended analysis of May Joyce's place in her son's art and life.

were, like Nora, the living agents of the dead mother, executing her will upon the faithless son.[34]

✓ ✓ ✓

After this purgation of guilt, the correspondence settled down to the traditional business of love letters, mutual sexual excitation. Written under the pressure of a single powerful impulse, sexual need, the significant remainder of Jim's letters read like fragments of a single great confession. Unfortunately, a good deal of this confession is under an interdict imposed by the Joyce Estate and cannot be published. But, like women, who, as Bloom observes, lose a charm with every pin they take out, these letters, too, lose a great deal of charm with every passage made public.

A number of the letters were on-the-spot transcriptions masturbatory fantasies. Jim encouraged Nora to record her masturbatory fantasies as well, and she either complied with his wish or carried on a skillful pretence of doing so. Thus, the correspondence bore the aspect of improvised coitus at a distance, each partner making do with what he (or she) had at hand. The shape of thought and feeling in these letters is precisely what one might expect in such a situation. The erotic desires and their accompanying fantasies build to a frenzied climax, then trail off quickly into apologies, businesslike instructions, domestic remarks, or silence. No doubt, these letters served Jim years later as models for the technique of "Nausikaa," which he described to Stuart Gilbert as

34. Edward Brandabur has some nice observations about the internalized mother and the dynamics of filial guilt in "The Dead" and *Exiles*. See his *A Scrupulous Meanness: A Study of Joyce's Early Work* (Chicago: University of Illinois Press, 1971).

"tumescence, detumescence." And the letters in turn may be likened to Bloom's description of his own auto-sexual fireworks in that chapter, "Up like a rocket, down like a stick" (364/371).

The varieties of sexual play that find expression in them testify to a catholicity of taste not sanctioned by Jim's church. His propensities extended to both active and passive sexual postures, to masculine and feminine roles, to oral, anal, and genital activities, and to Nora dressed as well as Nora undressed. He played the voyeur, the fetishist (and true connoisseur of "drawers"), the coprophile (and lover of smells), the coprolalic (the devotee of the dirty word), the sadist, the masochist, and the homosexual. No part of the body, no human function, nor any variety of orificial contact seems to have lacked its libidinal valence. In short, these letters show Jim to have been, at least in his fantasies, a prototypical Bloom, a sexual Everyman. Insofar as we can identify his preferences at all, we may detect a special proclivity for the anal. No letter lacks its anal or excremental fantasy, and some of these fantasies are elaborate, extended physical conceits. And, though it is not immediately obvious, this anal obsession does have a special significance apart from the context of polymorphous sexuality in which it appears.

It seems odd that so guilt-ridden a man as Jim should have been so open with his wife about his uncommon sexual preferences. For intimacy in no way precludes sexual restraint or otherwise secretive and defensive behavior, and Jim was the most secretive of men in his dealings with the world at large. But with Nora he was candid in ways that few men are or can be with their wives, and in the mutual revelation of sexual fantasies, if not in real

sexual relations, Jim and Nora seem to have shared a
mutuality of desire, if not always of taste. This openness
may perhaps be understandable as a case of confessional
freedom, that sudden urge to talk that wells up in the
guilty child in the presence of a forgiving or appropriately punitive figure of authority. Yet Jim's primary object here seems to have been neither to secure forgiveness
nor to elicit punishment, though he did demand those
things at times. He seems rather to have wanted Nora's
complicity in his shame. He demanded that she be open
about *her* secret life (a subject which always fascinated
him) *and* that she promise full cooperation in future
perverse undertakings.

There is also a bit of sadism in these revelations, for
these expressions of aggressive and offensive fantasies
were attempts at verbal rape. These letters were designed
to degrade Nora, to reduce her to the level of proper erotogenic contempt. In most of them the characteristic vir-
gin/whore polarity of Jim's sexual imagination was
skewed almost wholly toward the whore phase. Only at
the very beginning and end of this correspondence did
the imagery and attitudes of the devotional phase appear,
a phenomenon that bears some discussion.

In the December 2 letter, at the very beginning of this
series of love letters, the virgin/whore syndrome was
present at its ambivalent best (pp. 268–269). Jim imagined relations with Nora that were at once devotional
and abusive. He addressed her once again as "My beautiful wild flower of the hedges" and announced that he
was preparing a present for her, a handwritten copy of
Chamber Music, "and it is a poet's present for the woman
he loves." But at that point the superego-ridden rhetoric
gave way before the tough language of the id: "But,

side by side and inside this spiritual love I have for you there is also a wild beast-like craving for every inch of your body, for every part of it, for every odour and act of it. My love for you allows me to pray to the spirit of eternal beauty and tenderness mirrored in your eyes or to fling you down under me . . . . " Here the scissors of censorship cut in, and we must plunder our store of euphemisms and approximations to outline the rest. What follows is the first of the polymorphous fantasies, an extraordinary fantasy of porcine love that is by turns violent, sentimental, passionate, excremental, and comical. He would bugger her violently, reveling in the smell of her anus and the openness of her shame. He would lie with her in sixty-nine position while each licks, fondles, feels, fingers, and fucks the other. He reminds her of the obscene noises he has taught her to make and recalls the glorious time when, with great shame, she consented to let him lie under her while she "did it." Whereupon the letter reaches its possessive climax and he cries out, "You are mine, darling, mine! I love you." Then, having crossed the summit and turned downhill, he murmurs gratefully, "All I have written above is only a moment or two of brutal madness . . . . " After one final phallic spasm, the fantasy resolves in a denouement of devotional music; "a faint hymn is heard rising in tender pitiful worship of you from the dim cloisters of my heart." Jim brought this letter to a close by invoking her as his whore and mistress and reassuring her once again that she remained, nevertheless, "My wild flower of the hedges, my dark-blue rain-drenched flower."

After this letter, Jim's aggressive erotism more or less dominated the correspondence for the next three weeks, during which time the rough polymorphous fantasies persisted. Even when the fantasies themselves were not sadistic, as often they were not, Jim's program of brutal honesty was certainly carried out with sadistic intent. But as his return to Trieste drew near, Eros became tinged with anxiety. On one occasion he cautioned Nora not to expect too much of him upon his return, for he would not be able to get himself up for a nightly performance (December 16; this portion of the letter does not appear in Ellmann's edition). And in a letter dated December 20, almost two weeks before his departure from Dublin, he transcribed his last sexual fantasy. In that letter the usual verbal rape gave way at the end to nervous demands. "For God's sake," he complained, "arrange that you and I can have a comfortable bed," and added defensively, "I have no great wish to do anything to you dear. All I want is your company" (pp. 276–277). Three days later he complained, "I am so tired after all I have done here that I think when I reach Via Scussa I will just creep into bed, kiss you tenderly on the forehead, curl myself up in the blankets and sleep, sleep, sleep" (pp. 278–279). And the next day, in his penultimate letter, he brought the correspondence full circle. He invoked her as his "beautiful wild flower of the hedges" and "my little mother" and implored her to "take me into the dark sanctuary of your womb. Shelter me, dear, from harm!" (p. 281). As their reunion approached, Jim's "beast-like cravings" retreated and his infantile yearnings for maternal protection reappeared. The progress of these very last letters follows his retreat from genitality and manhood to orality and childhood as the threatening possibility of performance drew near. Love may have been unhappy when love was away, but love was more confident of its powers at a distance.

It appears that Jim found coitus a poor substitute for masturbation. And his books seem to confirm what these letters suggest. There is Bloom's sexual situation in *Ulysses* and Stephen's theory of the autoerotic creator-God as well as the general milieu of masturbatory implication in the library episode. What we see in both the letters and the books is an ambivalent suspension of sexuality between mutual and self-sufficient modes, a suspension that inclines toward self-sufficiency unless certain special conditions (such as the "injured third party")[35] are present. And why not? Autoerotic satisfaction, after all, arouses less anxiety than mutuality by circumventing the real and imagined threats that may be contingent upon masculine sexual assertion. It also provides greater variety, through the agency of fantasy, and avoids complicating obligations and inhibiting dependencies. I suspect that these letters from Joyce to Nora show us freedom of expression that disguises and substitutes for inhibition of performance. If that is the case, then, these letters cannot be regarded as epistolary foreplay or preparations for an orgiastic homecoming but rather as primary sexual activities themselves as well as records and demonstrations of another primary mode of sexual behavior—masturbation.

CLINICAL NOTES

The standard Freudian footnotes to these aspects of Jim's erotic propensities: the virgin-whore polarization of the sexual object; the need for an injured third party;

35. See Freud, "A Special Type of Choice of Object Made by Men." *SE*, 11:165–175.

the multiform oral, anal, and genital sexuality; and the
withdrawal of libido in the presence of its object, all invoke the same childhood source, castration anxiety.[36] The
same anxiety that shows itself in the fetishism discussed
earlier can give rise to the whole range of sexual patterns
we commonly call perverse.[37] It is clear that for Jim sexual
arousal meant the activation of an entire sexual history
and the bringing into play of the whole spectrum of
pregenital propensities that are normally subordinated to
genitality in the course of male sexual development. In
itself this polymorphous sexuality is hardly extraordinary: regression is built into the ordinary operation of
erotic fantasy and is part of the normal business of
sexual foreplay. But we may guess that in Jim's case it
achieved an imaginative potency that at very least equaled
the ends it usually serves.

The most striking demonstration of this castration anx-
iety in the letters is the virgin/whore syndrome, which
Freud described in a classic paper, "On the Universal
Tendency to Debasement in the Sphere of Love."[38] Ac-

36. See Sheldon Brivic, "James Joyce: From Stephen to Bloom,"
in *Psychoanalysis and Literary Process*, ed., Frederick C. Crews
(Cambridge, Mass.: Winthrop, 1970). Also Otto Fenichel, *The
Psychoanalytic Theory of Neurosis* (New York: Norton, 1945),
passim.

37. *Perverse, perversion*, and *perversity* are unhappily crude
words out of context. Freud used them (or their German equivalents) more generously than we do to describe the components of
oral and anal pleasure in adult sexual behavior. *Perverse* in the
Freudian lexicon is a clinically limited and morally neutral word.
See Freud, *Three Essays on the Theory of Sexuality*, SE, vol. 7,
especially part 1, "The Sexual Aberrations."

38. *SE*, vol. 11. The title by which this paper is more commonly
known in English is "The Most Prevalent Form of Degradation
in Erotic Life."

cording to Freud, the dominant form of psychic impotence afflicting Western man is the requirement for two women to satisfy the full range of a man's libidinal needs: an exalted (or appropriately respectable) object of affection and a reduced object of sexual desire. In terms of turn-of-the-century, upper-middle-class Viennese society, this meant marriage to a "lady" and an affair with the maid.

In Freud's view, this divided love life is latent in the normal progress of sexual development; it originates at the point where the infantile coalition of affection and sexual desire for the mother encounters the incest barrier. Faced with the taboo against incest, a taboo that may be backed up by the threat of castration, a child has little choice but to maintain his love at the level of benign, "oral" affection, while repressing the wish to replace his father in the parental bed. For some children this dissociation of sensuality remains a permanent constitutional condition and the world of women becomes neatly bi-furcated into two categories: those who *do* and those who *don't*. The latter are to be treated with worship or shy deference, while one may exercise upon the former the full range of one's aggressive manhood. "Where such men love," Freud observed, "they have no desire and where they desire they cannot love." Alas!

And yet the mother, it seems, is really the prototype of *both* women, as Freud himself observed in an earlier paper, "A Special Type of Object Choice Made by Men."[39] He noted there that jealousy and degradation became conditions of love precisely because they fit the specifications of an oedipal formula. The other man, the injured third party, is needed to reconstruct the original

39. *SE*, vol. 11.

oedipal triad. Possession of the woman then promises not only love but triumph, and her attractiveness may vary with the intensity of the rivalry between the men. Male sexual fantasies and practices in which degradation of the woman is a condition of satisfaction make sense in an oedipal scheme where love is a function of retaliation.

While Jim in 1909 had no divided love life in fact, it would appear that he maintained one in fantasy. The unconscious recipient of both libidinal impulses may have been the mother, but in 1909, at any rate, the weight of his ambivalence fell heavily upon Nora. She was both his whore and the object of his most rarified devotion, his wild flower blooming in a hedge. This libidinal dialectic played the two Noras off against each other in Jim's mind. Each begot her opposite. Jim would abuse her one moment and atone instantaneously with a gesture of obeisance. The result is the same in the letters of 1909 as in the "Penelope" chapter of 1921, a psychosexual instability characterized by the alternation of impulse and defense, desire and worship, sadism and masochism, desublimation and resublimation.

As Freud also noted in the "Debasement" paper, where such a conflict becomes too violent to be managed safely by a beleaguered ego, it may be resolved through the total withdrawal from sexual activity in favor of fantasy and masturbation. These letters may show us a stage in that kind of withdrawal already in progress in Jim's life. In later years it does seem that his solution to the conflicts and anxieties attendant upon sexuality was precisely this: the withdrawal from women altogether and the reinvestment of sexual interest in himself. That is, as I have already suggested, much of what *Ulysses* is about.

✔ ✔ ✔

These letters are not a complete guide to *Ulysses,* but I believe that one must read and understand them in order to properly understand some of the deepest currents of human feeling in the book. It is a major assumption of this study that both the meaning of the book and its aesthetic appeal derive from the varieties of erotic and self-protective experience we discover in it. It is demonstrable, I believe, that the conflicts experienced by Bloom and Stephen, as well as the intellectual and stylistic surfaces of the book, take their power from the author's sexual and aggressive conflicts and his means of resolving or otherwise surviving them. Joyce's books themselves make sense as strategies for survival, as his arrangements for living both in the world and in himself at the brink— but always this side—of penury and breakdown. The bridge between the letters and the novels is the precarious psychic life they share. Everything in *Ulysses* bears the imprint of the same conflicts and binds and the same oedipal family that haunt the letters. Obsession, like charity, begins at home.

If ever there was a reason to disregard the obfuscating ideology of the impersonal artist expounded by Stephen at the end of *Portrait,* these letters are surely it. For the relationship between the man who wrote letters and the characters of Stephen Dedalus, Leopold Bloom, and Richard Rowan is all too plain. They are patently and, in the case of Richard Rowan, embarrassingly the same man. The masturbatory retreat from sexual mutuality suggested by the letters as well as the multiform perversity of the fantasies in them are reminiscent of Bloom. The de-

pendency, too, is Bloom's. The heroic poses are the poses
of Stephen and Rowan. The whining self-righteousness
is Rowan's as well, while the fear of isolation and betrayal is common property. Like Whitman, Jim contained
multitudes, all of whom upon examination turn out to be
the same man.

✓ ✓ ✓

We may agree with Jim when he told Nora that she had
made a man of him (August 7, p. 233). He may have been
melodramatic in saying so, but he was speaking the
truth. Nora never broke with the Church, as her husband
had, yet it was she, after all, who broke the hold of
Catholic idealism on his sexual imagination. It was Nora,
as well as a life of hardship in Trieste, that weaned him
of "gentle ladies" and "dark Rosaleens" and disabused
him of his adolescent illusions of love as a Tristanesque
Liebestod. Nora's common sense, her unselfconscious
acceptance of her own sexuality (and even, finally, of
his), and her peasant self-reliance liberated him from the
painful romanticism of his youth. Despite Jim's complaints about her girlish demeanor and girlish figure, Nora
seems to have been a woman and to have borne her womanhood well, though, as Lionel Trilling has observed,
"She was, alas, no lady."[40] But had Jim remained at home
and married a "lady," he could hardly have created Leopold Bloom or ever have developed a Bloomian understanding of Dublin. His early career as a singer of light
verses suggests that he might have become, in time, one of
those aging aesthetes who, like Pater or AE, is trapped in a

40. Lionel Trilling, "James Joyce in His Letters," *Commentary*
45 (February 1968):60.

permanent adolescence in which the swoon of ecstasy denotes all that is noble in art. Or perhaps the early realism of *Dubliners* would have congealed into a heavy, Zolaesque naturalism. But, most likely, his Catholic yearning after the evanescent and the Flaubertian style of scrupulous meanness would have converged in a fastidious literature of bitter ironies. But for the marriage to Nora, Jim might have become T. S. Eliot, who was, after all, the old age of Stephen Dedalus.

3. Whom the Lord Loveth: Five Essays on Circe

> And ye have forgotten the exhortation which speaketh unto you as unto children, My son, despise not thou the chastening of the Lord, nor faint when thou art rebuked of him:
>
> For whom the Lord loveth he chasteneth, and scourgeth every son whom he receiveth.
>
> If ye endure chastening, God dealeth with you as with sons; for what son is he whom the father chasteneth not?
>
> *Hebrews* 12:5–7

> Shame is pride's cloak. —WILLIAM BLAKE

THE BATTLE AGAINST REPRESSION

JOYCE ALWAYS saw to it that his private life was well-protected from public scrutiny. He stood aloof from private intimacies outside the family and carefully avoided the tempting but treacherous intimacies tendered by an idolatrous public. He was not, like Yeats, the smiling public man among schoolchildren, nor, like Dylan Thomas, the much adored public scandal. He habitually refused to pronounce upon issues of the day; he disliked crowds and was cold both to strangers and to many who thought themselves his friends. And, though Nora and the children were often with him in Trieste or Zürich or Paris, he did not parade his family about or seek openly to make public capital out of his private affairs.

Yet, having perfected an impenetrable coldness of manner in his personal dealings (the "spiritual-heroic refrigerating apparatus"), he courted the world furtively in his books with hints of rare intimacy with himself. *Ulysses* is an autobiographical *roman à clef* which promises to reveal to the assiduous reader, not the private shame of public men, but that of the author himself. It imitates the artificial inasmuch as the verbal texture of the book is a masterpiece of rhetorical and imagistic artifice. But under each cold artifact of style lurks a warm confession. The fantasia of "Circe" is the most daringly confessional chapter of the book, for it displays, under the guise of ribald comedy, the most anxiety-producing aspects of Joyce's psychosexual nature. "Circe" is self-revelation as slapstick, and if we have hesitated to recognize it as such before, it is because we ourselves have been uncomfortable at seeing the fabulous artificer self-caricatured as fetishist, masochist, onanist, public enigma, and private buffoon. Yet the letters to Nora confirm our suspicions about that chapter. Give or take a detail or two, the psychosexual fantasy life of Leopold Bloom is Joyce's as well, and, similarly, Bloom's real sexual life has close affinities with his creator's. "Circe" makes abundant sense as a public demonstration of Joyce's private reality and as an ambivalent proclamation of both the shame and the glory of it all.

Theodore Reik's excellent book on masochism argues at some length that the masochistic temper is ever in search of ways to proclaim itself.[1] Pride, observed Reik,

1. Theodore Reik, *Masochism in Modern Man* (New York: Farrar & Straus, 1941).

cometh *after* the fall. "Circe" would endorse that. We are confronted there with what appears to be not only a revelation but a celebration of Bloom's self-punitive fantasies. The longest and most spectacular of the chapters in *Ulysses* is a fantasy on masochistic themes which proclaims Bloom's moral heroism by way of his psychosexual perversity. Bloom's moral ascendancy is guaranteed by the painful intensity of his own fantasy life; he is canonized by self-affliction. On Joyce's part, "Circe" appears to be a covert boast, a serious self-justification by way of comic self-denigration. As Bloom, Joyce cast himself in the role of victim as fool, a comic Job, cursed and blessed by an agency of divine justice that happened to be himself. If the implication of moral heroism is drowned in frequent baths of irony and self-mockery, that, too, is an aspect of self-abasement behind which the sense of moral nobility is supposed to be visible.

We ought to note in fact that the techniques of the ironist and the strategies of the masochist are similar. In Joyce's case, especially, irony and masochism go hand in hand, for both involve a strategic self-abasement. The masochist courts pain in the interest of disarming his superego much as the ironist cultivates self-criticism for the purpose of disarming his critics. We have already had a glimpse in the letters of the fine art of self-deprecation as manipulation, and we shall see it in "Circe" as entertainment. "Circe" is Joyce's Gallagher and Sheen act, his translation of Irish wit into stand-up Jewish comedy.

"Circe," then, expresses a sort of proud contrition, being a boastful acknowledgment of sin. We know that Joyce, like Bloom, preferred love at a distance to real sexual engagement. We know, too, that he was ambivalent about his sexual role, that he had strong, if unenacted (read *latent*) homosexual impulses,[2] and that he indulged in Bloomlike transsexual fantasies in which he imagined himself beaten and sexually penetrated. All this is acknowledged in "Circe." Yet we know, too, that Joyce softened some of the details of his idiosyncratic fantasy life in writing *Ulysses*, especially those details involving his fascination with the eliminative functions of women. The language of desire is gentler in "Circe" than in the letters, and the fine points of the excremental vision in the book are deliberately blurred. But the general outline is bold enough, and an imaginative reader may infer all the right things from Bloom's stuttering confession, "I rererepugnosed in rererepugnant" (526/538). Yet, if the chapter is a confession, a simple unburdening before a fatherly public upon whom the author has devised the priestly power to bind and loose from sin, it is a most unusual one. For it displays none of the customary signs of contrition: reserve, humility, the uncertain voice, or the downcast glance. Those are Bloomian qualities the author does not appear to share. The chapter is, instead, a demonstration and a celebration, not just of Bloom's virtues, fantasies, and sexual "crimes," but of the author's powers in representing them.

The power that is being celebrated is twofold. One aspect of it is the artist's power over the material medium in which he is working, in this case, language. Joyce spent a lifetime establishing his control over language, and the entire body of his work can be seen as a public

2. Joyce once acknowledged to Frank Budgen (Budgen, p. 315) that there is an undercurrent of homosexuality in Bloom, though, indeed, we may discover hints of homosexuality in just about every male character in *Ulysses*. See Sheldon Brivic, "James Joyce: From Stephen to Bloom," in *Psychoanalysis and Literary Process*, ed., Frederick C. Crews (Cambridge: Winthrop, 1970).

display of craftsmanship. But "Circe" also celebrates Joyce's power over himself—specifically, his power over taboo and repression. Bloom's virtue, as we shall see, is the virtue of self-possession in threatening and unstable circumstances. "Circe" shows us that Bloom can hold out against the tides of life that threaten to overwhelm him, not from behind breakwaters of order and elegance, but by virtue of some indefinable inner strength compounded of endurance and self-irony and abetted by fantasy. It seems to have been Joyce's intention, too, to make a public show of a similar mastery—even daring—on his part. "Circe" appears to be a demonstration of Joyce's ability to do what had not been done before, to reveal all and to violate the canons of social and personal taboo without being struck dead by censorship or guilt. It was a challenge to the fearsome tides of life, a show of strength in the face of danger. On the public side, it seems that Joyce did court censorship for the purpose of triumphing over it, while, on the private side, he apparently engaged in a kind of moral bullfight, provoking guilt in order to face it down through art. Such acts of dubious courage involve a degree of masochistic provocation, and it is often difficult in Joyce's case to determine where moral courage ends and moral masochism begins.

Joyce's main audience for his show of daring was always himself. In "Circe" he undertook to make a show of his power as an artist to overcome repression and to face down insanity, and it appears that to some considerable degree he succeeded in doing just that.[3] His conscious in-

3. Since completing this chapter, I have come to believe that the significant threat that is faced down in "Circe" is no less than insanity. That, however, is another study entirely, and for now it must be passed over.

tention with regard to self-revelation in "Circe"—indeed, in all of *Ulysses*—was, I believe, threefold: to know himself completely, to confess all fully, and to do so with perfect artistic control over the materials of expression. The boast he later made in *Finnegans Wake*, "I can psoakoonaloose myself any time I want" (*FW*, 522), is put to the test in "Circe." The result is an epiphany gone mad, one hundred seventy-two pages of sudden spiritual manifestation.

Joyce's reasons for wanting to do battle with repression and to make a show of his courage in the face of guilt (see note 3) is a complex matter in its specifics but comprehensible in its broad outlines. He was conscious of the partial dependence of sexual and intrapsychic repression upon the political and religious institutions that sponsor it in Ireland. Seeing sexual repression primarily as a function of cultural oppression, he undertook a regime of personal desublimation as an act of cultural radicalism. The defeat of inhibition in expression was meant to be an act of rebellion against the repressive fathers and treacherous brothers in Ireland, Rome, and England. When Stephen taps his brow and utters enigmatically, "In here it is I must kill the priest and the king," he is contemplating the victory over self-repression as a political act. Of course, the political component of repression is most available to Stephen, as it is to all of us, because it is manifested in specific and visible acts of tyranny. But the repression of Joyce's (as well as Stephen's) sexuality by Church and state is at least as much a matter of Joyce's self-mythologizing reconstruction of his own youth as it is a matter of historical fact, since the familial components of that repression, those primordial influences that endow priest and king with their psychological authority, are hidden behind a veil of amnesia and are as unavailable to Stephen's scrutiny as they are to ours.

However much Joyce may have struggled against sexual repression and attempted to make a show of his power over it, his success, we know, was only partial and at least as much a matter of rhetoric as of reality. He was not a hedonist; his sexual excursions outside marriage were pretty pallid stuff in reality, however breathtaking he may have made them seem as literature. His dongiovannism seems to have been more an epistolary than a real success. Nor does he appear to have been a particularly attentive or sexually active husband. His triumphs over repression were registered in those modes of regressive and incomplete sexuality that he was psychically capable of engaging in, and to language, which functioned for him as a surrogate penis. He did not and could not evade or lift the repression of his sexuality. Were mere power of the will sufficient to the task of libidinal liberation, Joyce might have achieved it, but no amount of will power alone can accomplish that. In lieu of lifting inhibition of action, he attacked the culturally imposed inhibition of expression and that public aspect of mass self-repression that was subject to attack, the bias against imagination and creativity. Indeed, the intensity of his linguistic desublimation was more or less proportional to the intensity of his sexual repression, and we may speculate that had the latter been overcome, the former might not have been possible.

This skeletal analysis of the motive forces underlying Joyce's self-revelation make *Ulysses* sound like the work of a bitter and compulsive man, though it is really the least bitter of modern novels. We are still in need of a theory of the two qualifying features of this con-

fession: the wit and the art of it. The function of neither
is psychologically self-evident, nor are their relations to
the dominant affective qualities of the confession—
shame, guilt, and pride—immediately apparent. But a
germinal analysis, or at least a description, of Joyce's
wit and craft should emerge with some clarity from our
reading of "Circe."

BLOOM AGONISTES

For Bloom, as for Stephen, history is a nightmare. Bloom
is haunted by the betrayals of the past: his father's sui-
cide, his son's death, his wife's infidelity, his daughter's
sexual maturation, his own religious apostasies (three
baptisms) and erotic improprieties. In "Circe," this history is relived through a series of masochistic fantasies
in which Bloom's guilt is put to work in the service of
sexual arousal and messianic exaltation. There, as elsewhere, Bloom is systematically beset by threats; accusations are heaped upon his head, and punishment is
endlessly proffered. Only here the threats are all internalized and the punishment self-administered.

Early in "Circe," for example, Bloom is beset variously
by visions of his father, who upbraids him for his mone-
tary extravagance; of Molly, who mocks his impotence
and flaunts her sexual power; and of such minor phan-
toms as Bridie Kelly, Gerty MacDowell, and Josie Breen,
who gleefully accuse him of sexual improprieties. In
reality, meanwhile, he is beset by a dog that covets and
finally gets the sheep's trotter and pig's crubeen he has
been carrying all day. Bloom's trial fantasy begins just
then as he feeds the dog, for which he imagines himself
arrested for "prevention of cruelty to animals" (446/

454). Upon his arrest, the charges against him multiply rapidly, and Bloom finds himself self-accused of all manner of sexual indecencies, many of which involve or imply anal or excremental pleasures: "unlawfully watching and besetting" (447/455); having been drummed out of the army (448/456); "breach of promise" (448/456); plagiarism (450/458); surprising the scullerymaid "in the rere of the premises" (452–453/461); defecating in a plasterer's bucket on Beaver Street (454/462); writing anonymous letters "in prentice backhand" to which he signed himself "James Lovebirch" (457/465); sending to Mrs. Bellingham a bogus bloom of edelweiss that was in fact the blossom of a homegrown potato plant; calling her "Venus in furs" and urging her to commit adultery with him (457–458/466); sending dirty pictures to Mrs. Mervyn Talboys and imploring her to "soil his letter in an unspeakable manner, to chastise him as he richly deserves, to bestride and ride him, to give him a most vicious horse-whipping" (458–459/467). And finally he is accused of no less than his own cuckoldry, as though his wife's infidelity were somehow one of his crimes. By and large, these charges do not cause Bloom much anxiety, for they are not real threats so much as a masochist's fond memories. Even the fantasied promises of affliction that follow upon these accusations ["Thrash the mongrel within an inch of his life. The cat-o'-nine tails. Geld him. Vivisect him" (460/468)] are more a delight to Bloom than a horror.

But masochism calls for exquisitely calibrated punishment. Only a degree or two of pain or threat or reality separates excitement from terror. Thus Bloom's visionary torments after the trial fantasy are more fearsome and problematic than the titillating fantasies that precede it, for they take their cue from a real and present danger, the prostitute Zoe's sudden theft of Bloom's moly, his talis-manic potato. To be sure, even in the enchanted world of "Circe," the potato has no real magic for Bloom, only psychological magic. Zoe's snatching of the potato, to which Bloom is sentimentally attached, commits him to bondage. The potato had been his mother's—"poor mama's panacea," he calls it. It serves him as a symbolic and psychological connection with what little remains of the past, and its loss is a symbolic castration and sepa-ration from *amor matris*. His momentary unwillingness either to struggle to get it back or to relinquish it man-fully is a tacit submission to pornocracy, government by whores.[4]

It is at this point in "Circe" that Bloom's messiah fan-tasy intervenes. The sudden interruption of these fan-tasies of abuse by an extended messianic fantasy may violate the conventional logic of dramatic development, but not the psycho-logic of primary process thought. Masochism and messianism are intrapsychic partners, and there is good enough reason to regard the former as a condition of the latter, a matter that will be explored more fully later in this chapter. The psychological dia-lectic of loss, castration, and sexual submission, on the one hand and messianic self-glorification, on the other, should not surprise us. That Bloom's loss of his talis-manic potato should be a prelude to fantasies of power and exaltation may seem unmotivated and illogical, but

4. Harry Blamires has pointed out in *The Bloomsday Book* (London: Methuen, 1966) that Zoe's real name is Ellen Higgens, the name of Bloom's mother. But one must suppose that all the prostitutes, not just Zoe, are in some way mothers to Bloom and that Joyce's hidden joke does not give Zoe any special preeminence among them.

it is psychologically sound. If we consider the prevalence of messianic themes in nineteenth- and twentieth-century Irish literature as a whole, and consider, too, the situation of cultural bondage and political impotence out of which they arose, we ought to see clearly enough the dependence of messianism upon castration and futility.[5]

Bloom's return to reality at the end of the messiah fantasy finds him still with Zoe, who is trying to lure him into the musicroom, where love's old sweet song is a nightly refrain. The potatoless Bloom seems reluctant to follow, and as Zoe persists in enticing him, he retreats psychologically into a defensive state of infantile helplessness. "Come," she entreats, and Bloom reflects on motherhood, "The hand that rocks the cradle" (490/500). "Babby!" she calls, and Bloom becomes just that, *"in babylinen and pelisse, bigheaded, with a caul of dark hair,"* counting the buckles on her slip and lisping in numbers, "one two tlee: tlee tlwo tlone." At last the powerful Zoe leads the infant Bloom forward *"by the odour of her armpits, the vice of her painted eyes, the rustle of her slip in whose sinuous folds lurks the lion reek of all the male brutes that have possessed her."*

In this regressive and submissive position Bloom is beset by a specter of one of his own alter egos in the form of a lecherous grandfather, Lipoti Virag. Virag is the perverse and bawdy Bloom, and for a moment grandfather and grandson confront each other in Bloom's mind as bawd and cuckold. Bloom has been shrewdly studying

5. An excellent study of messianism and the impact of Parnell's fall upon Irish literature is Herbert Howarth, *The Irish Writers: Literature and Nationalism, 1880–1940* (New York: Hill and Wang, 1958). See also William Irwin Thompson, *The Imagination of an Insurrection: Dublin, Easter 1916* (New York: Oxford University Press, 1967).

the girls, though it is as Virag that he enumerates to himself their charms: "Inadvertently her backview revealed the fact that she is not wearing those rather intimate garments of which you are a particular devotee" (501/511–512). Of another, Virag/Bloom observes, "On her rere lower down are two additional protuberances, suggestive of potent rectum and tumescent for palpation . . . ." Apropos of Bloom's masochism and sexual ambivalence, this alter ego sneers, "Have you made up your mind whether you like or dislike women in male habiliments?" (503/514). Like Bloom, Virag is a theorist of the science of sexuality, having theories concerning aphrodisiacs, the sexual allure of feminine scents, and such points of folk wisdom as why snakes seek out cows' udders and women's breasts. He is the fulfillment of Bloom's wish to be an author, having written a textbook, *Fundamentals of Sexology or the Love Passion* (504/515), and an exposé of ecclesiastical lechery, an account of why he left the Church of Rome, entitled, *The Priest, the Woman and the Confessional* (508/519). No doubt, both are plagiarized. Virag, one of the many agents through whom the sins of the past are recalled to Bloom in Nighttown, demands of him accusingly, "Who's Ger Ger? Who's dear Gerald?" (505/516). The question goes unanswered, but Bloom later confesses under extreme duress to Bella/o Cohen that "it was Gerald converted me to be a true corsetlover when I was female impersonator in the high school play *Vice Versa*. It was dear Gerald. He got that kink, fascinated by sister's stays. Now dearest Gerald uses pinky greasepaint and gilds his eyelids. Cult of the beautiful" (524–525/536–537).

Through part of this scenario, Bloom's bawdy self, Lipoti Virag, is played off against his romantic self, a

personification of his adulterous nom de plume, Henry
Flower. Where Virag is lecherous, witty, ribald, and in-
sulting to all, Henry is a Latin Lothario, Don Giovanni
in a dark mantle and drooping, plumed sombrero. While
Virag gleefully proposes his irreverent theories of the
immaculate conception: "She sold lovephiltres, white-
wax, orangeflower. Panther, the Roman centurion, pol-
luted her with his genitories" (510/521), Henry Flower
croons to a severed female head (the disembodied Martha?), "Thine heart, mine love" (511/522) and plucks
an insipid lute. But lecher and lutanist, obscenist and sen-
timentalist, are types of each other, as they are aspects
of Bloom. For they are none other than the author of
"Circe" and the singer of *Chamber Music* writ small.

The imaginary Lipoti Virag and Henry Flower give
way to reality when the door to Bella Cohen's bedroom
opens and a sinister male form *"passes down the creak-
ing staircase and is heard taking the waterproof and hat
from the rack"* (513/525). Bella's "tipster," a mystery
man who has been supporting her son at Oxford, has
been with her. He is mysteriously familiar to Bloom, who
cannot identify him but is intrigued and threatened by
him nevertheless. He suspects variously "MacIntosh"
and Boylan. "If it were he? After? Or because not? Or
the double event?" (514/525). The mystery man, whoever he is, arouses anxiety in Bloom, who, sensing the
presence of a devil, tries to exorcise him, "Go, go, go, I
conjure you, whoever you are." But even when the unknown Satan disappears out the door, the ambient mood
of the brothel remains cold and sinister. For just as her
lover leaves, Bella herself appears, the phallic mother *par
excellence.* "Her eyes are deeply carboned. She has a
sprouting moustache. Her olive face is heavy, slightly

sweated and fullnosed, with orangetainted nostrils. She
has large pendent beryl eardrops" (515/527). Hot from
an evening's tumble with her tipster, she is cooling herself with a large fan. Bloom is intimidated by the sheer
massiveness of Bella and the phallic assertiveness of the
fan, which, he imagines, addresses him sharply. "Married, I see" (517/527). "Yes," he replies and puns, "Partly, I have mislaid . . ." meaning, one presumes, that he
has mislaid his key, his potato, and his wife. "And the
missus is master," the fan charges. "Petticoat government." "Exuberant female," he invokes the fan, "Enor-
mously I desiderate your domination" (516/528). The fan
complies, "Be mine. Now." In these terms, the terms of
ruthless domination and complete submission, the elements of an extraordinary scenario are laid out. Guilt and
fear, evoked by the appearance of Bella, drive the entire
syndrome of Joycean/Bloomian sexuality to the surface
of Bloom's consciousness. By turns, his masochism, copro-
philia, homosexuality, transvestism, fetishism, and voyeurism assert themselves in the context of terrible
physical threat and psychological anxiety. Bloom imagi-
natively assumes a submissive and feminine role and
projects upon Bella the role of a cruel and castrating
male figure, the monstrous Bello.

The scenario develops through a series of variations
on a theme of degradation. Bloom is cruelly subjected
to threats of castration and dismemberment. "Adorer of
the adulterous rump!" Bello roars at the feminized Bloom
(518/530). "Hugeness," Bloom responds. "Dungdevour-
er!" Bello bellows. "Magnificence," sighs Bloom, who
sinks to the ground upon all fours, porcine, a truffle
hunter. "Very possibly I shall have you slaughtered and
skewered in my stables," Bello promises, and the other

whores vie for the privilege of taking a shot at Bloom themselves. After giving Bloom a hard ride ("A cockhorse to Banbury Cross"), squeezing "her" testicles for extra speed and farting ferociously to conclude the gallop, Bello directs Bloom to don his/her "punishment frock," which consists of "vicelike corsets of soft dove coutille, with whalebone busk . . . nettight frocks, pretty two ounce petticoats," and so forth (523/535). Bloom, of course, has enjoyed such attire before, in the high-school play *Vice Versa* (when dear Gerald converted him to corsetloving) and years later, on Holles Street, when he tried on some of Molly's things as a prank. Also, one time in the Shelbourne Hotel he had bought a black operatop shift from a promiscuous neighbor, Mrs. Miriam Dandrade, and had clipped off his "backgate hairs and lay swooning in the thing across the bed" while imagining himself violated by a long line of phantom male lovers. At Bello's direction, the sins of the past rise en masse to confront Bloom. All are perverse sexual offenses, incomplete and furtive acts of infantile sexuality:

Unspeakable messages he telephoned mentally to Miss Dunn at an address in d'Olier Street while he presented himself indecently to the instrument in the callbox. By word and deed he encouraged a nocturnal strumpet to deposit fecal and other matter in an unsanitary outhouse attached to empty premises. In five public conveniences he wrote pencilled messages offering his nuptial partner to all strongmembered males. (525/537)

In addition, he had spied upon lovers in the park, had undergone clandestine marriage ceremonies with strange women, and had gloated over a bit of used toilet paper given him by a prostitute. A handsome array of sins indeed. At last, upon Bello's command, Bloom unwillingly and with much difficulty confesses his "most revolting piece of obscenity" (526/538). "I rererepugnosed in rere-rerepugnant." In effect, Bloom has been to confession with Bello who, as Father Confessor, makes him "puke it out" (remember the "squalid stream of vice" that trickles from Stephen's lips in *Portrait*) and proceeds to impose an array of sexual and excremental penances: smelling dirty underclothes, emptying pisspots, swabbing latrines, submitting upon command to strange men, and so forth. Bello's justice turns the *lex talionis* into a scheme of rewards. Bloom's punishments fit his crimes by imitating them. An eye for an eye, a pisspot for a pisspot.

Following that, in a quickly moving sequence of short scenarios, Bloom is put up for auction as a domestic animal and as a well-dressed courtesan and is mocked variously for his sexual incapacity, his cuckoldry, his years of sexual sleep, and for the many future embarrassments he must yet endure. "You have made your secondbest bed and others must lie in it. Your epitaph is written," Bello mocks (531/543). Then, most cruelly of all, the imaginary Bello pronounces upon Bloom's uselessness and isolation: "Die and be damned to you if you have any sense of decency or grace about you" (531/543), and Bloom breaks down and weeps tearlessly, "My will power! Memory! I have sinned! I have suff . . ." (531/544).

This imaginary (hallucinated?) encounter with Bella/o has a definite and significant form, that of the medieval auto-da-fé, the ordeal, at the hands of the Inquisition, of the heretic or one who has mortally sinned. The torture, the charge, the confession of guilt, the imposition of cruel penance, the final judgment, and final despair form an identifiable pattern. The dramatic action of Bloom's self-tormenting fantasies, it seems, imitates the cruel logic of medieval ritual, or perhaps it is really the other way around. For Bloom carries this inquisitorial apparatus around in his head. He is self-tormented, self-accused, and self-confessed. His penance is self-imposed and his despair self-contained. Bloom has gone forth, and it is to Bloom that his steps have tended. His fantasy submission to Bella/o is a dramatization of his intrapsychic power struggles, for it is the submission of one principle of his own mental functioning to another. In a word, it is the obeisance of a guilt-ridden ego before the terrible internalized parent, the stern superego, which in Bloom's fantasies is characteristically the phallic mother.

We must bear in mind, too, that this elaborate ritual is enacted on behalf of sexual motives. The appearance of the real Bella Cohen activates in Bloom's mind an ancient complex of sexual drives, guilts, and anxieties to which he responds with characteristic self-punitive fantasies. An ancient and hidden sexual crime, a love that dare not speak its name, is recalled, a confession extracted and penance exacted. The "sins of the past" that are conjured up in this psychic trial are not the crime itself, for it remains repressed. They are, rather, minor acts of furtive sexuality upon which the burden of a massive free-floating guilt and anxiety has settled. The real crime, some wish or act of infantile assertion, lies hidden behind that barrier of repression which Freud called the veil of amnesia. It is perhaps an oedipal crime, a seductive or parricidal wish or gesture, or perhaps some other criminal assertion of bodily pleasure. The evidence points ambiguously everywhere: in *Ulysses* we discover the art of confession as obfuscation. We are told entirely too much. The most consistent symptom in this rite of injured

sexuality seems to be the furtive anality, which may point
to a crime of anal assertion. It may also point to a phallic
crime that has forced a retreat to anal sexuality. As I will
show later, there is much evidence for the former, though
there is no reason to doubt the possibility of the latter.
To be a child in a repressive society is to encounter one's
guilt everywhere, in every emotional need and physical
self-indulgence.

Bloom's self-confessions and the attendant fantasies of
masochistic submission serve him as preemptive penance
for his sins. The anxious anticipation of real punishment
is alleviated, and the threats posed by the temptation to
seek out that punishment are reduced through self-
confession and self-punishment. These fantasies then are
therapeutic, since they rehearse and alleviate in fantasy
a sense of overwhelming guilt that would be self-
destructive if acted out in reality. Bloom is thus left
more or less free to cope more or less rationally with
situations that demand his attention and action. It is
Stephen, whose masochism is more perfectly repressed,
who provokes his own beating at the hands of the British
soldiers in Nighttown, while Bloom, who has preemptive-
ly punished himself, is able to come to Stephen's rescue.

The return of Bloom's rationality and self-possession
in the scene that follows the fantastic encounter with
Bello Cohen seems to confirm this theory that Bloom's
fantasy life is therapeutic. The immediate conclusion of
the Bello scenario is the death and burial of Bloom, whose
passing is memorialized by "The Circumcised," who
chant "Shema Israel" over his grave. But resurrection is
immediate, as Bloom is revived by a specter of the nymph
he had clipped out of *Photo Bits* and set on the wall
above his and Molly's bed. "Mortal! You found me in

evil company, highkickers, coster picnic makers, pugi-
lists, popular generals, immoral panto boys in flesh
tights and the nifty shimmy dancers, La Aurora and
Karini" (532/545). Bloom had borne her away (that is,
cut her out and framed her "in oak and tinsel"), made a
household goddess of her, and done homage in his own
distinctive way. "Unseen, one summer eve, you kissed
me in four places. And with loving pencil you shaded my
eyes, my bosom and my shame." She recalls that during
dark nights, too, she heard his praise, and one suspects
variously masturbation, nocturnal emission, or, as Bloom
hints, snoring. She has been witness, too, to the nameless
improprieties of the Bloomian boudoir, and nothing has
repulsed the chaste and sphincterless nymph more than
Bloom's anal obsession. She boasts loftily of her aloof-
ness from such concerns: "We immortals, as you saw
today, have not such a place and no hair there either.
We are stonecold and pure" (538/551). "O I have been
a perfect pig," Bloom acknowledges. "Enemas too I have
administered." "In my presence," the nymph recalls,
"The powderpuff" (538/551). And Bloom, confessing
for the millionth time the most rerererepugnant of his
crimes, admits wearily, "Yes. *Peccavi*! I have paid homage
on that living altar where the back changes name." "It
overpowers me," he goes on, "Even to sit where a woman
has sat," especially with uplifted petticoats. "It fills me
full." Finally, in the garb of a nun, the *Photo Bits* nymph
makes her last dreamy appeal on behalf of cold, pastoral
beauty and what Stephen Dedalus once called static art.
"No more desire," she sighs. "Only the ethereal. Where
the dreamy creamy gull waves o'er the waters dull." As
Bloom rises, possibly to follow her, his back trouser
button snaps "Bip!" tolling him back to his sole self

(539/552). The spell of fantasy and sexual submission is broken by this fortuitous event, and Bloom, asserting himself for the first time all day, roughly seizes his immortal tormentress, who viciously responds with a poniard to the loins and then flees before Bloom's newly found manhood. As the fantasy fades, Bloom finds himself still in the company of Bella, whom he advises contemptuously, "A raw onion the last thing at night would benefit your complexion. And take some double chin drill" (541/554). And, following a round of sharp banter, he turns to Zoe and gently demands the return of his potato, which he gets. He is ready now to look after Stephen, and just in time, for the latter's rapidly deteriorating finances are badly in need of hardnosed Jewish thrift.

We know from Joyce's letters to Budgen and his note for "Circe" that he intended this masochistic ordeal and its modestly triumphant conclusion to be a kind of moral allegory. The chapter was apparently meant to be a showcase for both Bloom's psychosexual weakness and his psychological strength. It was to be Bloom's justification, the chapter in which his heroism, broadly defined as self-possession, would be revealed under the pressure of those most potent of personal threats: masochism, despair, and insanity. The bout with insanity may in fact be the deepest of the conflicts in "Circe," for in that chapter both Bloom and Stephen are provisionally psychotic.[6]

6. Bloom and Stephen have had premonitory hints of this possibility at every turn throughout the day. As demonstrations of what can happen to the isolated man in Dublin, the margins of the social universe bring forth, for their edification, lunatics and queer, unhinged figures like Denis Breen, the blind stripling, and Cashel Boyle O'Connor Fitzmaurice Tisdall Farrell, whose emblematic presences mock Bloom and Stephen with intimations of

They hallucinate their reality. Boundaries evaporate; inner and outer interpenetrate, and identity becomes a flux of interlocking possibilities. Bloom may be Virag may be Rudy may be Henry Flower may be Don Giovanni may be Bloom. The logic of this reality follows the canons of dreamwork: condensation, displacement, and symbolization. The categories of experience by which the sane mind maintains itself are here fused in visual, verbal, and existential puns. Stephen's afternoon lesson is his evening's experience. He and Bloom enter a brothel where, surrounded by lascivious women, they become Shakespeare. Their minds are overborne. *They go mad.*

That threat was a constant presence with Joyce himself, who confessed to Jacques Mercanton some years after the conclusion of *Ulysses* that "the book was a terrible risk. A transparent leaf separates it from madness." Again, "It is absurd to say I have no skill. I have too much. But fortunately, no intellect. Otherwise I should have gone mad a long time ago."[7] But Joyce did not go mad; Bloom, in his image, is not quite Denis Breen, nor is Stephen quite the blind stripling. The thin leaf that separates them all from insanity is a quality of mind that Joyce knew himself to possess, though he was unsure of its nature and sought mightily to define it.

He was especially hard put to find a moral equivalent for moly, the herb given to Odysseus by Hermes as a charm against Circe's magic. The physical equivalent could have been anything, and Bloom's shriveled pota-

---

their own insanity. See David Hayman, *Ulysses: The Mechanics of Meaning* (Englewood Cliffs, N.J.: Prentice-Hall, 1970), pp. 44–46.

7. Jacques Mercanton, "The Hours of James Joyce," part 1, tr., Lloyd C. Parks, *Kenyon Review* 24 (Autumn 1962):700–730.

to, a symbolic relic of his mother, was a suitable moly.[8]
But the moral equivalent was a tough problem. The qualities of character and circumstance that render Bloom finally resistant to real dangers, both internal and external, had to be discovered or invented by Joyce, who had no clear and ready formula for them.

He wrote to Budgen: "As regards 'moly' it can be chance, also laughter, the enchantment killer. . . ."[9] In subsequent letters he theorized that moly might be an invisible influence that saves in matters of accident, which he thought might be viewed as prayer, chance, agility, presence of mind, or power of recuperation. "In this special case," he theorized, "his plant may be said to have many leaves, indifference due to masturbation, pessimism congenital, a sense of the ridiculous, sudden fastidiousness in some detail, experience."[10] Again he surmised, "Moly could also be absinthe, the cerebral impotentising (!!) drink or chastity" and concluded in weary frustration, "Damn Homer, Ulysses, Bloom and all the rest."[11] His notes for the episode disclose the same range of choices: absinthe, mercury, chastity, chance, indifference, beauty, laughter, satire, conscience, and two enigmatic entries, escape from poison and Met-salt.[12]

8. Joyce, too, often carried about a talisman against evil, a pair of Nora's soiled drawers.

9. Letter to Budgen, September 1920, *Letters* 1:144.

10. Letter to Budgen, Michaelmas 1920, *Letters* 1:147–148.

11. Letter to Budgen, October 24, 1920, *Letters* 1:148–149.

12. See A. Walton Litz, *The Art of James Joyce: Method and Design in Ulysses and Finnegans Wake* (New York: Oxford University Press, 1964) pp. 25–26. Of the mysterious "Met–salt," Litz suggests, "The simplest explanation of it is that Joyce intended to introduce common table salt as a physical equivalent for 'Moly'. 'Met' probably stands for 'metamorphosis', the technique governing this identification and the entire episode as well." And I sup-

In brief, Joyce seems to have conceived of the moral equivalents to moly in terms of three fundamental possibilities: chance, indifference, and, most significantly, a highly developed and most ironic sense of self. These were the Ulyssean virtues, as Joyce saw and admired them. Neither physical courage nor deep passion nor sheer intelligence nor even imagination, so much celebrated by Blake, was sufficient to ward off despair or madness. Detachment, indifference, wit, and a sense of the ironic became for the mature Joyce in Europe what silence, exile, and cunning had been for him as a young man in Dublin. For in leaving Ireland he successfully flew by the nets of nationality, language, and religion only to discover in exile that the nets of panic and emptiness were spread everywhere.

Bloom's masochism, by its very openness and proximity to consciousness, seems to function in positive ways, unlike Stephen's masochism, which is severely repressed and potentially more dangerous. Like Stephen, Bloom is given to provoking violence against himself, though, unlike him, Bloom doesn't wait around to enjoy the beating. Bloom's psychic equilibrium, like Stephen's, is precarious, but Bloom's ability to survive is never in doubt. His fantasy life is the mechanism by which control is maintained over dangerous impulses. His freewheeling masochistic fantasies gratify his guilt to a sufficient degree to keep it from destroying him. His fantasy life is the arena in which his real struggles are forever taking place and in which his anxieties, once aroused, can be resolved. This internal magic theater in fact recalls Stephen's theory of the transcendental artist. Like the transcendant

pose *mercury* here means both Hermes, who had given the moly to Odysseus, and mercury, a popular treatment for syphilis.

Shakespeare, whose art is the record of his intrapsychic struggles, Bloom is both bawd and cuckold, the hornmad Iago ceaselessly willing that the Moor in him shall suffer. A great part of "Circe" may be seen as Bloom's art, since it is the dramatic representation of his inner conflicts. He has internalized his relationships and, at least in fantasy, hermaphrodized himself. His fantasy conflicts and resolutions make it possible for him to maintain a convenient distance between himself and threatening sexual situations. Thus, he will never meet Martha Clifford and will never approach the many Gerty MacDowells he will casually encounter, for the imaginative reconstructions of these possible relationships are more valuable to him, and the honeymoon in the hand is his preferred mode of response. This unending indulgence in fantasy enables Bloom to steer a precarious course of sanity and safety between the Scylla of sex and aggression in the real Dublin and the Charybdis of guilt, shame, and anxiety in his own mind. Both "Scylla" and "Circe" can be read as celebrations of fantasy and arguments that the inner life is at once richer and safer and more gratifying than the outer.

LOCOMOTOR ATAXIA

Joyce's own theories about the moral equivalent of Bloom's moly are not really incommensurable with the idea that moly may be fantasy itself. There is small difference between Joyce's conjecture that moly might be "indifference due to masturbation" and the more generalized idea of it as indifference due to preemptive intrapsychic gratification. Many of Joyce's attempts at definition—presence of mind, power of recuperation,

laughter, satire, and a sense of the ridiculous—are qualities of character that are underwritten by the imaginative
rites of self-accusation, self-punishment, and self-
gratification which Bloom performs. The ability to be
suddenly detached from inner compulsions that is hailed
by Joyce as presence of mind makes considerable sense
as a consequence of a violent fantasy life.

Bloom's self-possession, fitful though it may be, is a
rare quality in Nighttown, a world in which self-control
is at a premium. Not only is psychic breakdown a threat
in Nighttown, but physical breakdown, as well. According to Joyce's famous schema, the dominant organ of the
chapter is the locomotor apparatus, and the rhythm of
action, as Joyce told Budgen, is the rhythm of "locomotor
ataxia," which is a turn-of-the-century medical term for
the breakdown of motor control associated with syphilis.[13] Thus, it appears that in this chapter, where both
Bloom and Stephen stumble through the heart of Irish
paralysis, the genitocracy of Mabbot Street, physical and
psychic self-control are equivalent moral virtues.

Motor control, sexual control, anal and urethral control, and psychic control all suffer functional breakdown
in this chapter. As Bloom enters Nighttown, he is almost
run down by two cyclists, and when he "halts erect stung
by a spasm" in the middle of the street, he is almost run
down again by a trolley. As he manages to blunder stiff-
legged out of the track, the motorman hollers, "Hey shit-
breeches, are you doing the hattrick?" (428/435). Later,
during his hallucinated ordeal at the hands of Bella/o, he
defends, on the grounds of neatness, his preference for

13. Budgen, p. 228. See also Norman Silverstein, "Evolution of
the Nighttown Setting," in *The Celtic Master*, ed., Maurice Har-
man (Dublin: Dolmen Press, 1969).

urinating while seated "because often I used to wet . . . ."
(525/537). Zoe also recalls a priest who visited the
brothel two nights before but "couldn't get a connection. Only, you know, sensation. A dry rush" (509/520).
Kitty responds by recalling the recent convulsive death of
a syphilitic child of one of the prostitutes. Florry nods
and mumbles, "locomotor ataxy." Bloom's sexual self-
control is called into question by Zoe, who suspects from
his glum demeanor that he either "got up on the wrong
side of the bed or came too quick with [his] best girl"
(489/499). "Circe" is also a chapter of Freudian slips
and botched truisms. "God help your head," Zoe remarks to Lynch in defense of Stephen, "he knows more
than you have forgotten" (494/505). Bloom especially is
liable to mistake an aphorism: "Better one guilty escape
than ninety nine wrongfully condemned" (448/456). The
list is indefinitely extendable, and while we must bear in
mind that mental and verbal lapses of this kind are prop-
erties of the book as a whole, it is clear that they do
achieve a kind of fruition in "Circe." "Bloom's bloopers,"
as R. M. Adams has called them, are everywhere and are
themselves a fit subject for a book-length study.[14]

It seems that the theme of motor dysfunction was at
the heart of Joyce's conception of *Ulysses* from the beginning. In a sketch for "Circe" which may have been
drafted as early as 1915 the theme of motor failure was
already well developed.[15] *Ulysses* itself developed out of

14. R. M. Adams, *Surface and Symbol: A Study of the Consistency of Joyce's Ulysses* (New York: Oxford University Press,
1967), pp. 159–189.

15. See Silverstein, "Evolution." This early manuscript is in the
Joyce collection at Buffalo. See Peter Spielberg, *James Joyce's
Manuscripts and Letters at the University of Buffalo: A Catalogue*
(Buffalo: University of Buffalo Press, 1962), #V.A. 19, pp. 47–48.

plans for a story for *Dubliners* and thus was presumably meant to be another exposé of Irish "paralysis."
Joyce had explained to C. P. Curran in 1904, "I call the
series *Dubliners* to betray the soul of that hemiplegia or
paralysis which many consider a city."[16] And to Grant
Richards he later announced, "I chose Dublin for the
scene because that city seemed to me the centre of paralysis."[17] From the real paralysis of the old priest in
"The Sisters" and the paralytic panic of Eveline to the
sexual failures of James Duffy and Gabriel Conroy, paralysis, impotence, moral failure, and failure of nerve
invest the stories with that special odor of corruption
which Joyce took to be a uniquely Irish scent. In *Ulysses*
Stephen's multiple incapacities are said to be symptoms
of a "general paralysis of the insane" (8/6), and Bloom
and Stephen together in "Circe," peering into a "mirror
held up to nature," are confronted with an image of
themselves in the form of a beardless Shakespeare, "*rigid
in facial paralysis, crowned by the reflection of the reindeer antlered hatrack in the hall*" (553/567).

On the face of it, the motor dysfunctions of "Circe"
would appear to be physical correlatives or imitations
of the moral condition of Dublin. In the approved lexicon
of literary interpretation, the morally crippled are known
by their limp. But psychoanalysis, which is inclined to
seek out the image of the body in the most abstract of
mental operations, recommends an alternative view of
the relation of Irish paralysis to Circean locomotor ataxia.
It recommends that Joyce's early studies of moral and
psychological dysfunction in *Dubliners* may refer to a
preoccupation with motor control and that this concern

16. June 23, 1904, *Letters* 1:55.
17. May 5, 1906. *Letters* 2:134.

with physical control is the paradigm for the psychological and moral patterns of the book, not the other way
around.

In fact, as we might expect of any product of a puri-
tanical culture in which physical failure may bear the
taint of moral error, Joyce's books are preoccupied with
the imperfect and self-willed operations of the body. His
anxiety over the effects of "swine love" was not born
with the writing of "Circe." We know from Stanislaus's
diary that at about the time Joyce was beginning work
on *Dubliners* he held, perhaps ironically, some peculiar
notions about syphilis, hemiplegia of the will, and Irish
paralysis. *Dubliners* was to be, or so he told Stanislaus,
a study of the effects of syphilis in Ireland:

Jim wants to live. Life is his creed. He boasts of his power to
live, and says, in his pseudo-medical phraseology, that it
comes from his highly specialized central nervous system.
He talks much of the syphilitic contagion in Europe, is at
present writing a series of studies in it in Dublin, tracing
practically everything to it. The drift of his talk seems to be
that the contagion is congenital and incurable and responsible
for all manias, and being so, that it is useless to try to avoid
it. He even seems to invite you to delight in the manias and
to humour each to the top of its bent. (*CDD*, 51)

To be sure, there is the smell of an Irish joke here, the
hint of a jocoserious James humoring his brother's mania
to the top of its bent. Stannie, who claimed to be uncon-
vinced, responded with characteristic self-suspicion: "I
see symptoms in every turn I take. It seems to be that *my*
central nervous system is wretched, and I take every pre-
caution my half-knowledge suggests to revive it." Of
such stuff was made the character of Mr. Duffy in "A
Painful Case."

But of such stuff, too, was Joyce's art made. From *Dub-liners* through *Finnegans Wake* we discover a medical fascination with dysfunction, paralysis, and hemiplegia. Control, in all its forms, is a problem. Stephen Dedalus, from *Stephen Hero* through *Portrait* and *Ulysses*, strug-gles, on the one hand, with the problem of political con-trol within the school, the family, and the state, and faces, on the other hand, the double bind of a sexual ap-petite that can be neither satisfied nor suppressed. In *Stephen Hero*, which is nothing if not an inventory of tirades against restraint, Stephen complains in a long peroration on Irish puritanism and its unnatural authority over his manhood that among the Irish "contempt of [the body] human nature, weakness, nervous tremblings, fear of day and joy, distrust of man and life, hemiplegia of the will, beset the body burdened and disaffected in its members by its black tyrannous lice" (*SH*, 194).[18]

The manifold ramifications of control, including self-control, preside over *Portrait*, which begins with infant Stephen's wetting his diaper and ends with adolescent Stephen's preparations to fly by those famous aerial nets. Between these two events, the book develops around the irreconcilable antagonism between cultural and ecclesias-tical authority on the one hand and Stephen's instinctual and intellectual drives on the other, an antagonism that is finally resolvable only by flight. Stephen, as disobedi-ent subject, and his self-willed penis, as disobedient ob-ject, are in servitude to and rebellion against the same cultural authority. Stephen's "*non serviam*" becomes

18. Brackets in this sentence indicate Joyce's own substitutions in the text. Theodore Spencer, editor of *Stephen Hero*, has noted that the name *Gogarty* is scrawled across this sentence in the manuscript.

a psychological necessity only after it has become a physical one. To a great extent, however, Stephen's struggle is an internalized one, for cultural and ecclesiastical authority are ably represented in his mind by the fiercest of superegos. Thus, authority presents as much an intrapsychic as a social dilemma; the question "Who controls me?" interconnects with "Which part of me is in control?" As Stephen, who had decided upon his allegiances, acknowledges as he taps his brow in "Circe," "In here it is I must kill the priest and the king" (574/589).

In Stephen's imagination sin is the unrestrained flowing of waters, and the repressive struggle against affective threat, external or internal, is imagined to be a dam or breakwater weakly arrayed against an overwhelming tide. At one crucial moment, as Stephen finds himself unable to repress all that threatens him, he reflects on the futility of having armed himself against a sea of troubles: "How foolish his aim had been! He had tried to build a breakwater of order and elegance against the sordid tide of life without him and to dam up, by rules of conduct and active interests and new filial relations, the powerful recurrence of the tides within him. Useless. From without as from within the water had flowed over his barriers: their tides began once more to jostle fiercely above the crumbled mole" (*PA*, 98).

To be in mortal sin, to have a body and a mind that cannot be brought under repressive control, is to be inundated by the waters. And yet, when Stephen heads toward the brothel at the end of Chapter 2, the liquid metaphors yield to political ones: his sexual fantasies are "secret riots," his searches after sexual companionship are prompted by a "blood in revolt," and his encounter with the prostitute is a "surrender" and an "iniquitous

abandonment." In the brothel he commits a twofold
political sin: he surrenders control over his body to his
"riotous" lower functions, and he submits to the authority of false gods whom a jealous Church has forbidden
him.

The road back from such a state of sin is through a
program of intrapsychic counterinsurgency, the reestab-
lishment of control over the blood that has been in revolt,
and a resubmission of oneself to a parental authority.
Following the hellfire sermon and a spell of self-disgust
over his carnal sins, Stephen shrives himself at confession by submitting to an old priest and offering up his
shame. As Stephen imagines it, this confessional offering
is an inadequate oral-anal gift, a vomiting forth or moral
diarrhea. He submits by voluntarily surrendering all control over the contents of his mind, unlocking all repression and gushing forth a "squalid stream of vice" for his
confessor: "His sins trickled from his lips, one by one,
trickled in shameful drops from his soul festering and
oozing like a sore, a squalid stream of vice. The last sins
oozed forth, sluggish, filthy. There was no more to tell.
He bowed his head, overcome (*PA*, 144)."

The effect of this submissive and shameful opening up
is temporary superego reinforcement. Stephen does, in
effect, identify with his confessor and internalize him,
"let him in" to turn off the faucet of rampant sexuality.
Having done that, he submits to a self-imposed regimen
of sensual deprivation and mortification and emotional
self-control. In time, however, the tides of life begin to
move once more against his breakwaters of moral resolve,
and he finds himself given to gratuitous outbursts of
trivial anger. In the face of renewed sexual desire, his
struggle against masturbation becomes a source of pride

and a bracing sense of power as he provokes and then faces down the temptation to touch himself.

It gave him an intense sense of power to know that he could by a single act of consent, in a moment of thought, undo all that he had done. He seemed to feel a flood slowly advancing towards his naked feet and to be waiting for the first faint timid noiseless wavelet to touch his fevered skin. Then, almost at the instant of that touch, almost at the verge of sinful consent, he found himself standing far away from the flood upon a dry shore, saved by a sudden act of the will or a sudden ejaculation: and, seeing the silver line of the flood far away and beginning again its slow advance towards his feet, a new thrill of power and satisfaction shook his soul to know that he had not yielded nor undone all. (*PA*, 152)

This struggle for and against continence, renunciation, and self-control precipitates an intense intrapsychic power struggle, which in turn brings to the fore a nascent sadism and a "thrill of power"—characteristic anal qualities. In the same vein, one can't help noticing the peculiarly peristalic action of temptation and the nicely counter peristaltic "ejaculations" that magically cause the tides of Eros to recede. If one did not come to this passage knowing that Stephen was a masturbator whose specific temptation was to touch, ever so timidly at first, his own fevered skin, one might well imagine these advancing and receding waves to be part of some eliminative, anal or urethral struggle.

In this case, the end of the struggle is never in doubt. If Stephen is to renounce instinctual pleasure, it will not be at the behest of anyone but himself. Not even the threat of eternal damnation in the worst of all possible hells is sufficient to enforce the bans of religious authority upon his bodily functions. Stephen will submit to tyranny, as his situation in *Ulysses* shows us, but that tyranny

will be self-imposed. The price of his freedom will be
endless self-oppression. Similarly, we may guess that
his solution to the conflicts posed by forbidden sexual
desires will be, like Bloom's, an ambiguous mode of self-
control that admits of abstinence, satisfaction, and preemptive self-punishment all at once. We know that
Stephen will catch hold of himself sooner or later and
that when he does he will shamefully, and in sly agony,
write books about it.

To continue from this point requires a theoretical, and
perhaps imaginative, leap. It is necessary to invoke Freudian originology and suggest that there lurks behind this
struggle over Stephen's instinctual pleasures an earlier
one in which similar issues were at stake and similar
ambivalent solutions worked out. The tides of life that
advance and recede, the inadequate breakwaters of order
and elegance, the shameful streams of confession that
ooze from Stephen's mouth, the prurient wavelets that
advance toward his penis, the wetness of sin, the dryness
of salvation, all suggest a complicated web of connections
between sexual, moral, and eliminative behavior. We
know that this struggle over recalcitrant bodily functions
has been fought before, and theoretical considerations
alone argue that traces of the first battle inform every
aspect of the second, from the shame with which it is
carried on to the images through which it is apprehended
and the nature of the compromises by which it is finally
solved. Nor do we need a crude determinism to understand that similar battles over similar forbidden bodily
activities are likely to imply each other in the mind and
that the mode of solution of the earlier will hold some
dominion over the terms of the later. In any event, if

we allow ourselves a theoretical leap across this narrow-
est of chasms (which is too narrow to swallow us up),
we can bring a number of disparate elements of Joyce's
writing into focus as independent functions of a single
anal equation.

If it is true that patterns of moral, psychological, and
artistic behavior may be systematically modeled after
primitive patterns of compromise around areas of bodily
conflict, then we should be able to discover a stylistic
paradigm in any artist's life and work that organizes
otherwise disparate aspects of behavior into ordered and
significant relations under the rubric of a bodily metaphor. I think that what Freud meant in calling the ego a
"body ego" is that we *can* talk about oral, anal, phallic,
and genital characters and mean something real and important.[19] In Joyce's case, the anal equation brings into
common focus a multitude of disparate features of his
life and work, including Stephen Dedalus's radical self-
isolation and the liquid advance of his repressed desires,
Bloom's cloacal obsession, the stylistic development of
Joyce's own writing, and the themes of paralysis and
locomotor ataxia.

In fact, we can construct a consistent and far-reaching
theory of Joyce's art around the dialectic of anal control,
the components of which are complex and various. In
terms of relationships (and all human relationships in
Joyce's books involve dominance and subordination), the
elements of the anal dialectic are submission and depen-

19. See Father Walter J. Ong, S.J., on the tactual and kines-
thetic nature of Freudian metaphors in *The Presence of the Word:
Some Prolegomena for Cultural and Religious History* (New
Haven: Yale University Press, 1967), pp. 92–110.

dence *versus* defiance and autonomy.[20] Its affective component is, roughly, shame *versus* self-esteem. Functionally
it splits up into incompetence *versus* competence and
elimination *versus* retention. Spatially we have the modalities open and closed.

From the beginning it seems that Joyce confronted the
matter of artistic control as though it were a personal
struggle. His early compositional techniques make abundant sense as his attempts to work out, upon linguistic
materials, the rules for a regime of self-restraint. His
creative propensities, especially after his mother's death
in August 1903, were expansive and garrulous. Yet, his
first serious literary productions were the tight, discrete
epiphanies which he carefully produced over a period of
three or four years, from about 1900 to 1903 or 1904.
His stylistic aim in the epiphanies, it seems, was to rea-
lize a fine hardness of detail in a "form so fluent," as he
proclaimed to Yeats in 1902, "that it would respond to
the motions of the spirit."[21] To that end, he told Yeats
also, he had finally thrown over metrical form, though
in fact, he was yet to write the *Chamber Music* poems
in which the liquid gestures of Jonsonian music would be
held in place by the metrical rigor of Elizabethan forms.
Once free of poetic form, in *Dubliners* Joyce learned to
control the expansiveness of his verbal imagination by
invoking the canons of Flaubertian taciturnity. The famous snowy incantation at the end of "The Dead" is an
excellent example of powerful emotion powerfully withheld, the result being a fine and sensuous music. Also in

20. I owe this theory and a good deal else to Erik Erikson's
Childhood and Society (New York: Norton, 1950). See especially
"Theory of Infantile Sexuality," pp. 48–108.

21. Ellmann, *JJ*, p. 106.

the interests of control, he rewrote *Stephen Hero* as *Portrait*, harshly reining in the garrulity and open emotionalism of the former in favor of the latter's spare style of symbolic implication. Later, when the creative conflict between his effusive and retentive tendencies began to break down during the writing of *Ulysses*, he produced caricatures of both open and closed modes of writing: monotonous music ("Sirens") and endless inventory ("Ithaca"). Yet, even the last represents a kind of letting go. It does appear that Joyce at some point during the composition of *Ulysses* ceased to be bothered by the problem of control and began to emancipate his expansive tendencies without anxiety, thereby producing the encyclopedic enormities of the last chapters of *Ulysses* and *Finnegans Wake*.[22]

In another arena, under the aspect of this same anal dialectic, we can use the spatial modalities of open and closed to construct a simple but useful character typology that throws light upon Stephen and Bloom. Stephen is a closed character, Bloom an open one. Bloom delights in expelling the contents of his body; Stephen, who suffered from the "wasting fires" of lust in *Portrait* (*PA*, 99), is still anxious in *Ulysses* about wasting his essence. Observe his lingering concern with the problem of masturbation (383/389). Bloom is always in an open frame of mind, and he regards the world not only as food for thought but as a delightful array of eliminative events. On the way to Paddy Dignam's funeral, for example, Bloom is in an alimentary mood, and as he meditates upon death he reflects upon the rightness of sealing up

22. See Litz's account of the stylistic revolution that took place in Joyce's work somewhere between 1916 and 1920 (*The Art of James Joyce*, pp. 44–75).

the orifices of a corpse with wax, for otherwise "the insides decompose quickly. Much better to close up all the orifices. Yes, also. With wax. The sphincter loose. Seal up all" (97/98). Seeing an empty hearse leaving Glasnevin cemetery, he muses, "Looks relieved." At the funeral Bloom notices the size of Father Coffey, "with a belly on him like a poisoned pup," and the sight puts a strain upon his eliminative temper, making him uneasy:

What swells him up that way? Molly gets swelled after cabbage. Air of the place maybe. Looks full of bad gas. Must be an infernal lot of bad gas round the place. . . . Who was telling me? Mervyn Brown. Down in the vaults of saint Werburg's lovely old organ hundred and fifty they have to bore a hole in the coffins sometimes to let out the bad gas and burn it. Out it rushes: blue. One whiff of that and you're a goner. (102/103–104)

There is, it seems, a plentitude of ways to describe Stephen and Bloom and the differences between them: artist and scientist, son and father, intellectual and sensualist, Holmes and Watson (after Kenner), Künstler and Bürger (after Levin), and so on. Our theory puts us in possession of one more perspective on this duality, one that regards Stephen and Bloom as character types, rather than abstractions in an allegorical drama (*the* son, *the* father, *the* artist, and so forth), as they are most usually regarded. Stephen is more or less a closed or "retentive" character and Bloom more or less an open one.[23] Stephen

---

23. The entire range of possibilities in this definition of Bloom and Stephen as contrasting anal types works out with reasonable consistency. Bloom, the open character, is the more dependent of the two, Stephen, the more defiant. Both have developed unstable schemes of autonomy, though Stephen's seems to be more radical

is guilty of his own definition of incest, an avarice of the emotions. To his dead mother only does he pretend to be emotionally bound, and even from her he has withheld sympathy. Bloom, on the other hand, can and does extend himself emotionally, even if he is as avaricious sexually as Stephen. When the two meet, it is Bloom who tenders all the overtures and Stephen who systematically declines.

It may be possible to see Joyce's emotional career as an evolution from identification with the closed character as an ego ideal ("silence, exile, and cunning") to identification with the open character ("laughter, indifference, wit"), however difficult he may have found it to effect such a conversion upon himself in reality. This shift of identifications, moreover, loosely parallels the stylistic revolution in Joyce's prose, from the exclusive prose of *Dubliners*, *Portrait*, and the early *Ulysses* to the inclusive styles of the late *Ulysses* and *Finnegans Wake*. It makes sense to think of Joyce's development as an artist as a movement from the Dedalian to the Bloomian—from a style of scrupulous meanness, both in manner and matter, to one of unscrupulous hilarity.

One last example of the anal dimension of tyranny and rebellion lies in one of the book's political gestures, Stephen's (and Joyce's) anti-imperialism. Among the

---

and self-isolating. Bloom is the less competent and more shame-ridden; Stephen, the more competent and more guilt-ridden.

I have hesitated to use the word *eliminative* to define Bloom's character, though he is that, since so many of his qualities are ones we tend to ascribe to the oral character, which Bloom is also. In fact, Bloom is perhaps best thought of as an "alimental" character, open and active at both ends. His personality, I think, reflects such an omnibus openness.

crimes with which Joyce indicted the Roman and British
Empires was cloacal imperialism, the imposition of the
watercloset upon their colonial subjects. In "Aeolus"
Professor MacHugh observes of the Romans:

—What was their civilization? Vast, I allow: but vile. Cloacae:
sewers. The Jews in the wilderness and on the mountaintop
said: *It is meet to be here. Let us build an altar to Jehovah.*
The Roman, like the Englishman who follows in his footsteps,
brought to every new shore on which he set his foot (on our
shore he never set it) only his cloacal obsession. He gazed
about him in his toga and he said: *It is meet to be here. Let us
construct a watercloset.* (130/131)

The ancient Irish, adds Lenehan, "were partial to the
running stream." For Stephen, the watercloset becomes
an emblem of oppression, standing both for British imperialism and a spiritual rebellion that failed, for it was
in a Greek watercloset that the heresiarch Arius breathed
his last, "stalled upon his throne, . . . with upstiffed
omophorion, with clotted hindparts" (39/38). Stephen
adverts to that event a second time while drunk and
oppressed in "Circe," where he calls it, without so much
as a smirk, "the agony in the closet" (512/523).

This agony in the closet and its oblique variations are
present, I believe, in the locomotor ataxia of "Circe." But
the associative links that bind locomotor ataxia and
paralysis to anti-imperialism, to Stephen's sexual double
bind, to Bloom's cloacal obsession, and to the problem of
formal artistic control are ordinarily not available to the
reader or to literary criticism in any of its customary
forms. For the unifying logic is not manifest in the literature itself; it exists unconsciously in the mind of the
artist. This is not to rob "swine love," sexual failure,
paralysis, and syphilis of their legitimacy either as motifs

in the book or as sources of anxiety for Joyce. Rather, I
am insisting that we see Joyce's concern with them as
overdetermined, reaching back to and gaining affective
power from a more primitive bout with functional failure. The unique power of psychoanalysis as literary criticism lies precisely in its ability to make these connections.
Its interpretive virtue lies not merely in its ability to lay
bare the deep structure of the artist's psychic processes,
but in its demonstrations that the manifest artistic and
behavioral materials of his life and work contain thematic
unities that are otherwise unrecognizable. In this case,
it demonstrates that a general theory of Joyce's art,
however partial in its conclusions, can be constructed
around the theme of locomotor ataxia and that "Circe"
can be brought into focus as a psychic hub around which
much else in Joyce's life seems to resolve.

DISCIPLINE IN BLOOMUSALEM
OR THE MASOCHIST AS MESSIAH

> O foenix culprit! Ex nickylow malo comes
> mickelmassed bonum.
> —*Finnegans Wake*

We don't know precisely how the vision of Nighttown
unfolded for Joyce. An attempt to trace the chapter
through its many stages of composition has been promised us, and when published it may deepen our insight
into the psycho-logic of Joyce's imagination.[24] We do
know that Joyce rewrote, reorganized, and expanded the
chapter many times over and was at work on it as late as
January 1922, a month before its publication, when he

24. The Silverstein essay (see note 13) is a preview of that
study.

added and revised extensively on the page proofs. We
know also that one of the last major insertions, if not
the very last to be made in the proofs, was Bloom's messiah fantasy. And, although it seems awkwardly placed,
arising as it does in the midst of Bloom's uxorious behavior toward the prostitute Zoe and surrounded on all
sides by a saturnalia of masochism, the psychology of it
is sound. For, as I have pointed out, Bloom's (and Joyce's)
self-affliction is best understood as an agent of self-
exaltation, or, put in other words, their masochistic tactics work in behalf of messianic strategies.

   The messianic fantasy begins at midnight, with Bloom
in the act of making a "stump speech" on the incorrigi-
bility of mankind (469/478). He is stopped in midpero-
ration by the steeple chimes, which hail him as Leopold,
Lord Mayor of Dublin. At his inauguration the Bishop
of Down and Connor presents him to an Irish crowd
as "emperor president and king chairman" (472/482),
and the mob responds "God save Leopold the First,"
whereupon Bloom, right hand upon testicles, swears that
he will cause law and mercy to reign in all of Ireland.
Then, having been raised to the peerage by the Arch-
bishop of Armagh, Bloom delivers his first public message, an announcement of domestic intentions: "My
subjects! We hereby nominate our faithful charger
Copula Felix hereditary Grand Vizier and announce that
we have this day repudiated our former spouse and have
bestowed our royal hand upon the princess Selene, the
splendour of the night" (473/483). At that announcement, "the former morganatic spouse of Bloom is hastily
removed in the Black Maria" (473–474/483). It is minor
but worth pointing out here that Molly, so far as we

know, is legally married to Bloom and therefore not a
morganatic spouse.[25] But James and Nora Joyce were, in
a sense, a morganatic couple, for their marriage was not
legal in the eyes of English law until 1931.

Everyman is revealed in this fantasy to be Everysavior
as well, "emperor president and king chairman," as he
is named at his inauguration. He is hailed by John How-
ard Parnell as "successor to my famous brother"; he
discloses himself to be a hero of the Boer War, of the Cri-
mean War, of Fenian agitation, and, at last, of the Mil-
lenium itself. This omnipresent and omnipotent Bloom
ushers in the dawn of the new era with an announcement
of the golden city, the New Bloomusalem, which arises in
his mind's eye as "a colossal edifice, with crystal roof,
built in the shape of a huge pork kidney, containing forty
thousand rooms" (475/484). This new Messiah then
dispatches his enemies, including the man in the macintosh, and proceeds to befriend, console, titillate, approve,
protect, invigorate, and advise the world. He reveals himself to be a bourgeois, ecumenical, and altogether progres-
sive savior who stands for brotherhood, esperanto, union,
a decent life for all, "free money, free love and a free lay
church in a free lay state" (480/490).

The inevitable denunciation of this new King of Kings
is led, predictably, by the Church. Father Farley (whom
Bloom recalls as having been unwilling or unable to get
Molly into a Church choir) sets off a general revolt by

25. Hélène Cixous observes acutely that nowhere in Bloom's
or Molly's recollections can we find the wedding day. Indeed,
though one finds marriage everywhere in Joyce's work, there is
nary a wedding ceremony. *The Exile of James Joyce* (New York:
David Lewis, 1972), p. 57.

denouncing Bloom as an "episcopalian, an agnostic, an anythingarian seeking to overthrow our holy faith" (481/ 490). The evangelist Alexander J. Dowie takes up the denunciation on the grounds of sexual immorality, reviling Bloom as "this stinking goat of Mendes" and "a worshipper of the Scarlet Woman" (482/492), true accusations, one supposes, but reminiscent again of the terms in which Parnell had been denounced. "Lynch him," the mob responds, "Roast him! He's as bad as Parnell was." Bloom protests his innocence and calls upon Dr. Malachi Mulligan, "sex specialist," to give testimony on his behalf. Mulligan, punningly attired in a "motor jerkin," declares Bloom to be "bisexually abnormal," chronically exhibitionistic, latently ambidextrous, prematurely bald from selfabuse, more sinned against than sinning, and *virgo intacta*. In short, as Dr. Dixon declares, "Professor Bloom is a finished example of the new womanly man. His moral nature is simple and lovable. Many have found him a dear man, a dear person" (483–484/493). It is discovered, in addition, that "he wears a hairshirt winter and summer and scourges himself every Saturday." To fill out the contours of Bloom's divine androgyneity, Dixon reveals that this savior has indeed been wife unto himself and is about to have a baby, whereupon Bloom is delivered of eight male yellow and white children, who disperse instantly to the corners of the earth to take charge of its entrepreneurial affairs.

But the fantasy quickly breaks down into an incoherent array of accusations and condemnations, as an imaginary rabble condemns this polymorphous God as a false messiah and burns him at the stake. His last words are a most heroic "weep not for me, O daughters of

Erin," whereupon the daughters of Erin kneel down to pray, "Kidney of Bloom, pray for us, Flower of the Bath, pray for us," and so forth, and a choir of six hundred voices intones the Alleluia Chorus (488/498).

The dramatic movement of the fantasy is familiar to readers of Joyce. In one form it is recognizable as the Icarian paradigm, the cycle of precocious aspiration and premature failure. It is also a familiar sexual theme, the cycle of *ejaculatio praecox* sublimated into political and messianic fantasies. "Circe" rehearses a more elaborate form of this paradigm, the myth of the tragic savior, the drama of election and betrayal. In this version of the fantasy a savior arises and labors to lead his people to the promised land. Before his work is complete he is betrayed and denounced by his own followers, who have been turned against him by an envious brother, a Judas, a Vincent Cosgrave or a Tim Healey. He is crucified and his work destroyed. In Joyce's fantasies the three most prominent figures associated with this mythic pattern of election and betrayal were Christ, Parnell, and himself. As for himself, to be sure, he had little reason to believe that he actually ever had been (or would be) hailed as the Irish messiah, but he did consider his books to be doctrinal to the nation and regarded all hostility to them and himself as acts of envy, and therefore betrayals. He regarded himself as a closet savior, a secret prophet who had been betrayed before he had even had the chance to arise. His crime, he felt, was premature erection and his natural fate, the fate of all prophets in Ireland, premature castration. (Conor Cruise O'Brien calls this pattern in Irish politics the 1891 treatment.) The castration of Parnell was symbolized for Joyce by the attempted blinding

at Castlecomer,[26] an event which struck at the very heart
of his own anxieties. He noted: "Twas Irish humour, wet
and dry,/ Flung quicklime into Parnell's eye."[27] Joyce
was peculiarly sensitive to the attack on the eye. Parnell's ultimate fate at the hands of the Irish people, as
Joyce saw it, was dismemberment. In an article for *Il
Piccolo della Sera* he charged: "In his final desperate appeal to his countrymen, he begged them not to throw
him as a sop to the English wolves howling around them.
It redounds to their honour that they did not fail this appeal. They did not throw him to the English wolves; they
tore him to pieces themselves."[28] Yet, in spite of this
threat, which Joyce understood to be a threat against himself, he resolved as a young man to "stand erect" or, as he
proclaimed in his poem "The Holy Office":

> Where they have crouched and crawled and prayed
> I stand, the self-doomed, unafraid,
> Unfellowed, friendless and alone,
> Indifferent as the herring-bone,
> Firm as the mountain-ridges where
> I flash my antlers on the air.[29]

But, as we have seen already and as others have pointed
out in some detail, betrayal, martyrdom, and castration
were apparently courted with at least as much passion as
they were feared,[30] and it may be assumed that the idea

26. See the essay Joyce wrote for *Il Piccolo della Sera*, "The
Shade of Parnell," in *CW*, pp. 223–228.

27. From "Gas from a Burner," in *The Portable James Joyce*,
ed., Harry Levin (New York: Viking, 1947), p. 660.

28. From "The Shade of Parnell," *CW*, p. 228.

29. From *The Portable James Joyce*, ed., Levin, p. 659.

30. See Richard Ellmann, "A Portrait of the Artist *as Friend*,"
in *Joyce's Portrait: Criticisms and Critiques*, ed., Thomas E. Connolly, and also Morton P. Levitt, "Shalt Be Accurst? The Martyr
in James Joyce," *James Joyce Quarterly* 5 (Summer 1968):285–297.

of the fall from grace was every bit as attractive to Joyce as the dream of the rise to glory. As we can see in *Ulysses*, Bloom's moral preeminence is assured by his failures; he is a hero because he is a victim. He relives time and again in fantasy his personal version of the fortune fall, as though the theological pattern of sin, fall, redemption, and glorification were a law of his own psychical functioning. Joyce learned well the lessons of martyrdom, that "felixed is who culpas does" (*FW*, 246).

Bloom's messianic fantasies register the desire for spiritual election; his fantasies of affliction are his personal confirmation, if not of blessedness, at least of moral superiority. His masochism mediates between the desire and the confirmation by calling down evidence of election in the form of imaginary punishment. The betrayal of the savior, his ordeal at the hands of those whom he would deliver, and his final crucifixion are all part and parcel of the messianic dream. They bring the messianic paradigm to its necessary conclusion. The savior's betrayal and apparent failure are, for him, the stamp and assurance of his divine election, his castration the proof of his erection. The "Cyclops" chapter contains, in comic reduction, the whole paradigm of messianic affliction. Despite the obvious comedy of Bloom's martyrdom, flight, and Elijahlike ascent "to the glory of the brightness at an angle of fortyfive degrees over Donohoe's in Little Green Street like a shot off a shovel" (339/345), the underlying fantasy of triumph is a most serious one. It may be desirable for a self-elected saint to look to his works for confirmation of his authenticity, but where his works are nonexistent or have come to no good, he must look to his afflictions. This was certainly the case with Joyce before 1914, as it is with Bloom.

Bloom's masochistic and messianic fantasies come together because his sexual desires and those we might call
political or perhaps egotistical are answerable to the
same conditions. The job of exciting himself and that of
rescuing his people (Irish, Jews, mankind) demand submission to discipline and the cultivation of affliction. In
psychoanalytic terms, the audience for a masochistic
show of submission is oneself—specifically, one's own
superego, the internalized parent who autocratically ad-
monishes and justifies, chides and rewards, gives and re-
ceives. In sexual masochism, this harsh parental aspect
of the self may be projected upon a friend, a lover, or a
proper stranger, while in messianism, the object of submission is more appropriately a fierce and vindictive God
—a Jahweh, Jehovah, Lord of Hosts, or Almighty Father.
In Bloom's case the very pervasiveness of this strategy of
success by failure shows it to be a psychic cliché, a
ritualistic response of an anxiety-ridden ego which has
discovered an all-purpose weapon to do battle on many
fronts.

Theodore Reik has argued that masochism is really a
kind of strength, which imitates weakness for tactical
reasons but should not be mistaken for weakness.[31] Indeed, the historical phenomenon of early Christianity
argues well for the political and rhetorical force of submission. Peter's exhortation to all good Christians to
"be clothed with humility: for God resisteth the proud,
and giveth grace to the humble" (I Peter 5:5) may or may
not have been a correct reading of divine purposes, but it
was an excellent reading of the political necessities of a
new era. The conversion of a great military empire to the

31. See Reik, *Masochism.*

praise, if not always the practice, of meekness is testimony to the rhetorical power of masochism.

To be sure, Christian humility is not quite the same thing as Bloomian masochism. The one aims at the enforcement of continence and discipline in the face of threat, the other at the achievement of orgasm. Bloom may enjoy a good scourging now and then, but it is designed to make sexual gratification possible, not to do penance for desiring it. (Or, *first* the penance, *then* the pleasure.) This may serve to point up the tactical nature of pain in masochism, confirming Reik's view that it is a means and not an end. Thus, we may be able to view it, as I have already noted, as a stereotyped response of a particular ego, a routine posture which may be struck on behalf of a number of different ends. But, then again, we may also be able to view ascetic self-denial or self-mortification as ultimate forms of masochistic suspense whose aim is not to deny orgasm forever, but only to postpone it until after death, when it may be enjoyed as the eternal orgasm of divine love. As Reik has pointed out, the Medieval Church was obliged to place controls upon self-flagellation when too many monks discovered its delights.[32]

"Circe," finally, is an ambiguous document of Catholic thought. On the one hand it *is* a type of Christian martyrology and Bloom *is* a type of Christian saint. On the other hand, it is a comic critique of both asceticism and

32. Philip Slater thinks this extreme asceticism "the most pathological and bizarre of narcissisms," for its goal, like any narcissistic behavior, remains pleasure and self-aggrandizement. "The pilgrim," he observes, "brutally abandons his earthly family to aggrandize his immortal soul" (*The Glory of Hera: Greek Mythology and the Greek Family* [Boston: Beacon Press, 1968], p. 456).

martyrdom. Bloom's promise of "free money, free love and a free lay church in a free lay state" is a clear enough statement of his, and Joyce's, opposition to ascetic and religious principles. His refusal in "Cyclops" and "Circe" to allow himself to be a victim of violence is also a sign of his aversion to real martyrdom, however much it may appeal to him in fantasy. A modern man, he is willing to settle for the lesser martyrdoms of the bedroom. A sensible man, he will settle for those lesser salvations a man may find on the beach, in the bath, or some other private and furtive place.

EPILOGUE: THE DIALECTIC OF MOTIVES

It is by no means easy to account for the full range of Joyce's purposes in writing this comic fantasia on his own psychosexual themes. As befits the work of a complicated and devious man, the psychodynamics of "Circe" are inordinately complex, and in the attempt to summarize them we must limit ourselves to a few simple and reductive observations. In "Circe" we have two characters, each of whom both is and is not the author, and whom the author at once identifies with and holds at an ironic distance. We have also the author himself, the great fantast in whose mind the whole scenario takes place and who is present in it under several different aspects: as the dreamer, as the characters in his own dream, as the ironic interlocutor of that dream, and as the fabulous artificer who organizes the materials of the dream into a lucid and shapely artistic whole. Like Shakespeare, Joyce is all in all. The totality and complexity of his presence betrays an elaborate dialectic of motives and countermotives that proceeds from the depths of pure eros through the intervening medium of masochism to the heights of Daedalian indifference by a series of strategic reversals.

At very bottom there is Bloom's and Joyce's erotism, the physical drive toward sexual union with another. That sexuality, however, never declares itself in the form of direct and unconditional phallic potency. The direct expression of sexual desire is under intrapsychic prohibition and has been interdicted at its source by a repression with which it must negotiate for its release. Thus, the sexuality that does find expression in Bloom's and Joyce's psychic lives is a partial and regressive sexuality which has succumbed to repression and which, even in its admissable forms, is accompanied by shame, guilt, and anxiety.

No affective dispositions are quite so native to Joyce's characters as these three; they invade every relationship and paralyze every act. In *Ulysses*, as in *Dubliners*, Dublin is the center of paralysis, and the agent of that paralysis is the sexual guilt that is fostered in the home and sponsored by a church which has discovered its utility as an instrument of political control. Bloom's masochism serves this guilt and, as I have noted, is his defense against total sexual and behavioral paralysis, for his masochistic fantasies alleviate his guilt sufficiently to allow him a narrow range of anxiety-free activity. This same guilt, not unmixed with pride, underlies the Joycean confessional here and elsewhere. For "Circe" is, at bottom, a *mea culpa*, an admission of a great burden of sin that is struggling for expression. Yet, the precise nature of that sin remains hidden. We have Bloom's admissions, under self-imposed duress, of perverse and comic crimes against love, and there is Stephen's self-consuming guilt over the betrayal of his mother, a crime against the

only love that is real for him, *amor matris*. Yet, it is
a distinctive feature of guilt that it can produce the sins
to which it attributes itself in consciousness, and we need
not believe that the sins of the past that confront Bloom
and Stephen in Nighttown explain *Joyce's* guilt. Somewhere in the background, unwillingly and uneasily repressed, is a crime against love. Yet, despite the ubiquity
of confession in *Ulysses* and Joyce's other books, that
crime remains as mysterious as Earwicker's crime in
Phoenix Park. For between the sin and the guilt falls
the shadow, that veil of forgetfulness that stands between
infantile sin and adult consciousness. We may suspect,
on theoretical grounds, the classical oedipal crimes of
incestuous and parricidal desires, but should be cautious
in insisting on them alone. Infantile guilt antedates the
oedipal crisis and may be well developed and highly overdetermined by the time that crisis takes place.[33] We *can*
say with some certainty in Joyce's case that an oedipal
crime is strongly suggested and also that the sense of
guilt attaches itself to the anus and anal behavior. Bloom's
fantasies and Joyce's letters bear witness to that.

The exposure of Bloom's guilt in "Circe" gives rise to
at least two affective responses on Joyce's part: a sense
of pride and power in having overcome repression and a
helpless sense of exposure or shame—the feeling of
being watched and judged inadequate. It is for that reason that the confessional seeks the protective cover of a
comic saturnalia. Joyce presents Bloom's fantasy life as
an entertainment in which desire, guilt, pride, fear,
despair, and shame are all part of the same vaudeville

33. See Melanie Klein, *Contributions to Psychoanalysis 1921–
1945* (London: The Hogarth Press and The Institute of Psychoanalysis, 1948), *passim.*

routine. The fantasies are real but theatrically overdone, as if in apology for the truths they contain. We may expect in such a circumstance that the comedy will be most hilarious wherever the fantasy is most revealing, and such a formula does seem to describe Bloom's fantasy life in "Circe." The deeper we go, the funnier it gets. This confession bears its own formidable armor, an Olympian humor which denies Joyce's shame even as it snickers over Bloom's.[34] Joyce shows us in no uncertain terms: *Bloom did it!!*

The third step in this dialectic of shame in art is the application of ego controls to the whole process by the organization of the comic *mea culpa* into a work of impersonal craftsmanship. The Dedalian forge shores up the pose of ironic detachment by making it possible to confess guilt while minimizing shame. The elevation of guilt and masochism and their ironic defenses into great art is the weapon by which Joyce did battle with the syndrome of negative feelings associated with confession and derepression. For through art shame may be transformed into aggressive self-exhibition and the show of guilt may become a display of stigmata, the signs of spiritual election. Art bribes the superego by insisting on the artist's ability to exercise manipulative control over the sources of his own shame and guilt.[35] The artist manages them by translating the burden of affect from fantasy onto style, structure, and language wherein bad feelings assume the wholeness, harmony, and radiance of

34. Lionel Trilling has complained about this translation of Joyce's erotic fantasies into comedy in his review of Joyce's letters in *Commentary* 45 (February 1968):60.

35. George Devereaux, "Art and Mythology," in *Studying Personality Cross-Culturally*, ed., Bert Kaplan (New York: Harper and Row, 1961), p. 372.

good form. Art thus used is a program of salvation
through good works, for in art, as in religion, original sin
is undone by the show of a job well done. In this dedication to good works, the artist's unconscious aim is to
make a show of self-discipline to the cruel old Nobo-
daddy within, the superego, which apparently despises
life but is a collector of fine erotica.

4. Nausikaa:
The Anatomy of a Virgin

You will never go wrong in concluding
that a man once loved deeply whatever
he hates, and loves it yet. . . .
                                    —GEORGE GRODDECK

They are not all free men who mock
their chains. —LESSING, *Nathan the Wise*

THE BROTHERS CAFFREY:
A NOTE ON FRATRICIDE

IN THE "Cyclops" episode Bloom encounters in Barney
Kiernan's pub the Irish Polyphemus, Michael Cusack,
known to his cronies as the Citizen. The pub is the den
of such one-eyed Fenians and pubsters as Alf Bergen,
Ned Lambert, Joe Hynes, J. J. O'Malloy, Bob Doran, and
the Citizen himself, all drinkers, all boasters, all praisers
of their own past.[1] At the end of the chapter, Bloom, at
his most harried and Christlike, is hounded from the pub
by the Citizen and the dog Garryowen and escapes only
by virtue of a mysterious ascent "to the glory of the
brightness at an angle of fortyfive degrees over Donohoe's in Little Green Street like a shot off a shovel"

1. This analogizing of the Citizen to the Cyclops emphasizes
the savagery of his temperament and the carnivorous quality of
his politics. It implies also that Irish chauvinism is "one-eyed,"
lacking in vision and perspective. But it is also a joke and an
insult. The Citizen is a one-eye in the standard American slang
sense of the epithet—he is a prick.

153

(339/345). By the opening of "Nausikaa," he has made his way to Sandymount beach at sundown, where he finds himself within spying distance of three girls: Gerty Mac-Dowell, Cissy Caffrey, and Edy Boardman, and their young charges: eleven-month-old Baby Boardman and the noisy twins, Tommy and Jacky Caffrey. Assembled nearby is the men's temperance retreat receiving the Benediction of the Blessed Sacrament under the guidance of the Reverend John Hughes, S.J.

"Nausikaa" begins with a composition of place. The language and conception are Gerty's:

> The summer evening had begun to fold the world in its mysterious embrace. Far away in the west the sun was setting and the last glow of all too fleeting day lingered lovingly on sea and strand, on the proud promontory of dear old Howth guarding as ever the waters of the bay, on the weedgrown rocks along Sandymount shore and, last but not least, on the quiet church whence there streamed forth at times upon the stillness the voice of prayer to her who is in her pure radiance a beacon ever to the stormtossed heart of man, Mary, star of the sea. (340/346)

This is a domestic and sentimental sunset. The domestic world is being put to bed while the proud, fatherly promontory of "dear old Howth" guards the waters of the bay and the maternal summer evening enfolds the world in a final, mysterious embrace.[2] This sunset is a ceremonial changing of the guard in which the loving care of the sun that guards the sea and strand by day

2. Hugh Kenner has a more apocalyptic view of this sunset in *Dublin's Joyce* (Boston: Beacon Press, 1956), p. 231. Richard Ellmann, too, has some nice observations upon this *paysage sexualisé* in *Ulysses on the Liffey* (New York: Oxford University Press, 1972), pp. 126–127.

yields to the pure radiance of the Virgin, man's guide through the dark hours of the spirit.

The three girls are habituées of Sandymount "where they were wont to come" to "discuss matters feminine," such as romance and children. Cissy and Edy are the older sisters of the children, and older sisters, like summer evenings, are wont to fold the objects of their care in mysterious embraces: "Cissy Caffrey cuddled the wee chap for she was awfully fond of children, so patient with little sufferers and Tommy Caffrey could never be got to take his castor oil unless it was Cissy Caffrey that held his nose and promised him the scatty heel of the loaf of brown bread with golden syrup on. What a persuasive power that girl had!" (340/346).

The twins, being Irishmen, are prone to fight. Under the gentle aspect of motherhood, the aggressive chauvinism of the previous chapter returns in the form of a "slight altercation" between Master Tommy and Master Jacky over a sand castle that Jacky has built and Tommy wishes to improve by the addition of a front door "like the Martello tower had" (341/347). "But if Master Tommy was headstrong Master Jacky was selfwilled too and, true to the maxim that every little Irishman's house is his castle, he fell upon his hated rival and to such purpose that the wouldbe assailant came to grief and (alas to relate!) the coveted castle too" (341/347). Tears flow copiously, and Cissy Caffrey, like a beacon ever to the storm-tossed heart of man, hastens to console Tommy, for Cissy "was a past mistress in the art of smoothing over life's tiny troubles." But she who comforts can also be stern. The soft, maternal heart does not, as a rule, take kindly to youthful aggressiveness.

"—Nasty bold Jacky! she cried."

As Cissy scolds, Edy tries her had at comforting Tommy with talk of love. "—Tell us who is your sweetheart, spoke Edy Boardman. Is Cissy your sweetheart?"

"—Nao, tearful Tommy said."

"—I know . . . I know who is Tommy's sweetheart, Gerty is Tommy's sweetheart."

But Tommy just now can have no thought of sweethearts, and Cissy, perceiving what the trouble is, tells Edy "to take him there behind the pushcar where the gentleman couldn't see and to mind he didn't wet his new tan shoes."

This vignette, above all, is a comic rehearsal of Joyce's fratricidal obsession. Tommy and Jacky are miniatures of Stephen and Buck Mulligan, of Shakespeare and brothers Richard and Edmund, of Bloom and Boylan, of Joyce and Gogarty/Cosgrave, of Richard Rowan and Robert Hand, of old Hamlet and Claudius, of Shem and Shaun. Just as Stephen and Mulligan struggle silently for the key to the Martello tower, Tommy and Jacky come to grief over the door to a sand castle.

Most immediately, this interlude recalls the preceding chapter; Tommy and Jacky are Bloom and the Citizen writ small. The gigantism of "Cyclops" is undercut by the infantilism of "Nausikaa." In the former, the Dubliners' heroic illusions about themselves and the Celtic past strive toward a sort of sublimity; their language and the language of Joyce's interpolated strophes are two kinds of heroic overstatement. The beginning of "Nausikaa" is Joyce's revenge upon the Citizen, the deflation of the one-eye. In Homer's *Odyssey* the symbolic castration of the Cyclops takes place when Odysseus and his men drive a hot stake through his eye as he lies in a drunken sleep. Joyce performs the castration verbally, reducing the Citizen's bravado to a child's crankiness and depicting Irish manhood in general as subject to the soothing ministrations of all-enfolding motherhood. The stylistic technique of the chapter is "tumescence, detumescence," and this is detumescence with a vengeance. On Bloom's behalf, the Citizen's threat is neutralized as both men are reduced to infantile equality. Thus, the irony is double-edged, for the castration is general and includes Bloom. Yet "Nausikaa" represents a triumph for him, the triumph of the wounded. Bloom gains maternal favor as a consequence of defeat. Like the offended Tommy, he has been cruelly beset, and, like him, he is about to be offered solace of a sort by one of those lovely seaside girls. Again like Tommy, who finds relief behind the pushcar, Bloom relieves himself by masturbating behind a rock. And in this universe of embracing maternal evenings and radiant virgin comfort for storm-tossed hearts, a man's only care is to mind he doesn't wet his new tan shoes.

This playlet may also be read as a pocket history of Irish politics, a comic allegory of the fall of Parnell and the defeat of Home Rule in 1891. Jacky Caffrey, the builder of the sand castle (Ireland), is perhaps the Irish Catholic Church, and Cissy perhaps the Virgin, that rock upon which the Church is built. Tommy may be Parnell's Irish Party, in particular, or Irish Republicanism, in general. For, as Joyce surely knew, one Tom Caffrey was among those implicated in the Phoenix Park murders.

But, however we read the episode, the Joycean gesture remains the same. In reducing conflict, be it personal or political, to child's play, Joyce was responding to the threat by distancing himself from it, denying its value. As such, the scene is an example of Joyce's aggressive irony, the revocation of anger and passion through wit. Like all of "Nausikaa," the Caffrey affair is Joyce's comic reduction of his own major obsessions. Joyce often likened his creative office to that of the priesthood and regarded his work as a secular transubstantiation of common reality into art. But in the ironic reduction of his own fantasy life, he seems to do something of the reverse. This slight altercation of the brothers Caffrey represents a substantiation of Joyce's inner life, the body and blood of real terror becoming the water and wine of a comic subplot. This is the method of "Nausikaa" as it is that of all of *Finnegans Wake*. "History repeats itself comically"; Joyce once told Jacques Mercanton, "this is our funnaminal world."[3]

THE MALICE OF HIS TENDERNESS:
THE CASE AGAINST GERTY

> Yet must thou fold me unaware
>   To know the rapture of thy heart,
> And I but render and confess
> The malice of thy tenderness.
>   —*Chamber Music* 27

It is the task of psychoanalytic criticism to bring to light the uneasiness beneath the finished surface of a work of art and to map out the connections between that dis-ease and the more coherent and self-assured "artistic vision" and aesthetic surface in which it finds expression. For it is characteristic of the best literature that graceful and orderly surfaces conceal massive subterranean unrest. This is doubly the case with good satire, in which

3. Jacques Mercanton, "The Hours of James Joyce," part 2, *Kenyon Review* 25 (Winter 1963):96. The phrase comes up somewhat altered in *FW* 244.

the artist's defensive posture of creative competence is reinforced by the authority of moral rectitude. "Nausikaa" is good satire. The stylistic virtuosity brought to bear upon Gerty MacDowell is one of the best examples in *Ulysses* of the reductive and aggressive powers of Joyce's wit. This wit is not exactly the *saeva indignatio* of Swift, which is, perhaps, more Irish, nor is it quite the red-faced male chauvinism of the pub, which is most Irish of all. But in its imitation of the sharp gentility of British wit, "Nausikaa" closely resembles *The Rape of the Lock*, being a middle-class variation on Pope's courtly satire.

The consensus of received critical opinion is that "Nausikaa" is an attack on popular culture and bourgeois romantic sensibility and that Gerty is the epitome of vulgar sentimentality. As Richard Kain has put the charge in his *Fabulous Voyager*, "We see the romantic soul of Gerty MacDowell probed with astringent wit."[4] And Hugh Kenner, with characteristic chivalry and forebearance, condemns her as "a secular perversion of 'the Virgin most Powerful, Virgin most merciful' " and "a massive epiphany of second-hand living."[5] Darcy O'Brien sees her in more or less the same terms, as "a collection of pulp-fiction clichés" whom Joyce is using "as a means of mocking certain ridiculously sentimental distortions of reality."[6] To a point, there are commonsense judgments which command our assent. And yet it is hard to accept either Gerty or sentimentality as worthy objects of Joyce's satire. One of *Ulysses*'s most acute

4. Richard Kain, *The Fabulous Voyager: James Joyce's Ulysses* (New York: Viking, 1959), p. 114.

5. Kenner, *Dublin's Joyce*, p. 257.

6. Darcy O'Brien, *The Conscience of James Joyce* (Princeton: Princeton University Press, 1968), pp. 157–158.

readers, S. L. Goldberg, has accused "Nausikaa" of "breaking a butterfly upon its wheel," and he is surely right, despite O'Brien's complaint that Goldberg doesn't understand the prerogatives of satire.[7] Gerty, after all, is an easy mark for Joyce, and the contest is strictly no contest. A tiger stalks a lamb. Stanley Sultan, a later entry in this minor debate, has acknowledged the justice of Goldberg's complaint and answered it with the observation that Gerty is not herself the primary object of the satire, for that, indeed, would be breaking butterflies.[8] The real indictment, he claims, is against the romantic novel in general and Maria Cummins in particular, whose *Mabel Vaughan* and *The Lamplighter* are primary sources of the style and vocabulary of Gerty's narrative. And Miss Cummins, as Sultan sees it, is an object worthy of Joyce's satire. Most recently, Richard Ellmann has wisely stood aloof from the debate over Joyce's motives and has simply and rightly pointed out that there is praise in this satire and that Gerty's apparent lack of taste displays a genuine impulse toward art.[9]

With all good intent and solemn reverence, some of the critics have trivialized Joyce's concerns by portraying him as a simple moralist and culture critic with a special vendetta against romanticism, sentimentality, and the sexual illusions of unsatisfied young ladies. Such explanations contain, at best, partial truths but hardly touch upon the reasons for the special animus in "Nausikaa." Nor does the chapter itself contain its own justifications.

7. S. L. Goldberg, *The Classical Temper: A Study of James Joyce's Ulysses* (London: Chatto & Windus, 1963), pp. 140–141. See O'Brien's rebuttal in *Conscience*, pp. 156–157.

8. Stanley Sultan, *The Argument of Ulysses* (Columbus: Ohio State University Press, 1964), pp. 272–273.

9. *Ulysses on the Liffey*, p. 130.

It is, on the face of it, a gratuitously peevish, if entertaining, gesture. "Nausikaa" must be accounted an overreaction to the apparent object of its satire—the debris of the romantic tradition in popular Victorian culture.

There are clues to this overreaction elsewhere in Joyce's writing, especially and significantly in things he did not himself publish which have come to light only since his death. Specifically, they are *Stephen Hero* and its ur-text, the 1904 "Portrait of the Artist" essay, the *Giacomo Joyce* manuscript, the notes for *Exiles*, and, of course, the letters.[10] The message of these notes, manuscripts, and letters is that Gerty is a mirror held up to Joyce's own erotic nature and that the sentimental fiction he plundered for her vocabulary is only an accessory to the fact and not the thing itself. Joyce was playing in this chapter, but the game involved his own erotic propensities, his libidinal clichés. Gerty is the *reductio ad absurdum* of a particular phase of his own erotic life, and the chapter is an act of exorcism that affirms an old commitment even while denying it.

While Gerty may not be a virgin in fact, a curious matter which I'll take up momentarily, she is nonetheless a type of Joycean woman who is best understood as the virgin-temptress. This virgin-temptress is the narcissistic phase of Irish Catholic adolescence whose primary role in Joyce's life and fantasies was to provoke desire and deny fulfillment. Gerty, in light of her exhibitionistic

10. "A Portrait of the Artist," eds., Richard M. Kain and Robert Scholes, *Yale Review* 49 (Spring 1960):355–369. It is reprinted in Kain and Scholes, *The Workshop of Daedalus* (Evanston: Northwestern University Press, 1965), pp. 56–74, and in the Viking Critical Library edition of Joyce's *Portrait of the Artist as a Young Man* (New York, 1968), pp. 257–266. See also, *Giacomo Joyce*, ed., Richard Ellmann (New York: Viking, 1968).

propensities and her strong desire to be violated, seems
the least frigid of the virgin-temptresses we encounter in
Joyce's work, but she owes her literary existence to other
women who won't or can't surrender. Her literary genealogy reaches back to Emma Clery (E. C.), Mangan's sister, the birdlike girl, the dark lady of *Giacomo Joyce*,
Beatrice Justice, and their real prototypes: May Murray
Joyce, the B. V. M., Eileen Vance, Mary Sheehy, Amalia
Popper, Marthe Fleischmann, and, perhaps, several others
whom we do not and shall not know. If Gerty is a joke,
she is nevertheless the *reductio ad absurdum* of a long
line of virginal villains who are implied in her portrait.
As Ernst Kris has pointed out in an essay on the psychology of the comic, "What was feared yesterday is
fated to appear funny when seen today."[11] Or, in the
words of another psychoanalytic theorist, Martin Grotjahn, "Jokes grow best on the fresh graves of old
anxieties."[12]

AMOR VINCIT OMNIA

But we are getting ahead of ourselves. The immediate
question is who is Gerty?

Gerty MacDowell is described for us in her own language, which is the language of her favorite reading matter, the popular sentimental fiction of the nineteenth
century:

Her figure was slight and graceful, inclining even to fragility
but those iron jelloids she had been taking of late had done
her a world of good much better than the Widow Welch's

11. Ernst Kris, "Ego Development and the Comic," *Psychoanalytic Explorations in Art* (New York: Schocken, 1952), p. 213.
12. Martin Grotjahn, *Beyond Laughter: Humor and the Subconscious* (New York: McGraw-Hill, 1954), p. 115.

female pills and she was much better of those discharges she used to get and that tired feeling. The waxen pallor of her face was almost spiritual in its ivorylike purity though her rosebud mouth was a genuine Cupid's bow, Greekly perfect. Her hands were of finely veined alabaster with tapering fingers and as white as lemon juice and queen of ointments could make them though it was not true that she used to wear kid gloves in bed or take a milk footbath either. Bertha Supple told that once to Edy Boardman, a deliberate lie .... (342/348)

But though the style may be a pastiche of sentimental clichés, the content is original Joycean wit. No heroine of a Maria Cummins novel ever suffered from debilitating discharges or needed a hormonal supplement to control them. Gerty is an incomplete woman. Her vigor is chemically enhanced; her beauty is manufactured. Her feminine image, imperfect from the beginning, has been refashioned according to a mélange of romantic genres: Renaissance milkmaid, Virgin Mary, seductress.

Why have women such eyes of witchery? Gerty's were of the bluest Irish blue, set off by lustrous lashes and dark expressive brows. Time was when those brows were not so silkyseductive. It was Madame Vera Verity, directress of the Woman Beautiful page of the Princess novelette, who had first advised her to try eyebrowleine which gave that haunting expression to the eyes, so becoming in leaders of fashion, and she had never regretted it. (342–343/349)

Madame Vera Verity is the Daedalus of the Dublin exotic, the fabulous artificer of the haunting expression. Her medium is the collage, the conceit, the violent yoking of feminine opposites. Those eyes of witchery under dark, expressive brows are mated to a waxen pallor of ivorylike purity and hands of finely-veined alabaster. Gerty is a sexual oxymoron, a feminine version of limbo, defined by Temple in *Portrait* as "neither my arse nor my elbow" (*PA*, 237). As such, she reminds us of Chaucer's Prioress, another supersublimated female whose repressed sexuality shows forth from beneath the spiritual camouflage. In both women the delicacy of feature is reactive, revealing by indirection a ripeness it pretends to conceal.

Contradictions of all kinds lie at the heart of Gerty's narcissistic self-portrait. The terms of her self-adoration crystallize around two nuclear ideas of female beauty: grace, delicacy, and aristocratic hauteur on the one hand, and sensuality, witchery, and fetishistic appeal on the other. Nor are these ideas, as she sees them, really at odds. For example, "There was an innate refinement, a languid queenly *hauteur* about Gerty which was unmistakably evidenced in her delicate hands and her high-arched instep" (342/348). "[Her] crowning glory," we are told, "was her wealth of wonderful hair" which "nestled about her pretty head in a profusion of luxuriant clusters" (343/349). In her courtship fantasies "patrician suitors" or "beau ideals" genuflect endlessly at her feet, a part of her anatomy that particularly fascinates her (342/348; 345/351). She adorns them with shoes that "were the newest thing in footwear . . . with patent toecaps and just one smart buckle at her high-arched instep (344/350). "Undies," of course, ". . . were Gerty's chief care" (344/350) and furs another regal obsession. She imagines a wedding ceremony featuring herself and Reginald Wylie (who has just jilted her) and sees herself arrayed for the bridal in "a sumptuous confection of grey trimmed with expensive blue fox" (345/351).

We have encountered the now-familiar furs and drawers many times over already. The hair, shoes, and high-

arched instep are mere anatomical and sartorial variations on the same erotogenic theme. It seems that those
qualities which Gerty is apt to regard as evidence of regal
hauteur are no more than the most hackneyed of fetishistic commonplaces. The critics are right. Gerty has no
taste. But what then of Bloom, her admirer, who has a
"touch of the artist" in him? And what of Joyce, who
was not himself immune to such forms of the beautiful?

Bloom is no paragon of good taste, but his bad choices,
aesthetic or otherwise, are invariably based upon an
intuitive rightness of impulse. Gerty is not unattractive.
Nor is her notion of high style, which amounts to an
accumulation of fetishes, wholly ignorant. As Ellmann
says, "Gerty is untrained, but her impulse to art is as
genuine as Homer's."[13] And in light of what we know
about Joyce, we do have to agree that all the elements of
the true and the beautiful are here in "Nausikaa," however comical, ill-matched, and misproportioned.

Not the least of those elements is the familiar paradox,
the virgin/whore syndrome, of which Gerty partakes in
an unusual way. For, though it is nowhere made explicit,
it is probable that she is a prostitute.[14] The book contains
a number of sly, circumstantial hints that this may be
so. For one thing, she seems to be the roommate of Bertha
Supple (what's in a name?), who spreads those malicious
rumors about Gerty's bedtime habits and who shows up
as a prostitute in Nighttown (424/431). More striking are
the appearances of Cissy Caffrey and Edy Boardman as
prostitutes at the very beginning of "Circe" (423–426/

13. *Ulysses on the Liffey*, p. 130.
14. I owe this insight to Sheldon Brivic, who first pointed out
to me certain suggestive incongruities in the portrait of this supposed virgin.

430–433), and as the fellow travelers of Privates Comp-
ton and Carr at the end (572–586/587–603). Gerty appears in Nighttown also, but she may be only a halluci-
nation of Bloom's (434–435/442). The discharges Gerty
used to get may well be symptoms of a notorious disease
of the trade and the iron jelloids she now takes are perhaps pep pills to keep her going on an all-night job.
Similarly, the waxen pallor of a face that was almost
spiritual in its purity may be the sallow dullness of an
indoor complexion. The rosebud mouth that was a genuine Cupid's bow, the alabaster fingers, white as ointment
could make them, and the dark and haunting eyes of
witchery, are all characteristics of the cosmetic over-
elaboration that is the prostitute's stock-in-trade. As for
Bertha's nasty rumor that Gerty used to wear kid gloves
to bed, we *know* how Joyce felt about gloves. And her
display of her drawers to Bloom is admirably professional.
Yet, nowhere in her reflections does Gerty consider her
line of work, and if she is in fact a prostiute by night,
she is most thoroughly an ingénue by day. The very
naïveté and adolescent mawkishness of her thought
belies the notion that she works at the most hardening of
feminine employments. And while her friends appear in
Nighttown, she herself does not (see above), though her
menses are upon her and she may be taking a night of sick
leave from work.

It seems, finally, that the matter of Gerty's relative
virginity and the question of her profession are two
more mysteries to be added to the many that have already
been catalogued by R. M. Adams in his book of mysteries, *Surface and Symbol*.[15] Yet this puzzle, insoluble

15. R. M. Adams, *Surface and Symbol: The Consistency of
James Joyce's Ulysses* (New York: Oxford University Press, 1962).

in terms of the book, is no puzzle at all in light of what we know about Joyce. For Joyce, we can guess, contrived to have it both ways with Gerty, to have her both virgin and whore. In Gerty, the virgin/whore syndrome is writ small, reduced from a personal dilemma to a literary puzzle. By the transformation of his own ambivalence into Gerty's ambiguity, Joyce threw the burden of love's bitter mystery onto the reader of *Ulysses* in the form of a game of "does she or doesn't she." Gerty, like all Joycean women, proffers a riddle, though in her case nothing of substance hangs upon the solution.

A RADIANT LITTLE VISION:
A NOTE ON LOVE AND WORSHIP

Gerty just took off her hat for a moment to settle her hair and a prettier, a daintier head of nutbrown tresses was never seen on a girl's shoulders, a radiant little vision, in sooth, almost maddening in its sweetness. (354/360)

While some kinds of sexual activity are truly private affairs, marriages unto oneself, exhibition is incomplete without a witness to the exhibit. Gerty's accidental encounter with Bloom is a happy event for both. Exhibitionist meets voyeur and it is love at first sight. Bloom's eyes receive erotogenic impressions and are also organs of active sexual transmission.[16] They "burned into her as though they would search her through and through, read her very soul" (351/357). Bloom again eyes Gerty "as a snake eyes its prey. Her woman's instinct told her

16. Joyce's habitual use of eyes as genital substitutes has already been studied. See Richard Wasson, "Stephen Dedalus and the Imagery of Sight," *Literature and Psychology* 15 (1965): 195–209.

that she had raised the devil in him and at the thought a burning scarlet swept from throat to brow till the lovely colour of her face became a glorious rose" (354/360). In passive interludes the visual rapist turns pilgrim, "drinking in her every contour, literally worshipping at her shrine" (355/361). Meanwhile, at another shrine nearby the Star of the Sea Church, another visual love feast is being enacted en masse. "Queen of angels," prays the congregation, "queen of patriarchs, queen of prophets, of all saints . . . queen of the most holy rosary. . . ." (353/359). And as the tide of Bloom's desire rises, the contrapuntal interplay of the two events grows tighter: "Gerty could see without looking that he never took his eyes off of her and then Canon O'Hanlon handed the thurible back to Father Conroy and knelt down looking up at the Blessed Sacrament and the choir began to sing *Tantum ergo* and she just swung her foot in and out in time as the music rose and fell to the *Tantumer gosa cramen tum.* Three and eleven she paid for those stockings in Sparrow's of George's street" (353/360).

The benediction concludes with Psalm 117, *Laudate Dominum omnes gentes*, just as the bazaar fireworks begin down the strand. Cissy and Edy hurry with the children to see the show, but Gerty stays behind to put on a private show for Bloom, who, partly concealed behind a rock, has taken matters into his own hands. She imagines him to be "a man of inflexible honour to his fingertips" as she leans back to give him a good glimpse of thigh and petticoat. Down the strand a long Roman candle goes up over the trees as Gerty leans farther back and Bloom watches and works:

She would fain have cried to him chokingly, held out her snowy slender arms to him to come, to feel his lips laid on her white brow the cry of a young girl's love, a little strangled cry, wrung from her, that cry that has rung through the ages. And then a rocket sprang and bang shot blind and O! then the Roman candle burst and it was like a sigh of O! and every-one cried O! O! in raptures and it gushed out of it a stream of rain gold hair threads and they shed and ah! they were all greeny dewy stars falling with golden, O so lovely! O so soft, sweet, soft! (360/366–367)

Their final contact before Gerty departs is a meeting of their souls in a "last lingering glance" as "the eyes that reached her heart, full of a strange shining, hung enrap-tured on her sweet flowerlike face" (361/367).

Hugh Kenner has noted, I believe rightly, the ingenious correspondence between this visual orgy and the bene-diction taking place nearby: "The religious ceremonial synchronized with this episode is the Benediction: the sacrament, like Gerty, is exhibited but not eaten."[17] Though literally correct, however, this observation is psychologically naïve, for both Gerty and the sacrament are, in a sense, being eaten. For voyeurism partakes of the displacement of oral sexual tendencies into the realm of the visual. Such visual "eating" takes place both on the beach and at the benediction. And eating, like looking, is a primary mode of Bloom's sexuality. Later in the chap-ter, Bloom formulates his distaste for adultery in an oral metaphor: "Glad to get away from the other chap's wife. Eating off his cold plate" (364/370). Moments later, reflecting on all the amour Howth has witnessed, he thinks, "Lovers: yum yum" (370/377). This concur-rence of eating and sexuality is everywhere in "Lestry-

17. Kenner, *Dublin's Joyce*, p. 258. Ellmann puts the case this way in *Ulysses on the Liffey*: "Both Gerty and the men seek to receive an imagined body, communion being as illusional as mas-turbation" (p. 128).

gonians," where Bloom admires naked statues at the museum in digestive terms, calling them "aids to digestion." And late that night, when the wanderer comes home to Ithaca, the promised land is epiphanized as his wife's melonous buttocks, "the plump mellow yellow smellow melons of her rump," which provoke first "melonsmellonous osculation" and then a meager "proximate erection" (719/734–735).

COMFORTRESS OF THE AFFLICTED

Through the open window of the church the fragrant incense was wafted and with it the fragrant names of her who was conceived without stain of original sin, spiritual vessel, pray for us, honourable vessel, pray for us, vessel of singular devotion, pray for us, mystical rose. (350/356)

Gerty is a secular analogue to the Virgin, and much of the effect of this portrait of motherhood, as we have seen, lies in the contrapuntal interplay of the Gertean narrative and the devotional litany that emanates from the church. The Reverend Father Hughes reminds the congregation of what Saint Bernard said in his prayer of Mary, "that it was not recorded in any age that those who implored her powerful protection were ever abandoned by her" (350/356). Outside, on the beach, Baby Boardman wets himself and cries obstreperously until "Ciss, always readywitted, gave him in his mouth the teat of the suckingbottle and the young heathen was quickly appeased" (351/357). Gerty contemplates a melancholy Bloom on whose face "the story of a haunting sorrow was written" (351/357). She feels herself becoming maternal and protective: "There were wounds that wanted healing with heartbalm. She was a womanly woman . . . and she just yearned to know all, to forgive all if she could make him fall in love with her, make him forget the memory of the past" (352/358). And from the church nearby the litany responds, "Refuge of sinners. Comfortress of the afflicted. *Ora pro nobis*. Well has it been said that whosoever prays to her with faith and constancy can never be lost or cast away" (352/358).

The three girls are all versions of the Blessed Virgin, for each in her way brings comfort to the afflicted. The mysterious embrace of the summer evening, with which "Nausikaa" begins, is the powerful protection of Marian intercession, which is, in turn, the soothing teat of the Caffrean suckingbottle and, if we assume the girls to be prostitutes, the warm boudoir of a Dublin brothel. From beginning to end, a strange alliance of motherhood, virginity, and prostitution broods over the chapter, pregnant with parthenogenetic meaning.

Bloom, then, is a counterpart of Baby Boardman. He is also a version of the Irish oral archetype, the alcoholic, though he drinks only with his eyes. The men's temperance retreat fills out the pattern by being a ritual of therapeutic orality, for the strategy of temperance through faith depends upon the substitution of one mode of dependent orality for another. Religion and drink are two opiates of the same sullen Irish masses who, as weekend penitents, drink in the Virgin's every contour as they worship at her shrine.

It should be clear that Joyce, who understood well the erotic and maternal appeal of the Virgin, undertook in "Nausikaa" to undercut the popular dogmas involved in mariolatry by verbal and visual puns.[18] Gerty is a double

18. A detailed analysis of virginity as a condition of motherhood lies beyond the scope of a study of Joyce. Such an analysis

entendre: she is a genuine object of sexual desire in whom Joyce has invested all the significant qualities of an old erotic ideal and is also, by virtue of those very "charms," the iconic Virgin without stain, the tower of ivory. On the other hand, her adolescent banality is the measure of Joyce's protest against both mariolatry and sentimental idealism, which are the religious and secular expressions of the same denial of sexuality. If this attack on the virgin (and the Virgin) seems harsh, we must credit the harshness of the taboos upon which her cult depends, as well as the harshness with which the Church fosters self-repression among its members. The sexual critique of religious pieties may be merciless, but it is really no more severe in its defiance than the repression with which it is at war.[19] As Stephen discovers in *Stephen Hero*, the iron law of virginity is painfully inhuman and is finally an agent of fraud, for it forces love into the marketplace to be bartered for the impossible conditions of a Catholic marriage (*SH*, 200–203).

But, as *Stephen Hero* points up also, the strength of Joyce's old erotic commitments underlies the satiric gusto of this chapter. "Nausikaa" presents the author under two very different aspects, both of which are wholly au-

---

in depth is more appropriate to a critique of Christianity and the Catholic cult of the Virgin than to a reading of *Ulysses*. See, however, these three essays by Ernest Jones: "The Madonna's Conception Through the Ear," "A Psychoanalytic Study of the Holy Ghost," and "The Island of Ireland." All three may be found in Jones's *Essays in Applied Psychoanalysis* (London: International Psychoanalytic Press, 1923). The little-known essay on Ireland is a brief but excellent speculative excursion into the sociology of the Irish commitment to the Virgin.

19. See Philip Rieff's remarks on sexuality as a critique of culture and religion in Chapter 5 of his *Freud: The Mind of the Moralist* (Garden City, N.Y.: Doubleday, Anchor, 1961), pp. 163 ff.

thentic. Bloom's admiration is just as genuine a Joycean response to Gerty as the author's reduction of her to foolishness. In Bloom's act of masturbation, Joyce's antithetical attitudes toward old enchantments of the heart are momentarily reconciled, for that act is a sexual pun which expresses both Bloom's admiration and Joyce's criticism.

VIRGIN AS TEMPTRESS:
THE BACKGROUND OF NAUSIKAA

Despite the stylistic revolution in his art that took Joyce from *Portrait* to *Finnegans Wake* in just nine years, we can recognize in his fantasy life an extraordinary consistency of purpose. Gerty MacDowell and the various prototypes of her are ingredients of that consistency, and their repeated appearance makes possible a psychic biography of Gerty. She represents an old anxiety, and Joyce's art in "Nausikaa" is a formula for managing her. We can, I think, measure Joyce's growth as a man and as an artist by following the progress of these ur-Gerties from one book to the next and plotting the movement from anger to irony in Joyce's portraiture. However, a psychic genealogy or ideal history of Gerty is necessarily complicated by the appearance of a real Gerty in Joyce's life in 1918/19 when he was pondering "Nausikaa." Like her soul sister in *Ulysses*, Marthe Fleischmann walked with a limp, displayed her underclothes for a voyeur's delectation, and was regarded by her admirer as a type of the Virgin Mary, not to say the virgin Nausikaa.[20] Yet, we

20. Four of Joyce's letters to Marthe Fleischmann have survived. They were first published, with an informative introduction by Professor Heinrich Straumann, in *Tri-Quarterly* 8 (Winter

can claim, in good scholastic language, that those features which Gerty owes to Marthe are accidental, not essential. The essential Gerty is a creature of Joyce's boyhood among curious, grave beauties, real and imagined.

The combination of virginal sentimentality and sexual allure in the characterization of Gerty is a comic rendering of the same complex of qualities that appear in Emma Clery of *Stephen Hero*, a devout, stainless, and most seductive young lady. "By all outward signs [Stephen] was compelled to esteem her holy. But he could not so stultify himself as to misread the gleam in her eyes as holy or to interpret the rise and fall of her bosom as a movement of a sacred intention" (*SH*, 156). Her strategic virginity is an instrument of sexual domination over repressed young men, like Stephen, who must finally either "do the proper thing" (propose marriage), become guilt-ridden masturbators, prowl about in Nighttown, or languish in frustration. In "The Boarding House" Bob Doran does what is only right by Polly Mooney, and we know what happens to him. Stephen sees this domination-by-denial as part of a conspiracy by the Church to use the bodies of women as instruments of control over the souls of men. And he despises women for their easy submission to clerical seduction:

The general attitude of women toward religion puzzled and often maddened Stephen. His nature was incapable of achieving such an attitude of insincerity or stupidity. By brooding constantly upon this he ended by anathemising [sic] Emma

1967):177–188. They may also be found in *Letters* 2:424–436. However, the *Tri-Quarterly* publication is especially useful because it is accompanied by Frank Budgen's "Joyce and Marthe Fleischmann: A Witness's Account," a chapter from his autobiography, *Myselves When Young* (London: Oxford University Press, 1970). See also Ellmann, *JJ*, pp. 462–467.

as the most deceptive and cowardly of marsupials. He discovered that it was a menial fear and no spirit of chastity which had prevented her from granting his request. Her eyes, he thought, must look strange when upraised to some holy image and her lips when poised for the reception of the host. (*SH*, 210)

In a phrase, her heart belongs to daddy, and her eagerness to open up for the host, set off against her sexual denial of Stephen, amounts to a betrayal and a confirmation of the conspiracy of adulterous priests and their sly, deceitful women to rob him of his manhood. Stephen's response to this ecclesiastical primal scene are variations on a theme of impotence: anger, despair, disgust. He complains that he cannot survive where his body is not his own and his penis must serve an impossible law. "Impossible that a temperament ever trembling towards its ecstasy should submit to acquiesce, that a soul should decree servitude for its portion over which the image of beauty had fallen as a mantle" (*SH* 193–194). In a moment of profound frustration, he imagines this sexual conspiracy to be a plague upon Europe which clogs up the passages of sexual release with a deluge of excrement: "In a stupor of powerlessness he reviewed the plague of Catholicism. He seemed to see the vermin begotten in the catacombs in an age of sickness and cruelty issuing forth upon the plains and mountains of Europe. Like the plague of locusts described in Callista they seemed to choke the rivers and fill the valleys up. They obscured the sun" (*SH*, 194). In another fit of despair, Stephen visits a cemetery to contemplate bitterly the dead and their less fortunate brothers, the living: "The vision of all those failures, and the vision, far more pitiful, of congenital lives, shuffling onwards amid yawn and howl, beset him with evil: and evil, in the similitude of a distorted ritual, called to his soul to commit fornication with her" (*SH*, 162).

Even in the graveyard his thoughts turn to the bedroom. His lesson is not a contemplative *memento mori* but an agitated *memento sexualis*. Had the *Stephen Hero* fragment not survived, we could scarcely have imagined the depth of feeling behind Joyce's view of virginity as an agent of Church domination, nor could we have imagined the intensity of the psychic and sexual frustration associated with the figure of Emma. For, while frustration and disgust are very much a part of the later *Portrait*, Emma herself is a thin and shadowy figure who hardly seems capable of evoking such titanic emotions. Yet it is precisely such domination as this, perpetrated by this most "cowardly of marsupials" and her clerical co-conspirators, which later provides the motive for the satire on Gerty MacDowell.

Gerty's naïveté and sentimentality also recall Emma, for both are young ladies who grasp at clichés to express profundities. "I love the Irish music, [Emma] said . . . inclining herself towards him with an air of oblivion, it is so soul-stirring" (*SH*, 156). But the primary source of the "namby-pamby jammy marmalady drawsery"[21] style of "Nausikaa" is not the fictive Emma or the real Mary Sheehy, but Joyce himself. It is a reduction to banality of the obfuscating and embarrassing prose of his romantic youth. The attack on old enchantments of the heart in "Nausikaa" is accompanied by an attack upon their stylistic correlative, the purple passage, the quintessential examples of which are to be found in the

21. This is Joyce's own description of the style of "Nausikaa." From a letter to Budgen, January 3, 1920 (*Letters* 1:134–135).

narrative essay "A Portrait of the Artist," which Joyce
wrote in January 1904. The essay is a strange and all-but-
impenetrable document of self-analysis which Joyce
conceived and wrote only a few months after his mother's
death. Its style, turgid and devious throughout, achieves
total opacity in an apostrophe to an ambiguous "dearest
of mortals," a sexual tutor and spiritual *alma mater*
whom he invokes as "beneficent one" and describes as
"an envoy from the fair courts of life." The language of
the apostrophe is basically the language of aesthetic
idealism that Joyce had meticulously culled from Pater,
Newman, Yeats, Mallarmé, and the Church, but pushed
beyond the bounds of both the beautiful and the intelligible in a spirit of adolescent precocity and, one suspects, guilt. The passage recalls, in coded language, a
sexual and spiritual awakening through visits to brothels
("the yellow gaslamps . . . gleaming mysteriously there
before that altar"). Yet, while this mysterious tutor may
be a prostitute, she implies a number of other figures as
well: Emma, the birdlike girl, the B. V. M. All are implied, and more than one may in fact have been intended.
And behind these, subtle, hidden, but insistent, looms
the dead mother, the dearest mortal of them all. "Thou
hadst put thine arms about him and, intimately prisoned
as thou hadst been, in the soft stir of thy bosom, the raptures of silence, the murmured words, thy heart had
spoken to his heart." And again, "Thou wert sacramental, imprinting thine indelible mark, of very visible grace.
A litany must honor thee: Lady of the Apple Trees, Kind
Wisdom, Sweet Flower of Dusk." Finally, the young
Joyce epiphanized the relationship in a nympholeptic
fantasy of oral union that was orchestrated by the sounding of harps: "The blood hurries to a gallop in his veins;

his nerves accumulate an electric force; he is footed with flame. A kiss: and they leap together, indivisible, upwards, radiant lips and eyes, their bodies sounding with the triumph of harps! Again, beloved! Again, thou bride! Again, ere life is ours!"

The similarities between this turgid fantasy and Gerty's daydreams in "Nausikaa" are too many to be accidental. The dream of ideal maternal care has its comic counterpart in Gerty's fantasy of caring for Bloom. "The very heart of the girlwoman went out to him, her dreamhusband, because she knew on the instant it was him. If he had suffered, more sinned against than sinning, or even, even, if he had been himself a sinner, a wicked man, she cared not" (351–352/358). She also has her version of the oceanic kiss in which the young Joyce imagined himself soaring heavenward, mouth to mouth with his demonlover. She dreams of a hero who will "take her in his sheltering arms, strain her to him in all the strength of his deep passionate nature and comfort her with a long long kiss. It would be like heaven" (345/351–352). And the litany in honor of this dearest of mortals reverberates throughout "Nausikaa": "Refuge of sinners. Comfortress of the afflicted. *Ora pro nobis*" (352/358).

Some time between the abandonment of *Stephen Hero* and the completion of *Portrait* Joyce had a romantic dalliance of sorts with a Triestine student. Every aspect of this affair is shrouded in mystery. We know for sure neither when it took place nor the degree of intimacy it achieved nor the identity of the young woman, though Richard Ellmann's guess that it was Amalia Popper seems to be well founded.[22] Most of what we do know about

22. See Richard Ellmann's introduction to *Giacomo Joyce* and also *JJ*, pp. 350–360. The question of the young woman's identity

this delectably enigmatic affair is contained in the *Giacomo Joyce* manuscript, in which Joyce secretly memorialized it by fashioning the details of an intense and unstable attachment into a verbal scrollwork of baroque sexual fantasies. Like Emma, the young woman (let us call her Amalia) is virginal, provoking, exhibitionistic, and, ultimately, cold and malicious. And, like Emma, she contributed to the portrait of Gerty MacDowell. Her carnivorous "long lewdly leering lips: dark-blooded molluscs" conjure up most immediately the ghostly May Dedalus of "Circe" but have their comic counterpart, too, in Gerty's "rosebud mouth" that "was a genuine Cupid's bow" (342/348). Her threatening, serpentine locks of "slowly uncoiling, falling hair" are recapitulated in miniature in Gerty's alliterative "wealth of wonderful hair." Her underclothes hold the same fascination for the pseudonymous Giacomo that Gerty's do for Bloom; she shyly reveals a lace hemline and a web of stocking for *suo maestro inglese:* "A skirt caught back by her sudden moving knee; a white lace edging of an underskirt lifted unduly; a legstretched web of stocking." And in helping her hook the neck of her gown, he glimpses her orange shift, which is ominously draped over a reptilian body "shimmering with silvery scales." In *Giacomo Joyce,* as in "Nausikaa," the eroticized environment is interfused with the liturgy and ceremony of the Church. "Giacomo" recalls a Good Friday Mass attended with Amalia and recalls the voice of an unseen reader "intoning the lesson from Hosea. *Haec dicit Dominus: in tribulatione sua mane consurgent ad me. Venite et revertamur ad Dominum . . . .* " But, unlike the masturbatory events cele-

---

is reviewed in an exchange between Ellmann and Helen Barolini in *The New York Review of Books* 13 (November 20, 1969):48–51.

brated by the litany of Our Lady in "Nausikaa," this
service commemorates an erotic crucifixion. "Her flesh
recalls the thrill of that mist–veiled morning, hurrying
torches, cruel eyes." It is Joyce who is being crucified by
those cruel eyes. Hence, the thrill.

Those eyes are weapons in a struggle for sexual dominance that brings the affair to its climax and conclusion.
The benign visual love feast of "Nausikaa" has its malign
counterpart in this affair. "Giacomo," unable to have the
lady physically, loves her and leaves her in a fantasy
of visual impregnation:[23] "Her eyes have drunk my
thoughts: and into the moist warm yielding welcoming
darkness of her womanhood my soul, itself dissolving,
has streamed and poured and flooded a liquid and abundant seed . . . . . . Take her now who will! . . . . " (*GJ*, 14).
Consummatum est and, so it seems, without the laying
on of hands.[24] It is the rape of an angry voyeur, the
"dirty look" being the aggressive counterpart of the passive Joycean scoptophilia. But the lady does not take
this attack lying down, at least, not for very long. With
the affair in the last stages of breakup, she counterat-
tacks, eyes first: ". . . as I halt in wonder and look about
me she greets me wintrily and passes up the staircase
darting at me for an instant out of her sluggish sidelong
eyes a jet of liquorish venom" (*GJ*, 15). This exchange

23. For a curious parallel to this situation in Christian liturgical
history, see Jacob A. Arlow, "The Madonna's Conception Through
the Eyes," *Psychoanalytic Study of Society*, ed., Warner Muensterberger, 3 (New York: International Universities Press, 1964):
13–25. See also Wasson, "Stephen Dedalus."

24. This is certainly an ambiguous passage. It is not beyond
question that real coitus is being described. However, the imagery
most immediately suggests that what took place was a visual
imitation.

of spurting visual currents seems to be a curious phallic/ urinary duel with a virgin most powerful. Like all women in Joyce's work, the young woman here is likely to possess a penis, or a symbolic equivalent, and to know how to use it aggressively. But Joyce, by the time he had this affair, or surely by the time he had written about it (1909? 1912? 1914?), was no longer the passive victim of the "bright-eyed" Emma, as he had been in *Stephen Hero*. His defense here is a surprisingly tough offense. For that reason the imagery of *Giacomo Joyce* is the imagery of conflict and the atmosphere of the piece as tense and explosive as anything he ever wrote. His contemptuous envoy: "Love me, love my umbrella."

It is probably premature to caption this affair with Bloom's summary judgment of his encounter with Gerty, "Anyhow I got the best of that" (361/368), but that statement does suggest an emerging pattern of relationships, both in Joyce's work and in his real encounters with his dark ladies, all "virgins" and all temptresses, whether they would be or not. The struggle in *Giacomo Joyce* marks perhaps a turning point in his relations with the virgin-temptress and her various incarnations, real and imagined, for two of her next literary incarnations, E. C. in *Portrait* and Beatrice Justice in *Exiles*, are insubstantial figures. The former has been shorn of her full name and much of her charisma, while the latter slides quietly out of the center of the play, a victim of Joyce's indifference.

The formal situation of *Exiles* is a balanced quadrilateral affair involving Richard Rowan, Bertha Rowan, Robert Hand, and his cousin Beatrice Justice. But this fearful symmetry is quickly reduced to the familiar marital trio of husband, wife, and the ubiquitous other man,

as the old obsession whom Beatrice embodies in the play
fades into impalpability, becoming a ghost by indifference.
In his notes for the play Joyce describes her with weary
malice. "Beatrice's mind is an abandoned cold temple in
which hymns have risen heavenward in a distant past
but where now a doddering priest offers alone and hopelessly prayers to the Most High" (*E*, 119). This priest
within the temple of Beatrice's mind might once have
angered and threatened Joyce. For it is the same adulterous priest for whom Emma's eyes are upraised and lips
poised in *Stephen Hero*. But now Beatrice and her doddering priest are coldly employed as mere material in a
more intriguing version of the oedipal drama, the drama
of marital infidelity and fraternal betrayal.

E. C. in *Portrait* is a ghostly figure who flickers back
and forth across the borders of Stephen's consciousness.
Lacking even the substance of a last name, she has reality
only as an obsessive, if infrequent, image in his mind.
Like her predecessor in *Stephen Hero*, she is a coquette
who arouses Stephen only to deny him, but Stephen's
response is more dynamic than the bitterness and physical disgust of the earlier book. He is moved to various
imperfect modes of sexual release, both voluntary and
involuntary: whoring, masturbation, nocturnal emission,
and poetic composition. He masturbates with degraded
images of Emma in his mind's eye (*PA*, 115) and also
offers up to her his first "serious" poems: his youthful
"To E——— C———," which "told only of the night
and the balmy breeze and the maiden lustre of the moon"
(*PA*, 70), and the "Villanelle of the Temptress" ten years
later (*PA*, 217–224). In the latter poem he universalized
her as *temptress*, the Eve through whom man first fell
and continues to fall. Yet he addressed her in the language

of Catholic devotion, his poem being a Mass, a "eucharistic hymn." As in Gerty MacDowell's self-portrait, the language of spiritual devotion here is put to work in the service of the erotic, with the effect of blurring the differences between these supposedly distinct modes of love.

Most important, however, is the fact that the pain and frustration evoked by Emma are under control in *Portrait* and have artistic consequences. Stephen's dream of seraphic ecstasy may leave his soul "all dewy wet" in the morning, but it also sets him to writing his villanelle. The genesis of the poem in his mind is portrayed as a confused and shadowy insemination and embryonic gestation, with Emma and Stephen and the Virgin and the seraph Gabriel all tumultuously wrapped up in the miasmal mist of poetic creation. But stripped of its sexual and liturgical mysteries, this fantasy recalls the last page of *Giacomo Joyce*, where Joyce commemorated the end of the affair, as well as the end of youth, with this exhortation to himself: "Youth has an end: the end is here. It will never be. You know that well. What then? Write it, damn you, write it! What else are you good for?" By 1914 he had learned well the Shakespearean lesson that failure, especially failure in love, was the grist most suited to his artistic mill.

He had learned, too, the use of art as an instrument of transcendence and control. The villanelle to Emma may extol her powers, but it also circumscribes them with his own growing powers as an artist. He brings her under control by reducing her to a formula (Virgin and temptress) and calms his own dewy emotions by translating them into rhythmic language. Thus, the psychological function of *Portrait* and *Giacomo Joyce* is significantly

different from that of *Stephen Hero*. For the later writings
are acts of mastery, attempts to transcend and control
the magic of the temptress by surrounding it with the
more potent magic of language, while the earlier book
is simply a complaint, an admission of bafflement and
anger. Joyce's exhortation to "write it" is a psychological
imperative, his art being a promise of order amid chaos
and safety in the face of danger.[25]

This linguistic magic falls a bit clumsily on Gerty, as
we have seen, but it works with a nicer delicacy on another of her forerunners in *Portrait*, the birdlike girl on
the beach. The well-known description of her is one of
the originals of Gerty's self-portrait. "Her thighs, fuller
and softhued as ivory, were bared almost to the hips
where the white fringes of her drawers were like feath-
erings of soft white down. Her slateblue skirts were kilted
boldly about her waist and dovetailed behind her . . . .
But her long fair hair was girlish: and girlish, and touched
with the wonder of mortal beauty, her face" (*PA*, 171).
In the cool light of irony cast dimly backward by
"Nausikaa," this description cannot be read with the
hushed and prurient awe demanded by the language.
"The white fringes of her drawers" and "her long fair
hair" are self-deflating charms. The Pateresque language of the beautiful, which hallows the fetishistic attributes of the birdlike girl, is robbed of its virtue, and
the scene of its evocative power, by the later imitation.

25. Kristian Smidt has made some cogent observations of
Joyce's use of language as apotropaic magic in his *James Joyce
and the Cultic Use of Fiction* (Oslo: Oslo University Press, 1955),
pp. 67–78. He interprets *Ulysses* and *Finnegans Wake* as magical
incantation. "One is tempted to think," he surmises, "that to lay
the spectre of Ireland and the ghost of God, Joyce needed the
combined word-masses of *Ulysses* and *Finnegans Wake*" (p. 73).

The whole romantic aura of Stephen's vision is dimmed by irony. As the girl stands with her skirts drawn up, Stephen stares silently at her until "the first faint noise of gently moving water broke the silence, low and faint and whispering, faint as the bells of sleep; hither and thither, hither and thither: and a faint flame trembled on her cheek" (*PA*, 171).[26] And suddenly we know who this "angel of mortal youth" really is. We recognize none other than the young lady of *Chamber Music* VII, the one who "goes lightly, holding up/ Her dress with dainty hand." And, finally, Stephen's oceanic swoon in that same scene now arouses our suspicion, for the locutions of transcendental ecstasy most probably describe an act of masturbation.

This comparison of the two beach scenes, written some six or seven years apart,[27] brings the beautiful and the ludicrous into focus as two sides of the same thin coin. Gerty is the birdlike girl as ingénue and/or prostitute, and the style in which her character is revealed is the style of Joyce's own neo-Platonic youth filtered through the duller sensibilities of the popular novel. The difference is mainly a matter of language. Yet the language of Joyce's youth, as recreated in 1914, is itself sown with comic intent, as his language almost always is at its most solemn and exalted. It is Stephen in *Stephen Hero* who confesses that he "could not use [feudal termi-

26. Joyce apparently reworked this urinary incantation for the end of the Anna Livia Plurabelle section of *Finnegans Wake*. "Tell me, tell me, tell me, elm! Night night! Telmetale of stem or stone. Beside the rivering waters of, hitherandthithering waters of. Night!" (*FW* 216).

27. "Nausikaa" was written between fall 1919 and spring 1920. The final composition date of Chapter 4 of *Portrait* is unclear, but we may guess either 1913 or 1914.

nology] with the same faith and purpose as animated the feudal poets themselves [and] was compelled to express his love a little ironically" (*SH*, 174). Stephen was thinking no doubt of the *Chamber Music* poems, or perhaps his (that is, Joyce's) earlier "Shine and Dark" verses. But this confession reflects, as well, other romantic or exalted or self-consciously archaic writing. What *Ulysses* does is make manifest the subtle thread of irony that is latent in so much of Joyce's previous work, liberating it and giving it a voice of its own. "Nausikaa" frees the irony implicit in Stephen's worship of the birdlike girl by bringing to light Stephen's voyeurism (via Bloom's) and highlighting, via Gerty, the fetishistic and urinary charms of the girl. We should not be surprised to find that all of *Ulysses* is intelligible as a book of criticism in which Joyce's earlier work is reviewed and imitated and judged. For *Ulysses* is not only the Arnoldian criticism of life that Joyce intended it to be; it is excellent literary criticism as well, and in Joyce's self-regarding universe, the favorite object of critical study was always the book of himself.

The progress of the virgin-temptress in Joyce's life and work is complex but not impossible to follow. The strands of association that bind together the Blessed Virgin Mary, Mary Sheehy, Polly Mooney, Mangan's sister, Emma Clery, Amalia Popper, Beatrice Justice, E. C., the birdlike girl, Marthe Fleischmann, and Gerty MacDowell are rough and irregular, but form an intelligible enough pattern. If anything stands out in the general pattern of Joyce's changing relationship with this archetypal figure and her avatars, it is his inexorable shift from a passive position to an active one. This shift took place in the two arenas more or less simultaneously. The changing fantasy relationship that is reflected in the progress of Emma Clery to Gerty MacDowell is paralleled by the shift in Joyce's real relations—from adolescent submission to Mary Sheehy to middle-aged dalliances with Amalia Popper and Marthe Fleischmann.

The affair with Marthe, like "Nausikaa," was an exercise in mastery. Joyce's letters to her lack the emotional intensity of either the 1909 letters to Nora or the *Giacomo Joyce* manuscript. They disclose the artist at play, and if the game is not exactly a light divertissement, it is something undertaken with care and some degree of detachment. Joyce's dramatization of himself as a middle-aged Dante or Shakespeare or a poor seeker in the world who understands nothing of his destiny was not entirely disingenuous, but neither was it artless. It was his assumed dongiovannism. His sexual involvement in the game was genuine, but the passion seems to have been low-keyed and well controlled and the rake's progress well rehearsed.

What we know about the climax of the affair, a black Mass of sorts in Frank Budgen's studio on Joyce's thirty-seventh birthday (also Candlemas), confirms our sense of this affair as a well-made scenario. Joyce prepared the evening by bringing Marthe to the studio to show her Budgen's work, which included a quickly sketched, great-buttocked nude that the artist had done for the occasion as a favor to his friend-in-need. A symbolic and sentimental touch was added by a Jewish minorah that Joyce had borrowed for the evening to illuminate the studio. After a half-hour of banalities, "Wie schön! Wunderbar! Ein merkwürdiges Bild ist das!" Joyce and Marthe left. Joyce later told Budgen that "he had explored that evening the coldest and hottest parts of a woman's body."[28]

It is entirely conceivable that Joyce sought out this relationship for literary reasons. In need of a model for "Nausikaa," which he was soon to be writing, he was entirely capable of cultivating *l'affaire* Fleischmann as a strategic encounter with the reality of experience for the purpose of later artistic elaboration. That is what happens when you go around reading the book of yourself. And it seems that this Dedalian encounter also provided Joyce with an opportunity for self-experimentation and that he looked upon it as an exercise in self-containment. Not this time behind breakwaters of order and elegance, but naked, armed only with irony and art. The affair thus makes sense as the working out in reality of the same complex of memories and emotions which "Nausikaa" attacks through art. In the book of Joyce's life one finds the same text as in the book of his hand. In both books Joyce was attempting to free himself from the castrating tyranny of old romantic attachments through the conquest and degradation of some simulacrum or symbolic representation of them. The burden of this voodoo fell on poor Marthe, who was, like Amalia, "A sparrow under the wheels of Juggernaut" (*GJ*, 7). The success of the experiment may be measured by the ease with which Joyce engaged and disengaged himself from it and by the fact that the experience, so far as we know, had no sequels. After Marthe there were apparently no more excursions outside marriage for Joyce, no more dark ladies. But, though she disappeared from his life, the temptress remained a permanent fix-

28. Details culled from Ellmann, *JJ*, 462–467, and Budgen, *Myselves*, p. 194.

ture in his mind and reemerged, ever more tempting and ever more foolish, in *Finnegans Wake* as Issy (Izzy, Isabel, Isolde, Izod, and so forth), "a bewitching blonde who dimples delightfully and is approached in loveliness only by her grateful sister reflection in a mirror, the cloud of the opal" (*FW*, 220).

As Philip Rieff has observed, the temptress was a cliché of nineteenth-century Romantic culture.[29] As Astarte, Carmen, Anitra, Isolde, Hester Prynne, or Hetty Sorel (and one thinks of Marlene Dietrich as Lola Lola), she was the *primum mobile* in the erotic cosmology of the century. Even Freud was enchanted with the myth of the temptress, which accounts no doubt for his approbation of an otherwise mediocre book like Rider Haggard's *She*. Joyce did not invent the temptress; he found and adopted her. In this one aspect, at least, he is very much a writer of the nineteenth century and not of the twentieth. If the temptress has disappeared from our literature in this century, it is not because sexual temptation has disappeared from our lives, but because it has finally been dissociated from the concept of sin in a century that has invented sins far greater than mere adultery.

But the virgin-temptress is not merely conventional in Joyce's art. Like all men, Joyce assimilated experience by categories. The received categories or conventions of any age are psychologically functional for those who partake of them, being no less than the means by which men give name and form to otherwise inchoate desires and anxieties. It is no paradox that the most encyclopedic of modern writers turns out to be the most insistently categorical, for it was the scholastic spirit itself that made the encyclopedism possible. For Joyce, no idea or detail

29. *Freud: The Mind of the Moralist*, pp. 197–198.

of experience was unassimilable to his prefabricated categories. Gerty is *the virgin-temptress first* and a composite
portrait of Marthe Fleischmann and the others only by
accident. She grew by accretion, beginning with some
image of the first taboo figure, the forbidden mother, reinforced by the institutional forbidden mother of the
Church, and built up of borrowings from Shakespeare,
Dante, Homer, Sacher-Masoch, Maria Cummins, and innumerable encounters with the reality of experience. Yet,
from *Stephen Hero* to *Finnegans Wake* she is recog-
nizably one and the same.

The virgin-temptress is repetitive in Joyce's work to
the degree to which she was once threatening in his life.
This aspect of his art, the obsessive reweaving of old
themes in new and more complex variations, is like nothing so much as repetition-compulsion, and, like that
psychic phenomenon, it aims at mastery over a threatening image or impulse. In "Nausikaa," Joyce's strategy
for managing her involved the establishment of psychic
distance through the declaration of sexual independence.
The literary devices of the episode: irony, wit, and condescension, are, in their detachment, stylistic imitations of
that strategy. Bloom's masturbation is the objective correlative of Joyce's comic satire. It asserts masculine competence even as it acknowledges the power of that which
threatens it. Yet both serve the need for release and liberation, even if the relief afforded is only temporary and
the liberating act involves the payment of considerable
tribute to the oppressor. In *Portrait* Stephen himself is
aware that his mockery of Emma is an ambiguous act,
for "he felt that, however he might revile and mock her
image, his anger was also a form of homage" (*PA*, 220).
Or, in the words of the epigraph from Lessing that opens

this chapter, "They are not all free men who mock their chains."[30] Joyce was never wholly free, but he did mock his chains, and fortunately for us he sang in those chains like the sea.

30. Gotthold Lessing, *Nathan the Wise*, tr., William A. Steel (New York: Dutton, 1961), 4 (iv):189.

NOSTOS

5. Das Fleisch das Stets Bejaht

> Woman is an animal that micturates once
> a day, defecates once a week, menstruates
> once a month, and parturates once a year.
> —JAMES JOYCE

THE CRITICS

> . . . I wouldn't give a snap of my two
> fingers for all their learning why dont
> they go and create something. . . .
> —MOLLY BLOOM

UNDER THE scrutiny of psychoanalysis, the symbol, that artifact of human intelligence that transforms what is merely *actual* into what is significantly *human,* assumes the appearance of the Renaissance hieroglyph, the enigmatic figure in which a profusion of latent meanings is epitomized or writ small. It is as true of literary symbols as it is of dream symbols that they are, in Freud's words, "Brief, meagre and laconic in comparison with the range and wealth of the . . . thoughts" that find expression in them.[1] Molly Bloom is such a symbolic construct, and this is an essay on the economy of her portraiture—a demonstration of how a rich and contradictory array of psychic materials has been condensed into a few suggestive images.

As a character realized from within, Molly Bloom is the least complex and least important of the major actors

1. Sigmund Freud, *The Interpretation of Dreams*, SE 4:279.

in *Ulysses*. Though her soliloquy is great poetry and altogether a tour de force of Joyce's verbal artistry, it is,
after all, an addendum to the book. True, Joyce did call
"Penelope" the "clou" of the book, but he also regarded
it as a grand epilogue, a post-facto flourish. The chapter
clearly stands apart from the rest of the book and appears
to have a unity and insularity that should make it easy
to discuss. Yet, for the critics this apparently simple episode has been an enigma. Taken all together, the interpretive commentary that has sought to define Molly
Bloom since her debut in 1922 has been a genteel sort of
warfare. For in real criticism, as in the fictive Dublin,
Molly has been the object of many and diverse passions.
To those who deplore the use of criticism in our time as
an anaesthetic against feeling, I recommend the case of
Molly Bloom as evidence that critics may still be men.
From the beginning in the debate over her, disinterested-
ness has been a major casualty. Most criticism of "Penelope" is, I believe, best understood as an open letter to
Molly, for much that is puzzling as literary analysis
makes abundant sense as courtship or masculine protest. Indeed, psychoanalysis brings the extreme tactics of
this criticism into focus as the tactics of seduction—flat-
tery and assault. The phenomenon of transference is not
confined to the therapeutic couch; the dynamics of literary response depend on it.[2]

Though the history of commentary upon Molly is long
on passion, it is short on variety. Most of her interpre-

2. This is the conclusion drawn by Norman Holland in *The
Dynamics of Literary Response* (New York: Oxford University
Press, 1968). More recently, see his "Fantasy and Defense in Faulkner's 'A Rose for Emily'" *Hartford Studies in Literature* 4 (1972):
1–35.

ters have staked out positions in either of two opposed camps: the "earth-mother" camp and the more modern and ever-more-popular "satanic mistress" or "thirty-shilling whore" camp. Much of the criticism of the former group, moreover, is redundant, for its authority derives from one or two of Joyce's claims for Molly.[3] The major text to which this criticism appeals is a paragraph from a letter by Joyce to Budgen, written while Joyce was finishing the "Penelope" episode:

Penelope is the clou of the book. The first sentence contains 2500 words. There are eight sentences in the episode. It begins and ends with the female word *yes*. It turns like the huge earth ball slowly surely and evenly, round and round spinning, its four cardinal points being the female breasts, arse, womb and cunt expressed by the word *because, bottom* (in all senses bottom button, bottom of the class, bottom of the sea, bottom of his heart), *woman, yes*. Though probably more obscene than any preceding episode it seems to me to be per-

3. These writers are the following in order of their publication: Stuart Gilbert, *James Joyce's Ulysses: A Study* (London: Faber & Faber, 1930; reprinted New York: Random House, Vintage, 1956); Frank Budgen, *James Joyce and the Making of Ulysses* (Bloomington: Indiana University Press, 1960); Harry Levin, *James Joyce* (Norfolk, Conn.: New Directions, 1941; reprinted, 1960); R. P. Blackmur, "The Jew in Search of a Son," *Virginia Quarterly Review* 24 (January 1948):96–116; William York Tindall, *James Joyce: His Way of Interpreting the Modern World* (New York: Scribner's, 1950; reprinted, New York: Grove, 1960). It is significant that these are all early commentaries; only Tindall makes it into the fifties, and then just barely. All the major contributions to the "anti-Molly" school, beginning with Hugh Kenner's *Dublin's Joyce* in 1956, are products of the fifties and sixties. This is a curious episode in the history and sociology of taste in America. I would not be surprised to discover that even in such cultural backwaters as departments of English literature, the hardening of sensibility in postwar America has become visible in such aesthetic shifts.

fectly sane full amoral fertilisable untrustworthy engaging
shrewd limited prudent indifferent *Weib. Ich bin das Fleisch
das stets bejaht.*[4]

Elsewhere, at the end of the "Ithaca" episode, Molly's
position in bed is described by an astral voice:

In what posture?
Listener: reclined semilaterally, left, left hand under head,
right leg extended in a straight line and resting on left leg,
flexed, in the attitude of Gea-Tellus, fulfilled, recumbent, big
with seed. (721/737)

With few exceptions, the early glosses on Molly were
variations on the theme of idealized *Weiblichkeit*. The
Molly we encounter in the classic commentaries, those
of Gilbert and Levin, is drawn wholly in these terms. Both
men see her as Gea-Tellus, the fertile earth, the compliant
body, *mater omnipotens et alma*. But the most generous,
if not uxorious, version of this mythopoetic Molly has
been Tindall's:

> As fundamental and symbolic as her cat, she appears as
> "Gea-Tellus" or earth-earth, "fulfilled, recumbent, big with
> seed." By its redundancy this name expresses her meaning.
> Larger than individual Mrs. Bloom and far older, she is the
> Great Mother of the ancients. Her voice, the voice of the flesh,
> is endlessly affirmative. Her monologue which begins with
> "Yes," and uses "yes" as its refrain, suitably ends with "Yes."
> From its immediate reference to Bloom, this final word is raised
> by the chapter that precedes it and by the book that it ends
> to a general affirmation. The last two pages of her monologue
> and of the book are a hymn to God and nature. The center of
> natural life, she praises it.
>
> Bloom's equanimity resolves his private tensions. By her

4. From a letter to Budgen, August 16, 1921. Reprinted from
Letters of James Joyce, ed., Stuart Gilbert (New York: Viking,
1966) 1:169–170.

existence and her position at the end Mrs. Bloom resolves the tensions of the book. She makes the worries and frustrations of Bloom seem irrelevant and the problems of Stephen peripheral. Compared to her, nothing seems very important. By her irrationality she reconciles all rational conflicts. Stephen and Bloom, conflicting opposites, become one in her. As she thinks of them, their differences fall away to leave them united in a common being. She is the agent of reconciliation and its symbol.[5]

Whereas Stephen Dedalus and Leopold Bloom are the products of a history, be it racial, national, or individual, that resonates through *Ulysses*, Molly, in this view, is the end of history. The dialectical antagonisms that inform the book—fidelity *versus* infidelity, nationalism *versus* humanism, Catholicism *versus* catholicity, art and freedom *versus* home and dependence—are all resolved, not in historical synthesis but in ahistorical fusion in the person of Molly. And for Tindall, as for any Jungian, this is fusion by incorporation: history is swallowed up by the Great Mother. Molly's mind, like the grave or the womb or the Freudian id, contains no contradictions. She absorbs the world, and its manyness becomes ONE. In her imagination all men are he; the contradictions that plague the world of men are solved in the generic unity of *man*. And Joyce's letter to Budgen really implies it all. To read Joyce's "huge earth ball" as "the Great Mother" and "symbol of reconciliation" is only to make manifest the infantile oral ideal already implicit in his maternal Molly.

More recently, however, a number of revisionists, reacting against the sentimentality of these earlier readings, have taken a hard line on Molly. Some have done so with evangelical intent; others are merely second-generation

5. *James Joyce*, pp. 36–37.

New Critics and hard-nosed pragmatists of "the word."
Criticism makes strange bedfellows, and both evangelists
and close readers agree that Molly is to be disliked and
that "Penelope" is Joyce's devastating critique of her.[6]
This anti-Molly position was pioneered by Hugh Kenner,
who, in his *Dublin's Joyce*, anathemized her in a few
neat phrases. Dublin, he charged, is Hell, Molly its satanic mistress, and the previous generation of readers is "in
key with the animal level at which this comic inferno is
conceived." (Those readers, I gather, have forgiven him.)

The "Yes" of consent that kills the soul has darkened the intellect and blunted the moral sense of all Dublin. At the very
rim of Dante's funnel-shaped Hell is the imperceptible "Yes"
of Paola [sic] and Francesca; they are blown about by the
winds, but Molly lies still at the warm dead womb-like centre
of the labyrinth of paving-stones. Her "Yes" is confident and
exultant; it is the "Yes" of authority: authority over this animal kingdom of the dead.[7]

Though Kenner's critique, upon its publication, was a
challenge to thirty years of received opinion and the doctrinal authority of Joyce's friends, it did accept the level
of mythic abstraction as the appropriate grounds of un-

6. The major texts in this camp, again in order of publication,
are: Hugh Kenner, *Dublin's Joyce* (Bloomington: Indiana University Press, 1956; reprinted, Boston: Beacon Press, 1962); Erwin
R. Steinberg, "A Book with a Molly in It," *James Joyce Review*
2 (Spring-Summer 1958):56–62; J. Mitchell Morse, "Molly Bloom
Revisited," in *A James Joyce Miscellany, Second Series*, ed., Marvin Magalaner (Carbondale: Southern Illinois University Press,
1959), pp. 139–150; Robert O. Richardson, "Molly's Last Words,"
Twentieth Century Literature 12 (January 1967):177–185; Darcy
O'Brien, *The Conscience of James Joyce* (Princeton: Princeton
University Press, 1968). The latest Molly, that of Richard Ellmann
in *Ulysses on the Liffey*, is a revised, sentimental Molly. She
is a nice person, alive, with a heart of gold.

7. P. 262.

derstanding and argument. Between earth mother and mistress of the dead there is a broad gulf (though Kenner, for all I know, may think otherwise), but the universe of discourse is the same. Since Kenner, however, the case against Molly has fallen into the hands of the close readers like J. Mitchell Morse who have put the indictment on positive textual grounds. By means of a detailed analysis of Molly's recollections, attitudes, and fantasies, Morse has called into question the entire Gea-Tellus myth. His conclusions constitute a significant objection to the mythic Molly of Gilbert, Levin, and Tindall: "Molly is not honest, she is not kind, she is not creative, she is not free, she hasn't enough *élan vital* to get dressed before three P.M., and her fertility is subnormal."[8] Nor is she "big with seed" as the astral catechist of "Ithaca" tells us, but fat with drinking too much stout. Her lovers "do not take her seriously as a woman. She is a dirty joke. No one regards her as anything but a whore." Morse attacks directly the old view of Molly as an abundant earth goddess, giver of life, mother of all men. "Since when," he complains, "does an earth-goddess sneer at fecundity and practice coitus interruptus?" Finally, the indictment, feeding on its own indignation, rises to a truly Kennerian climax: "Molly's soliloquy is the bitterest and deadliest thing Joyce ever wrote. Without exhorting or haranguing his readers, observing strictly his own canon of reticence, he let Molly damn herself as the very center of paralysis."

As though such damnation were not a fitting epitaph upon a dead reputation, a more cunning attack has since been fashioned by Darcy O'Brien in *The Conscience of James Joyce*. O'Brien condemns Molly as a "distinctly

8. "Molly Bloom Revisited," p. 140.

lower-middle-class adulteress," which is probably the most damning of the anathemas yet pronounced upon her, for it denies her even the virtue of satanic potency.[9] Among her sins, O'Brien notes: "Molly's self-loving contempt for Bloom is monumental"; her measure of a man's soul is his sexual capacity; she is a jealous mother who regards her daughter with a mixture of exasperation and contempt; she is crude and venal, lacking any trace of delicacy and tenderness.[10] Yet the peculiar value of this attack lies not in the vigor of its scorn but in its frigid acknowledgment that Molly is not without charm: "One can be susceptible to Molly's charms without being entirely swayed by them. Her animal vitality is engaging, but her crudity repulsive. Her husband's sexual neglect of her invites sympathy but the virulence of her contempt for him seems malignant."[11] For O'Brien these charms are all the more reason for vigilance. His evangelical bias yields a medieval *caveat lector*: in a universe where beauty often masquerades as truth, a reader must keep his ethical sense (whose canonical authority is "the conscience of James Joyce") within easy reach. Thus, "For all of Molly's attractive vitality, for all of her fleshly charms and engaging bravado, she is at heart a thirty-shilling whore."[12]

Suitable terms for a negotiated settlement of this war

9. P. 150. O'Brien has recently had another go at Molly in "Some Determinants of Molly Bloom," in *Approaches to Ulysses*, ed., Thomas Staley and Bernard Benstock (Pittsburgh: University of Pittsburgh Press, 1970), pp. 137–155. In all, he is gentler with her there and has profited by the sporadic application of Freud. See also, in the same anthology, David Hyman's excellent study "The Empirical Molly," pp. 103–135.

10. Pp. 201–17.

11. P. 202.

12. P. 211.

have been offered by Phillip Herring, who has argued
that the Homeric Penelope is a historically bivalent figure and that Molly is ambiguous in her image.[13] He
points out the conflicts in Joyce's attitudes toward Nora,
Molly's immediate model, and notes that we can hardly
expect Molly to escape those conflicts. Herring insists,
however, that the apparent contradiction between the
symbolic element in Molly, her idealized *Weiblichkeit*,
and the realistic element, her vulgarity of thought and
promiscuity of manner, is traceable to an artistic program
of scrupulous realism on Joyce's part. In "Penelope," he
tells us, Joyce undertook to "portray the soul of a woman
in such nakedness and completeness as has never been
achieved before" in a spirit of ruthless realism which
compelled him to depict the vulgar along with the beautiful because both are indispensable elements of the
humanity of his characters and the comedy of his novel.

But, as we know from Joyce's letters to Nora, his creation of ambiguous Molly had little to do with an ethic of
scrupulous responsibility toward the truth of "humanity."
Rather, if there is a principled adherence toward any
sort of truth in "Penelope," it is to the subjective truth
of his own nature. And it is revelatory of Joyce's great-
ness as a writer that the terms of his ambivalence are
each so powerfully communicated that the two faces of
Molly have given rise to two coherent critical responses.
Finally, it seems that the significance of this critical cross-
fire is that both paeans of praise and anxious expressions
of contempt are plausible and intelligible responses to
Molly. And those responses have public value as mirrors
held up to the critics themselves and as clues to Molly's

13. Phillip Herring, "The Bedsteadfastness of Molly Bloom,"
Modern Fiction Studies 15 (Spring 1969):49–62.

character and Joyce's intentions for her. But the criticism that has sought to measure her has thus far been measured by her. Like the Theban Sphinx whom she so resembles, she confronts us with a riddle, and we must invoke the spirit of Oedipus to answer it.

THE RIDDLE OF THE SPHINX

Just as there are two Noras in the letters, there are two Mollys in "Penelope," a literal and a symbolic one, a woman who is wife to Leopold Bloom and *woman*, wife and mother to all men. She is both a maternal ideal and the epitome of bourgeois decadence, a goddess and a notorious virago. A symbol of fertility, she is, as Morse has pointed out, contemptuous of real pregnancy. What other married woman of her age in Dublin has had only two children? A paradoxical figure, she is Gea-Tellus as middle-class adulteress, the *ewig Weibliche* as Irish *Hausfrau*. The duality is reflected in the poetry of her monologue, which is both scatological and pastoral. Her inward speech is an uneasy mixture of obscenity and grace in which callousness and bad humor are played off against the most exalted expressions of physical and spiritual ecstasy to be found anywhere in literature. The same woman who proposes to extract information from her husband by tightening her bottom and letting out "a few smutty words smellrump or lick my shit . . . " (766/781) is authoress of "O that awful deepdown torrent O and the sea the sea crimson sometimes like fire and the glorious sunsets and the figtrees in the Alameda gardens yes . . . " (768/783).

Yet, in spite of these contradictions, Molly herself betrays few signs of personal conflict. Despite her furtive liaison with Boylan and the generally sleazy quality of her sexual life, her reflections betray little evidence of anxiety or guilt. A note of defensiveness does appear now and then, especially in her reflections on other women, but Molly is not much given to self-justification. The few occurrences of the psychopathology of everyday life in her monologue, the verbal slips and unintentional puns, reveal no severe opposition of psychic motives. And unlike Stephen, for whom history is a nightmare, or Bloom, for whom the past is a treasury of irrevocable failures, Molly is not committed to the past. She does recall lost possibilities with regret, but she is not obsessed or incapacitated by them. In short, she seems to be liberated from the characteristic paralysis of a Joycean character. Insofar as she is Irish, her life is unfulfilled, but she is not self-oppressed. She is free of the guilt, shame, and anxiety that beset Stephen Dedalus and Leopold Bloom and so many characters in *Ulysses, Portrait,* and *Dubliners.* Yet her liberated condition is not particularly admirable, for it has not been won. Molly has overcome no psychic or social barriers to gain her freedom. And whether it is more correct to say that she has no unconscious wishes or that those wishes enjoy free access to consciousness is indeterminable. But, clearly, her psychic processes are unitary; her motives are all in accord.

In short, the characterization of Molly is an expression of conflict, though she herself experiences none. And insofar as she exists in a realm beyond conflict, she is unreal. "Penelope" is a great poetic achievement, as anyone who has heard Siobhan McKenna's reading of it will agree, but the psychology of the chapter is superficial and cliché-ridden. When compared with "Proteus" or "Scylla and Charybdis" or "Circe," its inadequacies as psychology are self-evident. In spite of Carl Jung's praise of the chapter in a letter to Joyce[14] ("a string of veritable psychological peaches. I suppose the devil's grandmother knows so much about the real psychology of a woman"), R. M. Adams is closer to the truth when he observes that Joyce's vaunted understanding of the feminine psyche is not much in evidence here.[15] Doubtless, Jung's praise of Joyce's "psychological peaches" reflects his own inability to distinguish psychology from mythology, or perhaps his own subliminal rapture over Molly's physiological melons. But the end of this most psychological of modern novels is nonetheless a retreat from psychology into folklore and myth. Unlike earlier chapters, the interior monologue in "Penelope" does not constitute an analysis of real mental process, but is rather a stylized imitation of an analysis. S. L. Goldberg has observed that Molly lacks the odd moral contours of an individual, and he sees the chapter as a retreat from life disguised as a descent into its elements. "For all its earthiness and overt affirmation of life, much of 'Penelope' . . . paradoxically suggests a retreat in Joyce from living human beings toward dehumanized abstractions like Life and Humanity."[16]

Molly, then, is not a character whose psychic life has been revealed from within, but rather a nodal point of Joyce's masculine experience—a psychological category. The conflicting elements in her portrait call to mind familiar Joycean fantasies, while the abstractness of the image shows us what happens when erotic fantasies are

14. Letter from Carl Jung to Joyce, August ?, 1932, *Letters* 3:253.
15. *Surface and Symbol*, p. 40.
16. *The Classical Temper*, p. 299.

transformed into "characters." The erotic landscape of
the chapter recalls the clichés of Joycean love that we
find in the letters to Nora. There is the androgynous aspect of a phallic femininity, which shows itself both in
an aggressively masculine demeanor and in a multitude
of fetishes. Also, as we might expect, all of Molly's orificial activities, including her menstrual flow, are charged
with sexual significance. She is the object of oral and
anal erotic impulses on Bloom's part, while for the inevitable rival, in this case Boylan, she is an object of a
powerful, almost superhuman, genital drive. She is
Bloom's betrayer and his avenger. She is an adulteress
and a "fair tyrant" toward her masochistic husband
and, in terms congenial to both her husband and herself, the best of wives and mothers. And she is all
these things in the context of the familiar Shakespearean marital configuration of female viraginity, male
uxoriousness, wifely infidelity with the rival brother-
figure, and a husbandly impotence that is unrelieved by
assumed dongiovannism.[17]

This configuration, which resembles but is not identical with the classical oedipus complex, is the skeleton
upon which the emotional patterns of *Ulysses* are fleshed
out. The Boylan-Molly-Bloom triangle is a common
enough variation on the oedipal situation, and we perceive and respond to it characteristically from the view-
point of the injured son and lover, Bloom. Bloom is the
ardent but sexually incompetent son; Molly the wife who

17. The parallel of the Bloomian situation to the Shakespearean is a most elaborate one. For a catalogue of parallels, see
especially Schutte, *Joyce and Shakespeare: A Study in the Meaning of Ulysses* (New Haven: Yale University Press, 1957), pp.
121–135.

is made to perform the offices of the mother; and Boylan, the ubiquitous, treacherous brother. He is the indispensable catalyst in the book's erotic chemistry. When Joycean characters make love, no matter how private the circumstances, there are always three people present.

Molly serves two purposes in her husband's life: excitation and reassurance. The terms in which Joyce conceived her tend to highlight one or the other of these purposes, or, most often, one of them in the service of the other. Bloom's potency is severely inhibited by fear of castration, and he can, at best, achieve a partial liberation from anxiety under conditions which reassure him that his body is intact. Thus, he can achieve orgasm only when he can see or touch his penis and is incapable of climax within his wife, because the disappearance of his penis into her is a visual imitation of castration. For that reason, conjugal sexuality, for Bloom, is little more than masturbation in Molly's presence. He completes coition, if at all, outside her.[18] "I wonder did he ever put it out of sight," says Joe Hynes of Bloom (332/338). "Gob," laughs the narrator of "Cyclops," "there's many a true word spoken in jest." Molly, for her own reasons, is tolerant of her husband's perversity; she even solicits it in exchange for favors. Her tolerance allows for gentle punishment, "fair tyranny," the threat of which is another condition of Bloom's excitation. Molly's impulse to "bulge it right out in his face" (765/780) and mutter "smellrump or lick my shit" (776/781), is love's old sweet song in

18. More generally, Bloom's problem may be an aspect of the oral-narcissistic dilemma (see Philip Slater, *The Glory of Hera: Greek Mythology and the Greek Family* [Boston: Beacon Press, 1968]) and may betray a conflict over boundaries. Bloom's moly is the power to preserve ego boundaries, but that very firm sense of boundedness may be a sexually inhibiting quality of character.

Bloom's ears and in Joyce's. It is the paradoxical protective threat of the parent-lover.

This figure of the phallic mother in Joyce's writing is invariably a mature woman with maternal tendencies and capacities who is strong-minded, willful, and a bit cruel. Toward her husband generally she may be scolding and manipulative like Molly or cold and distant like Gretta Conroy or enigmatically noncommittal like Bertha Rowan. In any case, she is petticoat government incarnate, possessing in full the royal power to punish and reward. She is attractive and sexually alive, though she tends to deny her husband sexually and is suspected to (and sometimes does) harbor a desire for another man. Her husband's sexual disinterest is usually a mirror-image of her own. He keeps at a safe distance from her physically, while at the same time maintaining in his fantasy life an awesome passion for her that is transformable into real potency only upon the appearance or promise of the rival. Thus, he is dependent upon both her love and her defections.

She first appeared in Joyce's work as Gretta Conroy in "The Dead" and remained in it from there on as a common stock in his artistic trade, a category of the feminine in whom details of the real Nora Joyce were reconciled with fragments of an ancient infantile fantasy of maternal love and maternal duplicity. All of her incarnations are "essentially" the same: Gretta, Bertha, Molly, A L P. Motherness, Stephen would say, is the whatness of allmother.

As the epithet *phallic mother* implies, her attractiveness to men as well as her authority over them derive from what can only be understood as a phallic endowment. Thus, Bella Cohen, in becoming a man and tormenting a female Bloom in "Circe," is no more than a particularly malign manifestation of the bisexual potential in all of Joyce's women. She is, in a sense, the real, or latent, Molly. Molly herself, a somewhat modulated version of this figure, is equipped from hair to instep with the inevitable Joycean fetishes. She herself observes with mixed amusement and disgust how both Bloom and Boylan fix their attention on her shoes, stockings, feet, drawers, and gloves (729–730/744–745). The breast fixation her admirers share is, among other things, a fetishistic overvaluation of the most assertive part of her anatomy, or, as Lenehan the sponger says plainly, "Hell's delights! She has a fine pair, God bless her" (231/234). As we have already seen in some detail, these fetishes are standard equipment in every woman Joyce ever admired or created. Indeed, the fetish not only controlled Joyce's erotic responses but finally became, at some point in his life, the exclusive object of them. Joyce reportedly told Budgen (albeit ten years or so after the completion of *Ulysses*) that he no longer cared about women's bodies but was only interested in their clothes.[19] By clothes, Budgen reminded us unnecessarily, Joyce meant underclothing. Budgen also recalled that for Joyce the word *drawers* itself was "a word of power, and in it lay all the magic of the thing designated by it." Like Bloom, to whom Molly promised a pair of drawers "off my doll to carry about in his waistcoat pocket" (731/ 746), Joyce in Zürich "used to carry a miniature pair in his trousers pocket until one sad day, as he sadly informed me, he lost them."

As with the Joyces, the show of love among the Blooms requires the exchange of fetishes. Bloom demands draw-

19. Budgen, pp. 319–320.

ers from Molly; he gives her gloves, garters, or aprons in exchange. Though on June 16, 1904, his particular charm against evil is a potato (and Stephen's is a long stick, his ashplant), Bloom may just as often carry about a pair of soiled drawers as an anxiety-reducing talisman. In exchange for this borrowed potency, Bloom re-equips Molly with purchased fetishes. She recalls an early courtship present of Byron's poems and three pairs of gloves (728/743); on Lombard Street he had given her an apron (766/781), while more recently he has bought her violet garters (735/750), which she ironically and cruelly has just worn that afternoon to excite Boylan.

HER OMISSIONS

Of those female attributes which bear fetishistic import in *Ulysses*, the most curious and rich in implication is menstrual flow.[20] Molly's period comes upon her as she lies in bed, causing her some momentary apprehension and a moment, too, of unlikely fastidiousness ("O Jamesy let me up out of this pooh" 754/769). But although it is a source of discomfort, it is also an aspect of her allure, as she herself suspects. Anticipating her Monday date with Boylan and recalling how her menses affect Bloom, Molly ponders if Boylan, too, might like it: "wouldn't that pester the soul out of a body unless he likes it some men do God knows" (754/769). And Molly is not the only one under the lunar curse on Bloomsday, for Gerty MacDowell is, too, as Bloom, from behind his rock, happily infers from her behavior and the faint musky scent that drifts toward him up the beach. The

20. Ellmann teases us in his latest book with a chapter titled "Why Molly Menstruates." But he forgets to tell us why.

olfactory and imaginative apprehension of Gerty's blood excites him, adding one more element to her accumulated coquetries. "Near her monthlies, I expect, makes them feel ticklish" (361/368).

These menstrual heroines of *Ulysses* are not exactly novelties in the pantheon of Joycean women. In *Exiles* Joyce had made sly allusions to the menstrual charms of Bertha Rowan,[21] and, knowing him as we do, we can expect the worst of Stephen Dedalus's adolescent poem, "To E——— C———," which celebrates "the night and the balmy breeze and *the maiden lustre of the moon*" (*PA*, 70, italics mine). But though the fact of the menstrual attraction is clear, the psychology of it is not, despite Ellmann's recent illumination that the blood in the chamber pot is like the blood in the chalice. Any writer can turn a fetish into a sacrament—that is what art is all about. Other meanings suggest themselves. We note that blood almost always appears amid an abundance of frilly devices. In "Nausikaa," which is the bargain basement of Joyce's eroticism, Gerty MacDowell's menstrual flow lives in fit and harmonious company with her skirts, drawers, feet, and hair and appears to Bloom to be just another of her many seductions. At one point in "Nausikaa" Bloom's free associations casually slide from Gerty's menses to Molly's and thence to Molly's

21. Robert is always reminding Bertha that she is like the moon (*E* 31, 32, 48). "In that dress, with your slim body, walking with little even steps. I saw the moon passing in the dusk till you passed and left my sight" (*E* 31).

Joyce's notes (*E* 113) are explicit on that point. "Her age: 28. Robert likens her to the moon because of her dress. Her age is the completion of a lunar rhythm. Cf. Oriani on menstrual flow— *la malattia sacra che in un rituo lunare prepara la donna per il sacrificio.*"

itching foot, as though the association menses/foot might constitute for him a psychic constellation. "Devils they are when that's coming on them. Dark devilish appearance. Molly often told me feel things a ton weight. Scratch the sole of my foot. O that way!" (362–363/369). The sudden shift in attention from Molly's menses to her foot seems natural enough for Bloom and suggests the equivalence of the two as "phallic" presences.

Bloom's primitive olfactory longing is justified by Bruno Bettelheim and other anthropologists who have shown us that male menstruation envy is a common grudge that cuts across cultural lines and in some cultures forms the basis for male ceremonies of ritual mutilation.[22] Similarly, among adolescents whom Bettelheim has observed in clinical practice the onset of female menstruation is taken for a visible sign of maturation by boys who have perceived no such sign upon themselves and who thereby respond to it with awe and imitation. Quite simply, menstruation envy in men seems to be a common counterpart of the infamous penis envy that Freud observed in women. They share a common raison d'être. Blood is a presence that contrasts sharply with a corresponding absence in the opposite sex, and menstrual bleeding is a function which by its very nature is a reproach to the corresponding lack of such a function among men. Molly's menstruation, then, is a genital function that establishes and assures her supremacy over the genitally dysfunctional Bloom, and Bloom (and Joyce) respond to it as they do to that other wished-for genital "presence," the penis.

Another possibility, however, for interpreting this

22. Bruno Bettelheim, *Symbolic Wounds: Puberty Rites and the Envious Male* (New York: Collier, 1962).

menstrual fixation is raised by Molly herself, who associates bleeding with guarantees of virginity and fidelity:
". . . and they always want to see a stain on the bed to
know youre a virgin for them all thats troubling them
theyre such fools too you could be a widow or divorced
40 times over a daub of red ink would do or blackberry
juice no thats too purply . . ." (754/769). It may be that
Joyce, through Molly, is himself suggesting that the
association of ideas that eroticizes menstruation is: "she
bleeds—she bleeds for me—I am her first and only lover."
Inasmuch as this interpretation, however, runs counter to
what we know about the erotogenic appeal of infidelity
for Joyce, we may be suspicious of Molly's analysis. But,
then again, we also know about Joyce's ambivalent attraction to infidelity and virginity. And, since Molly
Bloom and Gerty MacDowell both partake of the virgin/
whore syndrome, it is not inconsistent to see the menstrual lover as an assertion of the virginal aspect of that
duality. But finally, of course, what really appealed to
Joyce was incertitude and the mysterious promise of both
virginity and infidelity in the same woman. And menstruation, like the fetish, is delightfully ambiguous. In
itself it neither confirms nor denies virginity; it merely
implies it by imitating defloration. Similarly, the classic
fetish neither confirms nor denies the existence of the
female phallus but merely, and provokingly, imitates it.

This fixation, then, may have several determinants,
and our analysis of it is not yet complete, for we haven't
taken up its obvious connection with Joyce's potent
urinary and excremental vision. Molly's menstrual activity in "Penelope," after all, is in sympathy with her
urinary virtuosity. As a urinary heroine, only the Irish

imagination has produced her like. Indeed, the Irish imagination has produced her betters. One thinks of the maids of honor at the Brobdingnagian court, who could "discharge what they had drunk, to the quantity of at least two hogsheads, in a vessel that held above three tuns."[23] And there is the "great-bladdered Emer" of Yeats's "Crazy Jane on the Mountain" and the woman in Irish myth who, as Yeats records, "was murdered by jealous rivals because she made the deepest hole in the snow with her urine."[24] Molly lacks their capacity. But she does seem, whenever we encounter her, to have a full bladder or to be in the process of emptying it (see *U*, 278/282, 729–730/744–745, 736/751, 755/770). The three-quarters mark in her soliloquy finds her stooped thoughtfully over the orangekeyed chamberpot. "O how the waters come down at Lahore,"[25] she muses grandiloquently (755/770). But Bloom earlier had thought of her cataract as more of a tinkle. He also had recalled for us (though obviously not for himself) one of Joyce's earlier excursions into the poetry of the bladder.[26]

23. Jonathan Swift, *Gulliver's Travels* (Boston: Riverside Press, 1960), 2(5):96.

24. W. B. Yeats, *On the Boiler* (Dublin: Cuala Press, 1939).

25. A reference to Southey's "The Cataract at Lodore." As Weldon Thornton has pointed out in *Allusions in Ulysses* (Chapel Hill: University of North Carolina Press, 1968), Molly's substitution of Lahore for Lodore is a nice self-incriminating slip (lahore ="la whore").

26. William York Tindall, in his edition of *Chamber Music* (New York: Columbia University Press, 1954), has read these lines as subtle urinary images, and I heartily concur in his reading.

> There, where the gay winds stay to woo
> The young leaves as they pass,
> My love goes slowly, bending to
> Her shadow on the grass;

"Chamber music. Could make a kind of pun on that" (278/282).[27]

Those critics who have read such displacements of interest from Molly's "soul" to her bladder as Joyce's attempt to present a degraded image of her are partly right. There is hostility in "Penelope," and the portrait is in some measure the fleshing-out of a formula that amused Joyce even in his mariolatrous youth: "Woman is an animal that micturates once a day, defecates once a week, menstruates once a month, and parturates once a year."[28]

> And where the sky's a pale blue cup
>   Over the laughing land,
> My love goes lightly, holding up
>   Her dress with dainty hand.
>
> (from *CM*, 7)

> Thou leanest to the shell of night,
> Dear lady, a divining ear.
> In that soft choiring of delight
>   What sound hath made thy heart to fear?
> Seemed it of rivers rushing forth
> From the grey deserts of the north?
>
> (from *CM*, 26)

27. According to Ellmann (*JJ*, p. 160), the pun had already been made by Gogarty. "Gogarty . . . had brought Joyce to visit Jenny, an easygoing widow, and while they all drank porter Joyce read out his poems, which he carried with him in a large packet, each written in his best hand in the middle of a large piece of parchment. The widow was pleased enough by this entertainment, but had to interrupt to withdraw behind a screen to a chamber pot. As the two young men listened, Gogarty cried out, 'There's a critic for you!' Joyce had already accepted the title of *Chamber Music* which Stanislaus had suggested; and when Stanislaus heard the story from him, he remarked, 'You can take it as a favorable omen.'"

28. Recorded by Stanislaus in his diary, *CDD*, pp. 10–11. Stanislaus's observation accompanying this remark that his brother "has lately become a prig about women" is dated September 26, 1903, in the middle of James's romantic *Chamber Music* period.

But in *Ulysses* micturation is another exciting orificial activity and is an item of Molly's allure. Yeats was right about love's mansion being pitched in the place of excrement. Yeats knew where to look for property. But it took Joyce to show us the true charm of the location.

These apparently secondary details in the characterization of Molly have stylistic consequences for the chapter. Molly's vaginal effluents, or omissions, as she calls them, influence the style of her monologue: the stream of her consciousness is the displacement to language of her urinary and menstrual flow. As Freud showed us, the mind is always punning on the body. A. Walton Litz, in a study of Joyce's notes for *Ulysses* in the British Museum, has called attention to a note for "Penelope" that characterizes the chapter as "gynomorphic," which suggests to Litz that "the form of the episode is shaped by the physical characteristics of the female sex."[29] Among those characteristics are Molly's omissions and her preoccupation with them, which invest her interior monologue with imagery of flow, wetness, roses, smell, and the sea and are the reasons for the liquid and ineluctable movement of her thoughts. We don't know whether Budgen was right by intuition or was using inside information when he said of the chapter, "Marion's monologue snakes its way through the last forty pages of *Ulysses* like a river winding through a plain, finding its true course by the compelling logic of its own fluidity and weight."[30] If the former, this characterization of "Penelope" is great unconscious wit; if the latter, it is another revelation of

29. A. Walton Litz, *The Art of James Joyce: Method and Design in Ulysses and Finnegan's Wake* (New York: Oxford University Press, 1964), pp. 45–46.

30. Budgen, p. 262.

Joyce's genius. For those who have taken seriously Joyce's disavowal of interest in Freud, the ingenious displacement of Molly's gynetropic preoccupations onto her fantasies is additional evidence of his sophisticated understanding of the determinants of human fantasy and the dynamics of what Freud called dream-work. One excellent example of this displacement is the reverie in which Molly recalls the end of her brief romance with Lieutenant Harry Mulvey in Gibraltar:

I could see over to Morocco almost the bay of Tangier white and the Atlas mountain with snow on it and the straits *like a river* so clear Harry Molly Darling I was thinking of him *on the sea* all the time after at mass when my petticoat began to slip down at the elevation weeks and weeks I kept the handkerchief under my pillow *for the smell* of him there was no decent perfume to be got in that Gibraltar only that cheap peau despagne that faded and *left a stink on you.* (747/762, italics mine)

It should be clear that Molly's preoccupations with smell, flow, and liquidity (bay, snow, sea, perfume, a handkerchief full of semen?!) are unconsciously displaced onto the Mulvey fantasy from her olfactory and coenesthetic awareness of the functioning of her body.[31] In similar fashion, we can read the lyric coda of the book as Molly's—and Joyce's—celebration of the menstrual cycle. Molly's famous ode to joy is a menstrual ode. Her flow, though uncomfortable, is welcome, for she is fearful of an unwanted pregnancy. "O patience above," she thinks, "its pouring out of me like the sea anyhow he didn't make me pregnant" (754/769). Relief and joy animate her

31. My friend and colleague Murray Schwartz has pointed out to me that since Bloom and Molly are lying head to foot, the images of smell that incessantly enter her monologue may have drifted there from her husband's unwashed feet.

bodily preoccupation, the result being a fluid fantasy of immersion, flowing currents, roses, and redness as she recalls, first her girlhood in Gibraltar and then her seduction of Bloom on Howth.[32] "I love flowers Id love to have the whole place swimming in roses God of heaven theres nothing like nature the wild mountains then the sea and the waves rushing . . . " and "O that awful deep-down torrent O and the sea the sea crimson sometimes like fire and the glorious sunsets . . . where I was a Flower of the mountain yes when I put the rose in my hair like the Andalusian girls used or shall I wear a red yes . . . . " The gathering rhythm of the last lines is a psychic response to the intensification of the flow as she drifts toward sleep.

LITTLE BOY BLOOM

If the portrait of Molly is really Joyce's version of "Love's Old Sweet Song," then that song is a lullaby, a hymn to regression. It portrays love as an attachment to infantile ways of affection, ways that prevailed in the dear dead days beyond recall. It reflects the refusal of genital sexuality in favor of earlier modes of libidinal organization, both oral and anal, and the patterns of marital organization

32. Another of the notes for "Penelope" uncovered by Litz makes the equation "rose-menses." Joyce's use of that equation is self-evident in this lyric coda, in which he celebrates his unique vision of the Homeric "winedark sea." In fact, *this* equation, "menses-sea," had been made by Stephen in "Proteus" as he watched the gypsy cocklepicker pass by. "Across the sands of all the world, followed by the sun's flaming sword, to the west, trekking to evening lands. She trudges, schlepps, trains, drags, trascines her load. A tide westering, moondrawn, in her wake. Tides, myriadislanded, within her, blood not mine, *oinopa ponton*, a winedark sea" (48/47).

appropriate to them. Bloom has not completed normal intercourse with Molly in the last ten years, five months, and eighteen days prior to June 16, 1904, and there is no reason to think he will do so in the future, for his one act of husbandly assertion at the end of his voyage is just another oral demand—that Molly bring him breakfast in bed the next morning. Since Rudy's death the relationship has settled into unhappy patterns, and where we should have husband and wife, we discover instead child and mother. Specifically, Molly is the androgynous phallic mother and Bloom the oral-passive son. Both view the relationship in this way, if not exactly in this language, and both accept it. Nor is such an agreement wholly disadvantageous for Bloom, for there are ways in which Molly's phallic endowment and her potency are active in his behalf.

Molly, who betrays her husband in fact, protects and even avenges him in fantasy. She dismisses John Henry Menton as a "big stupo" and Ben Dollard as a "balmy ballocks," while Lenehan, who brags to friends about having once fondled Molly in a coach, is passed off by her as "that sponger." And of Pisser Burke, who amuses fellow drinkers with stories about the Blooms in their City Arms days, she thinks, "You vomit a better face there was no love lost between us" (750/765). Even Boylan, whom she accepts as a lover, is compared unfavorably with Bloom: "Im sure hed have a fine strong child but I don't know Poldy has more spunk in him" (727/742).

She provides a similar service for Joyce himself. Outside the book, as well as in it, she is ever vigilant and aggressive in defense of her sons and lovers. Joyce's male alter egos are trapped in different modes of submission to a hostile Dublin; Bloom submits with a self-deprecating apology, Stephen submits in dubious battle with a lamp-shade. But Molly is immune to attack; her "woman's invisible weapon" (194/196) affords her a magical armor which no rumor can pierce and no reputation withstand. Thus it is that she is spokesman for Joyce's misogyny. She reels off a series of angry denunciations of other women —Mrs. Riordan, the maid that had been with them on Ontario Terrace, Mina Purefoy, Josie Breen Powell, even her daughter Milly and the cat. Lest there be any doubt about what Joyce is up to in this omnibus denunciation, we should remember that in at least one clear instance, that of Mrs. Riordan, Molly is paying off an old debt of Joyce's. For surely Joyce has brought the terrible Dante of *Portrait* into Bloom's and Molly's life in order to have Molly denounce her. Bloom, several years back, had plotted to become Dante Riordan's heir when she and the Blooms lived in the City Arms Hotel. Molly, recalling her now at the beginning of her soliloquy, slights this once-potent figure as "that old faggot Mrs. Riordan" (723/738). Nor is it strange that the exorcism of this most terrible of demons is performed by another woman. As the Christmas dinner scene shows us, Dante terrorizes men. But Molly can exorcise her and does it by calling her a faggot, denying her womanhood. Molly observes, "I suppose she was pious because no man would look at her twice," and Dante, shorn of her power, is dismissed.

On Bloom's and Joyce's behalf, then, Molly is the figure who confronts and defeats Ireland on its own terms: aggressive wit and the unselfconscious assumption of moral superiority. As the phallic mother, the un-differentiated parent of pre-oedipal fantasy, she wears and wields the paternal phallus. The critic of Irish manhood, Molly is also its rhetorical counterpart, for the bulk of her censorious monologue is like nothing else in the book so much as the anonymous narrative of "Cyclops." Most of "Penelope" (excepting, of course, the concluding hymn to sexual and menstrual joy) has a tone, a style, and a content that elsewhere in *Ulysses* are reserved for the meanest of male figures—the Irish pubster. Both are censorious, vulgar, and arrogant, and both take attitudes of critical superiority to the chaotic sprawl of sex and childrearing in Dublin. She sounds so much like the Irish wits in "Cyclops" because she is for Joyce, among a good many other things, one of the avatars of the father. Simon Dedalus, who ought to represent the vigorous father in *Ulysses*, is a limp figure when compared with his image in *Portrait*. The rhetoric is there but the vigor is not, and Molly, by a peculiar infusion of paternal authority, has inherited it.

Ulysses is *Hamlet* with a smile, a revenge comedy in which Molly Bloom is the agent of Joyce's vengeance. While she passes judgment *on* Joyce by judging Bloom, she also executes judgment *for* both of them by verbally slaughtering their enemies. She is the cutting edge of Joyce's wit, and her aggressive condescension cuts a broad swath through the alien corn of Dublin. In one sense, then, the gift of fetishes that Bloom regularly makes to her, as Joyce did to Nora, is the gift of weapons with which she can do battle for him. The gift of gloves, furs, aprons, garters, and the like is a transfer of potency from the vulnerable son to his champion, the invincible mother.

The phallic mother equation has a maternal side as well, which is every bit as important for Bloom as the phallic, though its ramifications for the chapter as a whole are less startling. They are important, but we expect them. Molly feels herself beleaguered by men who are fixated on her breasts; "They want everything in their mouth," she complains (739/754). For both Bloom, whom she reduces to "Master Poldy," and Boylan ("like some kind of a big infant I had at me") she is the dispenser of love and largesse and even milk—"he said it was sweeter and thicker than cows then he wanted to milk me into the tea well hes beyond everything I declare . . ." (739/754). She recalls, too, the time she wouldn't let Bloom lick her (758/773) and he, in a tantrum, slept naked on the floor and wouldn't eat breakfast or speak to her "wanting to be petted" until she relented. As though Bloom's infantility with respect to Molly were not obvious here and throughout, Joyce freezes it into tableau at the end of "Ithaca," where Bloom drifts off to sleep in a fetal curl, "the childman weary, the manchild in the womb" (722/737).

Beneath the surface simplicity of "Penelope" we find a complex image of womanhood. Molly is the phallic mother, but she is also the menstrual and alimental heroine and the infantile oral ideal. Boylan takes possession of her body while Bloom loves mainly what she wears upon it. She is an adulteress and a good wife, Bloom's betrayer and his avenger, and finally "the indispensable countersign to Bloom's passport to eternity."[33] In fact, as we pursue Molly her image dissolves in the multitudinousness of her qualities.[34] Just as Bloom is an Everyman, Molly approaches the condition of Everyparent.

33. Budgen, p. 264.
34. David Hyman observes the same omnivalence in ALP in *Finnegans Wake. Ulysses: The Mechanics of Meaning* (Englewood Cliffs, N.J.: Prentice-Hall, 1970), p. 36.

It appears, then, that Molly is a highly overdetermined figure in whom a multitude of Joyce's conscious and unconscious ideas have sought reconciliation. But it also appears that all have not been comfortably resolved in this image, for, as several readers, most notably S. L. Goldberg, have pointed out, "Penelope" is not internally consistent.[35] The ode to sexual joy at the end seems insincere, inappropriate, "tacked-on." The vulgar and censorious Molly of most of "Penelope" yields suddenly at the end to a priestess of love, and the transition is awkward. No more than twenty-three lines separate "then Ill wipe him off me just like a business" (766/781) from "I love flowers Id love to have the whole place swimming in roses." And in between only the increasing prominence of flowers, roses, and cherries gives any clue that a major change in the stream of Molly's consciousness is under way.

Joyce's conscious design in rendering this sudden shift can only be guessed at. I imagine it to be an attempt to render the psychology of approaching sleep by showing how Molly's aggression dissolves as sleep approaches, leaving only the coenesthetic awareness of menstrual flow and a wise, feminine passiveness. Under these conditions Molly's personality "peels away," revealing the essential and impersonal *Weiblichkeit* below. No doubt, too, it is Joyce's attempt to mythologize woman by demonstrating that all women are archetypally indifferent and receptive beneath the thin crust of character. Yet, how different this is from the unlayering of character in "Circe," where the psychic depths of Stephen's and Bloom's minds reveal, not an archetypal monism, but

35. S. L. Goldberg, *The Classical Temper: A Study of James Joyce's Ulysses* (London: Chatto & Windus, 1963), pp. 292–300.

an anguished and conflict-ridden dualism. Where personality yields to deep-psychic processes in "Circe," we
are confronted with guilt, remorse, masochism, infantilism, and anxiety. But the abysm of Molly's unconscious
greets us with simple, uncontested desire—yes.

The significance of this turnabout lies in the revelation of purposes of which Joyce may have been unaware.
It is a quintessential expression of an ambivalent relationship with Nora which we discovered in the letters and can
trace throughout his work. As the critics have told us,
the greater portion of "Penelope" is an act of hostility
on Joyce's part. And as the letters have shown us, it is
the hostility of the oedipal son and/or cuckolded husband
who has discovered himself betrayed in love.

But for Joyce, every gesture of hostility generated its
own antithesis, and the harsher his attack, the more lavish
the reparation. Thus, the mythic simplicity of Molly's
mind reflects, not Joyce's naïveté about female psychology, but his purposeful misrepresentation of it. Such misrepresentation discloses what Freud called infantile overvaluation—the exaltation and simplification of a parent
figure for religious purposes. As a Joycean act, Molly's
hymn to love and nature appears to be a sly penitential
gesture, and we have seen such gestures before in the
letters. Such a sudden turnabout, from insult to adoration, is also characteristic of those letters and, as in them,
derives from an unresolved quarrel of impulse and
apology. Thus, the last pages of *Ulysses* constitute a
gift offering to Nora of a verbal portrait of herself in
which she has been endowed with the lyric powers of
her husband's poetic imagination. The fine poetry that
Joyce has put into Molly's mouth at the end of the chapter makes sense as an act of restitution to Nora for the

degrading image of her he has created elsewhere. He not only recreates her as a "flower of the mountain" but makes of her the poet who can praise herself in such language. The end of "Penelope," then, is a devotional exercise in which the artist is discovered offering up his creative powers, much as Bloom offers up gloves and garters, to the object of his guilty adoration.

6. The Song of the Wandering Aengus: James Joyce and His Mother

> But thou hast suckled me with a bitter milk: my moon and my sun thou hast quenched for ever. And thou hast left me alone for ever in the dark ways of my bitterness: and with a kiss of ashes hast thou kissed my mouth.
>
> —STEPHEN DEDALUS

> The great danger against which mankind has evolved culture is that of object loss, of being left alone in the dark.
>
> —GÉZA RÓHEIM

THE SYLLOGISM of loss and gain that Stephen invents for his lecture on Shakespeare could well have been taken from psychoanalytic speculations upon creativity. As Géza Róheim and other like-minded anthropologists have insisted, nothing less than all of human culture is founded upon absence. "Civilization," says Róheim, "originates in delayed infancy and its function is security." He adds, "It is a huge network of more or less successful attempts to protect mankind against the danger of object-loss, the colossal efforts made by a baby who is afraid of being left alone in the dark."[1] In recent years, particularly

1. Géza Róheim, *The Origin and Function of Culture*, Nervous and Mental Disease Monograph No. 69, 1943 (Garden City, N.Y.: Doubleday, Anchor, 1971). Quote is from Anchor edition, p. 131.

among the British or "object-relations" schools of psychoanalysis, the idea has taken hold that creativity, especially, is arrayed against loss by restoring what is ab-
sent, reconstituting what is damaged, atoning for what
has been injured.[2] Hanna Segal has proposed that art
partakes of a ritual of mourning, being an internalization
and rerepresentation of whatever has been lost, ruined,
or destroyed. She quotes with approval Proust's view
that art is a response to loss and declares that "all creation is really a re-creation of a once loved and once whole,
but now lost and ruined object, a ruined internal world
and self."[3] Similar conclusions have been drawn by
William Niederland, an American analyst who observes,
"The mystery of death, the sudden disappearance of a
more or less ambivalently loved object, e.g., the death of
a sibling in childhood, seems to provide a powerful stimu-
lus for fantasies and strivings of a restitutive character."[4]
He points to K. R. Eissler's observation about Goethe,
that "the first spurt in Goethe's writing of *Wilhelm
Meister* . . . was initiated or precipitated by news from
home . . . that his father was a dying man."[5] Freud himself revealed the dynamic of loss and gain in his own life

2. See the panel discussion on creativity of the 27th International Psychoanalytic Congress, Vienna, July 29, 1971. *International Journal of Psychoanalysis* 53 (1972):21–30. See also Melanie
Klein, "Infantile Anxiety-Situations Reflected in a Work of Art
and in the Creative Impulse" and "Mourning and its Relation to
Manic-Depressive States" in her *Contributions to Psychoanalysis,
1921–1945* (London: The Hogarth Press, 1950).

3. Hanna Segal, "A Psychoanalytical Approach to Aesthetics,"
International Journal of Psychoanalysis 33 (1952):196–207. See also
Freud, "Mourning and Melancholia," *SE*, vol. 14.

4. William Niederland, "Clinical Aspects of Creativity," *American Imago* 24 (Spring–Summer 1967):6–34.

5. Ibid., p. 9. K. R. Eissler, *Goethe: A Psychoanalytic Study*
(Detroit: Wayne State University Press, 1963).

when he confessed in the preface to the second edition of *The Interpretation of Dreams*: "For this book has a further subjective significance for me personally—a significance which I only grasped after I had completed it. It was, I found, a portion of my own self-analysis, my reaction to my father's death—that is to say, to the most important event, the most poignant loss, of a man's life."[6]

In all these cases, artistic creation (and Freud's writing of *The Interpretation of Dreams* is surely that) is brought into focus as re-creation. What is made by the artist is a substitute object which bears a significance, not its own, that has been displaced onto it from something that is lost, ruined, or destroyed. The elegance of such a theory for the study of Joyce is self-evident, for it organizes *art* and *exile* into a single dynamic category. It tells us plainly what we have always understood intuitively: that what Joyce did with his art was to recreate a lost world in order to restore, preserve, protect, preside over, and control it. It proposes that the theme of sundering, which hovers about the end of *Chamber Music* and invades all of Joyce's books thereafter, is not just another leitmotif of *Ulysses* but a necessary psychological precondition for the book's existence. For Joyce, as for Shakespeare, loss was gain, and loss indeed may have been the single necessary condition for the lifelong gain of his art.

1903–1904 AND THE SOURCES OF ART

When the twenty-year-old James Joyce went auspiciously forth to encounter the reality of Parisian experience in December 1902, no real father or fabulous artificer stood

6. Freud, *The Interpretation of Dreams*, SE, vols. 4–5.

him in good stead. Nor need they have, for that flight was not so much an exile's renunciation as a bohemian's excursion, a young man's tentative surrender to the spell of arms and voices from abroad. And to the extent that Joyce did take his household gods with him, they were not images of the father. As Ellmann has said of the Stephen Dedalus who prepares to leave Ireland at the end of *Portrait*: "He buys his own ticket for Holyhead, but claims to have been deported. Yet his mother prepares his clothing for the journey; she at any rate does not break with him. Of this young man it may be safely predicted that he will write letters home" (*JJ*, 302). And those letters, we know, will be answered by a mother's admonitions not to drink unboiled Paris water (December 12, 1902, *Letters* 2:20) or wear the soul out with tears (December 18, p. 22).[7] Stephen Dedalus's painful lesson about *amor matris* as the only true thing in life was well taught by a mother who wrote to a son, scarcely eighteen days in Paris, "I only wish I was near you to look after and comfort you but we will be united very soon again thank God for *home you must come* if only for a week" (December 18, p. 22). Home he did come for one final Christmas in the bosom of the family before departing again to Paris, by way of London, near the end of January. More letters home, telling of literary ambition and personal anxiety, creative asceticism, and noble poverty ("Today I am twenty hours without food" [February 21, 1903, p. 29]) in a tone more dutiful than desperate, known to parents everywhere as the filial-heroic. "Do not despair though," she assures and advises him, "for I feel still

7. All letters quoted in this chapter, as in Chapter 2, are from volume 2 of Ellmann's *Letters* and will be cited only by dates and page numbers hereafter.

full of hope for you and this month will tell a great deal *keep all your friends* and in a suitable time call on Mrs. McBride who received you well. . . " (March 2, p. 32).

In one letter home, after announcing his literary time-table for the next fourteen years (his "book of songs," 1907; his first comedy and his "Esthetic" in subsequent five-year intervals), he begs her to respond to his adventures and schemes: "You will oblige me very much if you will write to me and tell me what you think of me. I shall read your letter with great anxiety" (March 20, p. 38).

That anxiety was, if anything, understated. Alone and hungry in Paris he dreamed of her, and because all events brought grist to his mill, even at twenty, he memorialized the dream in his growing collection of epiphanies.

She comes at night when the city is still; invisible, inaudible, all unsummoned. She comes from her ancient seat to visit the least of her children, mother most venerable, as though he had never been alien to her. She knows the inmost heart; therefore she is gentle, nothing exacting; saying, I am susceptible of change, an imaginative influence in the hearts of my children. Who has pity for you when you are sad among the strangers? Years and years I loved you when you lay in my womb.[8]

This mother most venerable was not only Mary Joyce but her blessed and virginal namesake as well. The tone of her reproach was gentle, for the son who had left Ireland, Church, and mother for Paris, art, and isolation was not in mortal sin—merely in danger of offending his mother. But early in 1903 May Joyce was alive and a

8. Kain and Scholes, eds., *The Workshop of Daedalus* (Evanston, Ill.: Northwestern University Press, 1965), p. 44. See Stanislaus's mention of it in *MBK*, pp. 229–230.

life in Dublin for her son still seemed a possibility. During the same sojourn, under the pressure of more violent dreams, he drafted a decidedly uncourtly poem which in later form he made the capstone of *Chamber Music*. The trauma of separation, of sundering, emerges suddenly from a vision of violent and irresistible masculinity. Joyce transcribed the poem in a letter to Stanislaus:

I hear an army charging upon the land
And the thunder of horses plunging, foam about their knees,
Arrogant, in black armour, behind them stand,
Disdaining the reins, with fluttering whips, the charioteers.

They cry amid the night their battle-name;
I moan in sleep, hearing afar their whirling laughter.
They ride through the gloom of dreams, a blinding flame,
With hoofs clanging upon the heart, as upon an anvil.

They come triumphantly shaking their long green hair,
They come out of the sea and run shouting by the shore—
My heart, have you no wisdom thus to despair?
Little white breast, O why have you left me alone?

(*Letters* 2, February 8, p. 28)

The version that was published in *Chamber Music* in 1907 ends with the incantatory "My love, my love, my love, why have you left me alone?" a powerful, melancholy, and more genteel lament than the naked and embarrassing little white breast of the original. What the later line lacks in specificity, and perhaps honesty, it gains in rhetoric. The image of the lost breast, it seems, has been suppressed and the affect associated with it invested in the language itself.

This anxious idyll of sympathetic alienation was interrupted by John Joyce's Good Friday telegram, "Mother dying come home father," which drew his son back to the center of paralysis to await, through an agonizing summer, his mother's death on August 13, 1903. We know from Stanislaus's account of the deathbed scene that Stephen's obsessive recollections of the event in *Ulysses* somewhat distort what really happened.[9] Contrary to Stephen's memory, it appears that both James and Stanislaus were ordered to kneel and pray and that it was not their mother but the hated maternal uncle, John Murray, who gave the order. It appears also that both brothers refused to make what they felt to be a gesture of false piety at this uncle's behest and that their mother was quite unconscious throughout this curious struggle. However that may be, Joyce's guilt over his mother's death and the circumstances surrounding it could not have been greater had he plunged a knife into her heart. He later confessed to Nora in a "courtship" letter, "My mother was slowly killed, I think, by my father's ill-treatment, by years of trouble, and by my cynical frankness of conduct" (August 29, 1904, p. 48). *Exiles* and *Ulysses* shows us this guilt growing more intense rather than less during the years in Trieste.

Soon after his mother's death Joyce wrote a poem which may have been an epitaph for her. It was first entitled "Cabra," later "Ruminants," and was still later rewritten as "Tilly."[10] It was a laconic, anxious, and

9. There is, of course, always a question about Stanislaus's accuracy. See *MBK*, p. 234.

10. There are two manuscripts of the "Cabra/Ruminants" version, one in the Lockwood Memorial Library at State University of New York, Buffalo, the other at Cornell University. Though the Cornell typescript is entitled "Cabra" and the Buffalo manuscript "Ruminants," the texts are identical. Both are signed "Dublin, 1904," though both are undoubtedly later transcripts, perhaps done in Zürich. The datings and meanings of all versions of the

moody poem, quieter than "I Hear an Army" but similar
in imagery. Because its music was somber and wintry
Joyce held it out of *Chamber Music* in 1907, proclaiming
to Stanislaus that his "dancing days" were over (*Letters*
2:181). It remained unpublished until it appeared in 1927
as "Tilly" in *Pomes Pennyeach*. The early "Cabra/
Ruminants" version reads:

> He travels after the wintry sun,
> Driving the cattle along the straight red road;
> Calling to them in a voice they know,
> He drives the cattle above Cabra.
>
> His voice tells them home is not far.
> They low and make soft music with their hoofs.
> He drives them without labour before him,
> Steam pluming their foreheads.
>
> Herdsman, careful of the herd,
> Tonight sleep well by the fire
> When the herd too is asleep
> And the door made fast.

Despite the apparent lucidity of the surface, the poem
is a mystery. The cattle drive is affectively neutral and

---

poem are presently in question. See: Chester G. Anderson, "James
Joyce's 'Tilly,'" *PMLA* 73 (June 1958):285–298; Robert Scholes,
"James Joyce, Irish Poet," *James Joyce Quarterly* 2 (Summer 1965):
255–270; John T. Shawcross, "'Tilly' and Dante," *James Joyce
Quarterly* 7 (Fall 1969):61–64; Scholes, letter, *James Joyce Quar-
terly* 8 (Winter 1971):192–193.

The earliest indication we have of the existence of "Cabra/
Ruminants" is at the beginning of Stanislaus's diary, which was
begun in late August or early September 1903. See *CDD*, p. 2,
and George H. Healey's note about the beginning of the diary,
p. x. The "Cabra/Ruminants" poem may have been in existence
by September 1903, the month after May Joyce's death, and while
it is even possible that it actually antedates her death, it surely
does not antedate the final stages is of her illness.

thematically nonsuggestive; the final apostrophe to the herdsman is ominous but nonspecific. Something threatens from without, but one can sleep before a fire within behind a door made fast. There is no obvious allusion to a mother's death, and yet—*and this is axiomatic*—we may assume its presence throughout. "Cabra" seems to be a winter poem, and winter 1903 is our best bet. Moreover, the poem's objectless anxiety, its joyless music in the context of Joyce's otherwise gayclad lutanist verse of the period, and its not being published for twenty-three years call special attention to its mysteries. But the imagery of the poem is scrupulously noncommittal. If the cattle drive is a funeral procession, it is not obvious. We are met by a seemingly real herdsman driving real cattle along a real red road in a poetic setting that does not appear metaphoric or symbolic. But, again, it is impossible for one who knows Joyce not to seek out the autobiographical, and specifically the familial, in such a poem. The tone invites speculation, as does our limited knowledge of the poem's circumstantial background. *We know Joyce*; he was always an "occasional" poet. And we know, too, that loss or the threat of it was his characteristic occasion. For myself, I cannot suppress the suspicion that it is John Joyce and the multitudinous children of his wifeless household who trudge here gloomily toward the house Stanislaus nicknamed Bleakhouse, 7 St. Peter's Terrace, Cabra.

All available evidence argues that the version we know as "Tilly" did not exist before 1916 and may be dated even later than that. And it is not improbable that the rewriting represents a response to a different situation and that "Tilly" is a different poem. Nevertheless, if we take the precarious liberty of reading "Tilly" as a gloss upon its predecessor, we get some interesting results. For if the family drama was ever there in "Cabra" to begin with, it has surely been highlighted in "Tilly."

> He travels after a winter sun,
> Urging the cattle along a cold red road,
> Calling to them, a voice they know,
> He drives his beasts above Cabra.
>
> The voice tells them home is warm.
> They moo and make brute music with their hoofs.
> He drives them with a flowering branch before him,
> Smoke pluming their foreheads.
>
> Boor, bond of the herd,
> Tonight stretch full by the fire!
> I bleed by the black stream
> For my torn bough!

The mourning which we had to infer from the mood and rhythm of "Cabra" is now manifest in the image of the tree bleeding for its torn bough. Given the economy of Joyce's art, that torn bough is surely the same branch that flowers in the herdsman's hand. That torn bough also, so blatantly and self-consciously a "Freudian" proclamation of castration, is perhaps a measure of Joyce's familiarity with the more obvious principles of dream interpretation and of his willingness to mythologize himself according to a prearranged program of symbolic meanings. And if I am right in seeing the imprint of the Joyce family upon the enigmatic cattle drive, what we have in "Tilly" is a lament for the loss of maternal care, as well as a dreary portrait of the Joyce family after May Joyce's death and an acknowledgment of a son's sense of castration by a malignant, boorish father.

But even if that is correct, it makes of "Tilly" at best a

retrospective lament. The 1903 "Cabra/Ruminants" may be built upon loss, but it is not, on the face of it, a lament. No wailing poet bleeds there for his torn bough, which is the real point of this digression. For what we have is not a young man's complaint but a young artist's work; a tough, controlled, and lucid poem. Joyce's mother dies, and he epiphanizes a random local event which appeals to his unconscious sense of his own situation. He experiences a deep loss and creates an image of Ireland. If that is in fact what happened, then "Cabra" was indeed auspicious. For it was precisely out of a sense of castration and abandonment, it seems to me, that Joyce's creativity finally and most suddenly emerged.

On January 7, five months after his mother's death, Joyce wrote in one day his narrative essay "A Portrait of the Artist," in which the central fantasy is one of ecstatic oral merger with an omnibus whore/Virgin/ saint/muse/temptress whose very ambiguity is emblematic of the missing mother. He submitted it to W. K. Magee (John Eglinton) and Frederick Ryan for their new journal of "free thought," *Dana*. Predictably, Ryan and Magee (whom Joyce had nicknamed "the horrible virgin" [*CDD*, 14]) rejected it because of its overt sexuality. Almost on the moment, Joyce began to expand it into the autobiographical novel *Stephen Hero*. This burst of creative labor by a young man who until then had little more than the Dedalian "capful of light odes" to call his genius father was stupendous. He finished the first chapter of *Stephen Hero* by February 10 (*JJ*, 153) and by the end of March had written eleven chapters (*CDD*, 19–20). Nor had he completely abandoned poetry. Though the greater part of *Chamber Music* was complete, he added in April three more poems to the collection (*JJ*, 155) and may have added yet others in the fall. Later that summer he was to write his Swiftian satire on the Irish literary scene, "The Holy Office," and begin work on *Dubliners*. In short, in the period between his mother's death and his flight into exile with Nora, Joyce was not the guilt-paralyzed Stephen Dedalus of *Ulysses*. Rather, he had discovered, or had been discovered by, that spring of creative energy that, with rare exceptions, stood him in good stead the rest of his life. If anything, he became like Stephen's Shakespeare, who transformed himself into the creator-God of the Elizabethan stage after his flight from Ann Hathaway and who, as if in imitation of the earlier sundering, wrote *Hamlet* in the months following his father's death. Whereas for Stephen the final separation from mother leads to guilt, melancholia, and paralysis, for Joyce in reality it seems to have yielded a creative mixture of desperation and hard work.

It does seem that May Joyce's death released her son from some long-standing inhibition against exploring the past in writing. One suspects on the basis of Stephen's sullen and irritable relations with his mother in *Stephen Hero* that the gentle tyranny of maternal disapproval constrained Joyce from beginning the task he had to undertake and finally did in his books—the task of descending into the nightmare of personal history in order to forge some durable sense of himself from the brittle and painful fragments of childhood. But he was not just liberated to work; he was compelled to. His writing makes sense as the effort to reconstruct in symbolic form what had been lost in reality: his mother and an entire environment that was infused with her presence and invested with maternal significance. Despite the disappointments of life in Ireland and the squalor and apparent disorder of the Joyce household, Joyce's ego and his sense of reality were stabilized and made coherent by his mother's ordering presence. Her death affected him not only as a loss of that ambiguous *amor matris*, but as a threat to his psychic integrity as well as his trust in the reliability of a stable, supportive reality. After her death, the center no longer held. For that reason, it seems that Joyce, starting in January 1904, gave up plans for the projected "comedy" and "esthetic" and set out instead to shore up the threatened inner and outer worlds by reconstructing them symbolically in the form of autobiography. If this is in fact the case, then Stephen Dedalus's magniloquent promise in *Portrait* to forge in the smithy of his soul the uncreated conscience of his race is no mean adolescent boast, but a statement of what he must do in order to survive.[11] Moreover, since Joyce's project of reconstructing the soul of Ireland went hand in hand with the remaking of his own, we find him in the first "Portrait" sketch entertaining fantasies of nympholeptic oral union with a maternal "dearest of mortals" and vowing to return to the past in order to plot the curve of his own emotional growth.[12] Later that year Stanislaus noted in his diary that brother Jim spoke admiringly of Ibsen as a "self-made man" (*CDD*, 52). That phrase, we now know, de-

11. Niederland has observed, appropriately: "In exploring the lives—and ills—of creative personalities, one becomes increasingly aware of the great amount of energy available to them. Their energies appear to converge on the creative process and seem to be regression not so much in the service of the ego, as in that of ego restoration, sometimes even of ego survival" ("Clinical Aspects," p. 21).

12. See the opening proclamation of the "Portrait" essay.

scribes a formula for survival that Joyce took in desperate earnest in the midst of the institutional and familial failures of life in Ireland.

To what extent this sudden creative burst also constitutes an act of restitution or atonement toward the dead mother for hostile acts or wishes, we can only guess. Atonement and undoing as manifested in creative activity are difficult motives to identify in art. Theory urges us to seek them out, and if we are lucky some of our discoveries may fit and confirm, prima facie, our theory. Joyce's first published prose fiction, for example, "The Sisters," a story by one Stephen Daedalus, appeared in *The Irish Homestead* on August 13, 1904, the first anniversary of May Joyce's death. Coincidence? Possibly.

Joyce's disposition to seek out symbolic solutions to real dilemmas did not always preclude his discovering in the world without as actual what was in his world within as possible. Thus, his drive to restore through fantasy and art losses suffered in reality did not prevent him from falling in love with Nora Barnacle and transferring onto her the burden of his need. As the 1909 letters demonstrate in detail, she was, willy-nilly, the lost mother come back, but ever on the brink of being lost again and thus ever to be wooed, chided, loved, admonished, injured, and wooed once more.

All evidence suggests that Joyce's commitment to Nora was instantaneous. Their courtship was troubled, but it demanded of him none of the agonizing, unending preliminaries that had soured his flirtations with the chaste beauties of middle-class Dublin. Their first date took place on June 16, 1904. Within a week Nora was addressing him confidently as "my precious darling" (June 23, 1904, p. 42), and he was discovering, more slowly, his own embarrassed language of endearment. The combination of Joyce's emotional and sexual isolation and Nora's openness to his advances allowed his libidinal trademarks to surface instantly. From the very beginning she was cherished as something less than the sum of her parts. His first note to her reads, "I may be blind. I looked for a long time at a head of reddish-brown hair and decided it was not yours" (June 15, 1904, p. 42). Even before their first date (the day before Bloomsday) he identifies her by her hair and is feeling betrayed. Another letter concludes with the synecdochic, "Adieu, dear little brown head" (July 8, p. 43). He appropriates one of her gloves for a bed partner and teases, "Your glove lay beside me all night—unbuttoned—but otherwise conducted itself very properly—like Nora" (July 22?, p. 43). Again with a sartorial eye, he entreats, *"Please* leave off that breastplate as I do not like embracing a letterbox," and elsewhere, with a rare attention to physical detail, croons, "I kiss the miraculous dimple at thy neck" (July 12, p. 43; July ?, p. 44).

The filial theme develops also. Predictably, Nora is the refuge of sinners and comfortress of the afflicted. The poet who had written, perhaps to her, "I would in that sweet bosom be/ . . . Where no rude wind might visit me" (*CM*, 6) anxiously writes to his beloved that he must see her because "I have been in such a whirl of trouble that I want to forget everything in your arms" (August 3, p. 45). But she is not only the mother come back to take him in her arms; she is even more surely an object of that cynical frankness of conduct which, he confided to her, had contributed to his mother's death. "There is something also a little devilish in me that makes me delight in breaking down people's idea of me and proving

to them that I am really selfish, proud, cunning and regardless of others" (September 10, pp. 51–52). Object
lessons abound: "How I hate God and death!" he proclaims to her. "How I like Nora! Of course you are
shocked at these words, pious creature that you are"
(September 1, p. 50). Such offense predictably yields to
remorse. The dialectic of attack and atonement appears
early in their relationship. "My dear, dear Nora I suppose you have been very much upset since last night"
(September 10, p. 51), is a standard greeting. "I will
not speak of myself for I feel as if I had acted very
cruelly." The sentence might stand as their insignia,
their coat of arms: vert, an artist couchant proper, bearing apologies. Like her prototype, whom a restive son
had cruelly dazzled with his erudition and accused of
stupidity,[13] she can only puzzle at such complexity of
emotion and subtlety of thought and is forced once to
confess, "I read that long letter over and over again but
could not understand it I think I may take it to you to
morrow eve—and perhaps you might make me understand it" (September 12, p. 52). Both discover in short
order that talk is not their métier. More and more he
finds himself wearily and regressively silent with her.
In one letter, which sounds like a confession of marital
boredom cast as a lover's homage, he writes, "The mere
recollection of you overpowers me with some kind of
dull slumber. The energy which is required for carrying
on conversations seems to have left me lately and I find
myself constantly slipping into silence" (September 26,
p. 56).

Whatever it was that brought and held Jim and Nora

13. See the letter from May Joyce, December 18, 1902?, *Letters*
2:22.

so firmly together may have been both physical and spiritual, but it was hardly intellectual. A marriage of bodies and souls, as they came quickly to understand, need not be a marriage of minds as well. But Jim did not want a marriage of minds. Intellectually he felt himself to be autonomous. His intellectual nourishment, moreover, was gotten from masculine sources, which he preferred to encounter indirectly, in libraries, those "painted chambers loaded with tilebooks." Nora's virtues were the maternal ones: a fragile constancy, honesty, a lack of education, a minimum of ideas, a simple Catholic piety, a readiness to condescend to him upon demand, and the possession of a secret life, however trivial it might have been.

The ambiguous fate of this project to install Nora in that ancient seat vacated by May Joyce is revealed not only in the 1909 letters from Jim to Nora but in his books, most especially *Ulysses*. The measure of its success is the relative stability of Jim's life: he stayed with Nora, raised a family, and wrote his books.[14] The mea sure of its failure is more omnibus, for its inscription is everywhere on his life, his family, and his art. The letters to Nora remain the clearest expression of the project and its insufficiency. The woman into whose "soul of souls" Jim would return in order to become the "poet of his race," whose death he mourns in 1909 even while she is alive, whom he calls "my strange-eyed Ireland" and "my little mother" was always a substitute figure.[15]

14. John Gross, in his excellent introduction to Joyce's work, *James Joyce* (New York: Viking, 1970), makes just this point. It cannot be overemphasized that Joyce could and did manage his life and his work admirably and that the abundant "evidence" of psychopathology must be weighed against his hard-won successes.

15. Gross, ibid., p. 18, draws that same conclusion.

Thus, the attempt to refashion her, to deck her in furs, to brighten her hair, to develop her breasts by having her drink cocoa, was a twofold and paradoxical project. On the one hand, it proposed to make manifest the restitution wish by making of Nora an appropriate mother. But Joyce's attempt to do so made him, in effect, her mother as well, a paradox Joyce seems to have understood. The fantasy that she would be his handiwork, a slow and painful creation of his own, a creature, even, of *his* womb, even as he retreated for emotional nourishment into the warm, secret gloom of *her* flesh, represents marriage as a job of mutual mothering.[16] If she would nurse him, he, in return, would do no less than give birth to her. Talk about *amor matris*! Everywhere in his letters to her his filial longings are laced with parental condescension. From the beginning she is his "Little Pouting Nora," "My dear little Goodie-Brown-shoes," and "My particularly pouting Nora." The phrase *my little mother*, which appears in the 1909 correspondence, is an epiphany. In the circularity of such maternal mutuality lies its economical wonder, since as the circle of co-maternity contracts about its thematic center Nora disappears and the allotropes of the mother whom he would recreate in art—Mary (May) Joyce, Kathleen ni Houlihan, the Bride of Christ, the B. V. M., Gretta, Bertha, Molly, ALP, and so on—dissolve in the masturbatory splendor of Dedalian self-sufficiency. The unconscious proposition he always made to Nora, "I will create you in order that you can nurse me," becomes "I will create myself in order to practice self-nurture." In the totalistic universe of the self-made man, maternity may

16. Note Robert Hand's insistence that Richard Rowan has created Bertha, *E* 62, 67.

take its place alongside paternity as a legal fiction. Yet, in Joyce's case the maintenance of this fantasy of self-generation and sexual (oral *and* phallic) self-sufficiency, which repeals motherhood in favor of total autonomy, required a real, quasi-maternal presence. The satisfactory introjection of the "idea" of the mother into the ego of the son required at all times the presence of some external analogue or simulacrum, for the dream of self-sufficiency would not work unless it was anchored to something in the real world. Nora had to exist in order that her husband could pretend not to need her.

COME THOU LOST ONE!

Attempts to restore lost objects by introjection or internalization or by re-creation or substitution are, at best, imperfect psychic stopgaps for anyone but the psychotic for whom reality is only a shadow on the wall of a cave. It is the very irreparability of loss that lies at the heart of *Ulysses*. The deepest movements in the book are the paired tropisms of Stephen and Bloom: the former's radical drive toward isolation and autonomy and the latter's need to be reconciled with all he has lost—his past, his present, his future, all of which is handily symbolized by Molly's afternoon tryst with Boylan. The isolation, or the threat of isolation against which Joyce's art is arrayed, is reflected in *Ulysses* in the general alienation of all his disheveled, wandering Dubliners. Their condition is the thematic heart of *Ulysses*. Beneath the mock-heroism, fetishism, nationalism, oedipal drama, irony, anticlericalism, sexual perversity, stylistic virtuosity, cloacal obsessiveness, fraternal rivalry, guilt, wit, shame, messianism, masochism—beneath all other thematic,

stylistic, and deep-psychic materials—is the fact of
sundering. Sundering is the ineluctable void upon which
Ulysses is built. *Ulysses* is a book of distances in which
all things proclaim their isolation. There is the distance of
the exile from home, of the prophet from the promised
land, of husband from wife, of father from son, brother
from brother, Dubliner from Dubliner, present from past,
comet from sun. Joyce's characters inhabit a universe from
which satisfactory human connections have been ex-
cluded. The marriage of Poldy and Molly would seem
to be the most enduring and gratifying of relationships
in *Ulysses*, and we know the price at which its sad and
fragile stability has been bought. In Dublin, breakup is
more than a habit; it is a cosmology. Dubliners meet
briefly like particles in space, reconnoiter in a formal
astral dance, then fly off into solitary orbit in the Irish
void. The very indiscriminateness of human dissociation
argues for the existence, somewhere, of a primal flaw
or flaws, a core of dislocation that invests all human possibilities with the assurance of failure. Somewhere at the
heart of this universe is a deep-psychic equivalent of
original sin.

We seem to be confronted by a failure of what Erik
Erikson calls mutuality.[17] Trust in the possibility of fruitful interaction between persons has been foreclosed, and
we find ourselves in a universe of defensively self-enclosed actors: autoerotics, automystics, automobiles,
autodidacts. The interior monologue in Joyce's books is
no gratuitous device of style; it is the stylistic correlative
of the self-enclosed mode of existence it represents. Such
a massive failure of mutuality in favor of total narcissism
makes a good deal of sense as an oral failure, and it is

17. *Childhood and Society* (New York: Norton, 1950), pp. 68 ff.

indeed around the ramifications of such an oral failure that the thematic structure of *Ulysses* is organized.

I believe it is fair to say that the book's variegated and encyclopedic surfaces and symbols are set down in sedimentary layers upon a psychic base of oral need and oral insufficiency. Moreover, if this claim errs at all, it is on the side of tautology, inasmuch as psychic development itself can be so described.[18] However, in the case of *Ulysses* this self-evident theorem has special critical usefulness, for without it we could hardly winnow meaning out of the chaos of conflicting psychic clues. In Bloom's case it enables us to see clearly that Bloom, despite his preference for anal sexual fantasies and (presumably) acts, is a classic oral character. His basic condition is his isolation and his all-pervading and indiscriminate hungers. Bloom leaves 7 Eccles Street in the morning in search of spiritual, emotional, sexual, and alimental nourishment. His passivity and dependency upon Molly testify to the same oral insufficiency, as do his voyeurism and his tendency to think of loving (as Stephen does) in terms of eating. But beyond Bloom's needs and tastes one finds the multiple ramifications or displacements of "the mother" projected everywhere into the ambience of Joyce's Dublin. As catastrophic mother, she is Bella Cohen, the ghost of May Dedalus, and the Dante of *Portrait*. As betrayer, she is Eve, Ann Hathaway, Helen, Devorghil, Kitty O'Shea, Molly. As temptress, she is the *Photo Bits* nymph, Josie Breen, Nurse Callan, Gerty MacDowell, and, of course, Molly. As savior, she is Gerty and Molly; as whore, she is Bella, Zoe, Kitty,

18. The sedimentary metaphor for psychic development was suggested by Freud in the first chapter of *Civilization and its Discontents*, *SE*, 21.

Florry, Cissy, Edy, perhaps Gerty, and in some ways
Molly. The lost mother is numinous and mythic—she
expands into every category of experience, investing an
entire universe with promises of love, abandonment, and
punishment, and an aura of bitter mystery. She is the
Church, Stephen's Italian master (why not mistress?),
"A crazy queen, old and jealous," as well as the Virgin.
She is present under the various aspects of Ireland: the
old sow that eats her farrow, Kathleen ni Houlihan, the
peasant milkwoman. She is the promised land toward
whom all voyages tend—Ithaca, Agendath Netaim,
Penelope, Molly's melonous buttocks, a lost Druidic Ireland. She is the white breast of the dim sea upon which
Stephen broods all day and the scrotumtightening sea
itself, or, as Algy calls her, the "great sweet mother."

The apparently overwhelming contradictions in the
image of this polymorphous mother are not unresolv-
able. The psychoanalytic schedule of psychic developmental events confirms what our intuitions tell us about
the mother in *Ulysses*. It insists that the level at which
she operates as a betrayer and threat to her son does not
run as deep as that upon which she is felt to be home,
paradise, the promised land, our great sweet mother. As
we have seen, Joyce's ambivalence toward Molly is resolved at the end of her soliloquy, albeit at the cost of
some dramatic credibility. But it should be clear from
Molly's casual demolition of Dante Riordan, from her
recitation of finer poetry than the lame temptress, Gerty, and from her ceremonial position at the end of the
novel that we are in a universe that is essentially comic,
one in which we can expect the good mother to drive out
the bad. *Ulysses* is a fairy tale, and in fairy tales, when
the dilemma over the identity of the mother moves toward

its regressive solution the nurturing mother wins out over the catastrophic, the numinous over the devouring. Mom gets the kids; stepmom gets the axe.

In *Ulysses*, as in the *Odyssey*, the grand dramatic movement, the exile's return, is an archetypal oral theme. The hero's situation is the same in each: he is an isolated, separated, incomplete man. It is this situation and the quest that issues from it that bound the *Odyssey* to Joyce's purposes, beyond any abstract formulas about historical parallelism or historic change. Whether the modern world recapitulates the ancient or represents its debasement is not to the point. Both epics are an expression of a universal, *individual* struggle—the struggle of the lost son to get back to the infinitely distant mother. And this may be the most primitive and universal literary theme of all, for its psychological origins antedate the oedipus complex, and its ramifications, correspondingly, are more pervasive. Thus, what lies at the heart of this correspondence of epics goes beyond the recurrence of discrete Homeric themes. What moves us dramatically is the single parallel: the lonely exile and the agonizing return, the isolation from and the quest for the nurturing mother. *Ulysses* extracts from its prototype the epic of regression. It yearns after a lost homeostasis and idealizes the pastoral. *Ulysses* highlights the oral paradigm in the *Odyssey*, which is why a passive and dependent middle-aged man seems an appropriate hero. Bloom's character is the sign of his quest. He wants only to be reattached to what has been taken from him: wife, son, daughter, the halcyon days of his childhood, mother, father, his people, Jerusalem. In short, Bloom would be restored to the entire nurturing reality that has fallen away from him. Such a passive hero in any other epic mode could only be a fool or a satiric butt. But a regressive hero can be a serious figure in a regressive epic. Joyce could not have recreated Achilles or Aeneas as oral-passive characters without satiric intentions, but an oral-passive Odysseus is only comic and is not without his measure of dignity.

Bloom and Stephen may not be the most errant of the many wandering Irish rocks in *Ulysses*, but they are the ones who hold our attention. S. L. Goldberg, using Joyce's own vocabulary of isolation and drift, describes the heroes as they appear in "Ithaca" as "wanderers like the stars at which they gaze."[19] And that does seem to describe their situation. Wandering Aengus meets Wandering Jew, and after a brief communion of coffee, cocoa, philosophy, and co-urination they drift apart, disheveled wandering stars. But this wandering is directed, purposive motion. Like the stars at which they gaze, Bloom and Stephen are in orbital flight. As they take leave of each other, Bloom stays on the inside of the threshold at 7 Eccles Street, a "centripetal remainer," and bids farewell to Stephen, the "centrifugal departer." Bloom, the regressive hero, is on the homeward leg of his daily orbit; Stephen is outward bound. This mutual orbital motion presumes a center of attraction, and in fact Stephen and Bloom do navigate about a common center. Schematically, in "Ithaca" it would have to be Molly, though more abstractly and correctly, it is the idea of the mother, of which Molly is but one incarnation. Bloom's path has been homeward tending since he left Eccles Street in the morning, for, as he puts it, "the longest way round is the shortest way home." Stephen, in radical flight from an external crazy queen and an internal ghostwoman is also

19. S. L. Goldberg, *The Classical Temper: A Study of James Joyce's Ulysses* (London: Chatto & Windus, 1963), p. 196.

homeward-tending via the same circuitous route. His path leads backward from the catastrophic mother to the primal oral ideal. He had told Davin at the end of *Portrait* that "The shortest way to Tara was *via* Holyhead," and we may guess that Stephen, as he leaves Bloom's house, is Holyhead-bound, having traveled that route once already in search of Tara. And Tara, to risk being tiresome, is one and always the same: the arms of the Druidic past, the bosom of Celtic Ireland, the heart of Kathleen, the womb of the mother. Music, please.

All this of course is *not* a simple consequence of May Joyce's death in 1903. That event alone, coming when James Joyce was already a young man of twenty-one, was not in itself likely to have given rise to a career of plaintive longing such as Joyce's work seems to represent. Rather, we have to look backward to more fundamental losses and separations—to the loss of primal oral unity that is the common experience of all children and to those subsequent serial losses of daily love and daily attention that are especially attendant upon growing up in a large family. Exile is built into childhood. In "Proteus" Stephen reflects on his mother's death as one of a succession of losses, each of which involves a bed: "Bridebed, childbed, bed of death" (48/47–48). For both Stephen and Bloom that bed is the place of betrayal, never the place of love.

May Joyce's death, then, has to be regarded, not as the cause of those lonely searches for love and anxious efforts toward restoration we discover in her son's books, but the special occasion for them. Her deathbed confirmed for him what her bridebed and a succession of childbeds had threatened: you can't go home again. The first loss, the loss of the primal mother, is the real one;

regard all others as imitations. It follows that the creative response called up in Joyce by his mother's death was there from the beginning, biding its time and awaiting its occasion.

Who, then, is really lost? If loss as a psychic condition precedes loss as reality, then we must ask who is real and who has faded into impalpability to become a ghost by absence—mother or child? What we know about the desperate dependence of ego-identity upon this often fragile relationship justifies the question. As Simon Dedalus sings the plantive aria from Flotow's *Martha* in the Ormond Bar, the listening Bloom silently identifies. "*Co-me, thou lost one!*" (271/275). The aria leaps, "*Co-me thou dear one!*" It holds its flight as it soars toward its resplendent climax, "*Come! . . . . To me!*," and plummets downward into smiles and applause. One reflects on lovelost Si Dedalus and lovelost Leo Bloom and recalls the chilling question Stephen had put to Cranly in *Portrait* after the latter's discourse on the wages of aloneness: "Of whom are you speaking?"

Selected Bibliography

PSYCHOANALYTIC PSYCHOLOGY

The use of psychoanalysis as a system of interpretation is no mere offshoot of a prior clinical practice but a basic and original task of psychoanalysis itself. Note the title of the first psychoanalytic book, *The Interpretation of Dreams*. And very possibly psychoanalysis is more successful as an interpretative instrument than as curative one. Certainly, in our time, while psychological therapies have multiplied beyond count, principles of psychological interpretation have remained more conservative and have tended to share a common body of postulates. The principle of psychic determinism, the belief in a dynamic unconscious, the theory of infantile sexuality, and a recognition of the authority of the past are held in common by all depth psychologies. Clearly, the interpretive gestures of psychoanalysis cannot be dismissed as casual by-products of a diagnostic art. Applied or critical psychoanalysis is as old as psychotherapy and boasts a sizable bibliography of important books. The bibliography included here provides only those crucial books that are essential reading for the beginning student of literature and psychology.

The study of psychoanalysis as an interpretive system begins with Freud and with the early, great books of interpretation: *The Interpretation of Dreams* (1900), *The Psychopathology of Everyday Life* (1901), and *Jokes and Their Relation to the Unconscious* (1907). Where possible, Freud should be read in the standard translation, *The Standard*

Edition of the Complete Psychological Works of Sigmund Freud, 24 vols., edited by James Strachey, Anna Freud, Alix Strachey, and Alan Tyson (New York: Macmillan, 1953–1966). All three are available in paperback in the same *Standard Edition* translations: *Psychopathology* and *Jokes* from Norton and *The Interpretation of Dreams* from Avon. Students who are unwilling to struggle through the monumental detail of *Interpretation* may find its essentials digested and condensed by Freud himself in his *A General Introduction to Psychoanalysis* (New York: Washington Square, 1952). One other essential early book, which, like *Interpretation*, Freud revised and kept current throughout his career, is the *Three Essays on the Theory of Sexuality* (1905), also an Avon book. Section 1, "The Sexual Aberrations," sounds creakily Victorian to the modern ear, but Freud's explanation of the "partial" sexual instincts has stood up remarkably well as psychosexual theory. Section 2, on infantile sexuality, is crucial and necessary reading. The beginning student can find the theory of infantile sexuality brilliantly schematized by Erik Erikson in *Childhood and Society* (New York: Norton, 1950), pp. 48–108.

Freud's occasional papers are often vehicles for his best discrete insights and most trenchant analysis, and they are available in two versions besides the *Standard Edition*. Basic Books publishes a five-volume edition of the *Collected Papers*, and Collier publishes a ten-volume paperback collection, edited and introduced by Philip Rieff. The student of psychoanalysis should own a set of the papers and work his way through them assiduously.

Freud's attempts at interpretation in literature and art are predictably uneven as criticism, and his choice of texts such as Jensen's *Gradiva* is sometimes disappointing. But some efforts, like the essay on Michaelangelo's Moses, are remarkable demonstrations of Freud's power to spy out motives in scattered and minute details. See especially "The Relation of the Poet to Daydreaming" (1908), *Leonardo da Vinci and a Memory of his Childhood* (1910), "The Theme of the Three Caskets" (1913), "The Moses of Michaelangelo" (1914), "A Childhood Recollection from *Dichtung und War-*

heit" (1917), and "Dostoevsky and Parricide" (1928). Take a look also at his remarks on Richard III, Lady Macbeth, and Rebecca Gamvik of Ibsen's *Rosmersholm* in "Some Character Types Met with in Psychoanalytic Work" (1916). *Leonardo* is published separately by Norton, and the others are available in the Collier paperback *Character and Culture*, edited by Rieff.

But these essays are special instances of a general habit of interpretation in psychoanalysis. The very heart of the psychoanalytic enterprise is the act of textual analysis. Freud did not distinguish in principle between the dream, the error, the symptom, and the joke. Each bears differently upon the tasks of the ego, but all share a common motivational structure: all originate in psychic conflict and are the product of psychic compromise. Each is a coded text that both conceals and reveals the motives it reconciles, and psychoanalysis, as Freud conceived it, is a universal scheme of cryptography which unmasks or decodes original messages. Indeed, textual interpretation and clinical diagnosis are perfectly fused in one of Freud's most famous case histories, that of Dr. Schreber, a subject he met only through a written memoir. See "Psychoanalytic Notes upon an Autobiographical Account of a Case of Paranoia" (1911), conveniently available in *Three Case Histories*, edited by Rieff (Collier). For a persuasive argument for psychoanalysis as an interpretive art, see Rieff, *Freud: The Mind of the Moralist* (Garden City, N.Y.: Doubleday, Anchor, 1961), especially Chapter 4, "The Tactics of Interpretation."

The student in need of an introductory outline of psychoanalytic theories of mind might well begin with Freud's posthumously published *An Outline of Psychoanalysis* (1940) or the earlier, more leisurely *New Introductory Lectures on Psychoanalysis* (1932). Both are Norton paperbacks. A more schematic outline of theory is Charles Brenner, *An Elementary Textbook of Psychoanalysis* (Garden City, N.Y.: Doubleday, Anchor, 1957). Robert Waelder, *Basic Theory of Psychoanalysis* (New York: Schocken, 1964), covers much the same ground as Brenner and is both more speculative about the status of psychoanalysis as an exact science and curiously

cranky about peripheral social issues. The only thoroughgoing attempt to flesh out the theory and provide a com-
pendium of psychoanalytic knowledge up to the mid-1940s
is Otto Fenichel, *The Psychoanalytic Theory of Neurosis*
(New York: Norton, 1945). Fenichel's extensive bibliography
is almost thirty years old but is still useful. His text too remains a serviceable guide to diagnostic commonplaces, though
it sounds archaic to a generation of readers unaccustomed to
the language of libidinal hydraulics, energic cathexis, bound
and unbound energies, and the rest of the medical jargon
of early psychoanalysis. The working bibliography of psychoanalysis is Alexander Grinstein, *Index of Psychoanalytic
Writings*, 14 vols. (New York: International Universities
Press, 1956–1972), which is now complete through 1969.

Psychoanalysis as history is in the process of being uncovered. Freud is always the appropriate starting point, and one
might well start with his early apologia for himself and complaint against Jung and Adler, *On the History of the Psychoanalytic Movement* (1914). See also his later *An Autobiographical Study* (1935). The standard biography of both
the man and the movement remains Ernest Jones's compen-
dious three-volume *The Life and Work of Sigmund Freud*
(New York: Basic Books, 1953–1957). The student curious
about the development of Freud's thought before 1902 ought
to look at his correspondence with his elder confidant, Wilhelm Fliess, collected in *The Origins of Psychoanalysis*, edited
by Marie Bonaparte, Anna Freud, and Ernst Kris (New York:
Basic Books, 1954). The intellectual and political complica-
tions of the middle years, 1906 through 1918, are visible in
The Minutes of the Vienna Psychoanalytic Society, edited by
Herman Nunberg and Ernst Federn, 3 vols. (New York: International Universities Press, 1962–1972). See also: J. A. C.
Brown, *Freud and the Post-Freudians* (Baltimore: Penguin,
1961); *Freud and the Twentieth Century*, edited by Benjamin
Nelson (New York: Meridian, 1957); Martin Freud, *Sigmund
Freud: Man and Father* (New York: Vanguard, 1958); *Letters
of Sigmund Freud 1873–1939*, edited by Ernst Freud (New
York: McGraw-Hill, 1964); Clara Thompson, *Psychoanalysis:*

Evolution and Development (New York: Grove, Evergreen, 1957); and Richard Wolheim, *Sigmund Freud* (New York: Viking, 1972).

Of course, psychoanalysis is no longer Freud's exclusive province, and the student will find much in the proliferation of post-Freudian psychological theories that is critically important for the study of literature and much, too, that is without value. By and large, Jung's theories of mind do not provide useful alternatives to Freudian analysis, at least for the student of literature, and anyone wishing to follow Jung or Erich Neumann into the forest of archetype in the belief that he'll find the human mind there should first consult Edward Glover, *Freud or Jung?* (New York: Norton, 1950). The so-called neo-Freudians Erich Fromm, Karen Horney, and Harry Stack Sullivan have done much to hone depth psychology into an instrument for social analysis, but at the considerable cost of Freud's dynamic theory of mind. Their psychohumanism has its virtues, but it has spawned no literary criticism to challenge the Freudian. See Herbert Marcuse's critique of the neo-Freudians in *Eros and Civilization* (New York: Random House, Vintage, 1962), pp. 217–251.

But the psychologies that have emerged in England under the aegis of Melanie Klein offer more serious challenges to "pure" Freudian perspectives. Klein, W. R. D. Fairbairn, Marion Milner, and, in a more mediated position, D. W. Winnicott, have produced a respectable and useful body of theories that have real consequences for applied psychoanalysis. But, since Kleinian and Freudian theories of mind hold somewhat divergent views of mental development, the student who looks toward British analysis for a guide to the interpretation of acts or texts should acquaint himself with the debate between the two psychologies. Above all, see Melanie Klein, *Contributions to Psychoanalysis: 1921–1945* (New York: McGraw-Hill, 1964); *The Psychoanalysis of Children* (London: The Hogarth Press, 1949), and Klein, Paula Heimann, and R. Money-Kyrle, *New Directions in Psychoanalysis* (London: Tavistock, 1955). The orthodox end of the dialogue falls to Anna Freud, whose papers are now in process of being collected and published. See *The Writings of Anna Freud* (New York: International Universities Press), especially volume 3, which covers the years 1937 to 1944, and volume 4, covering 1945–1956.

PSYCHOANALYSIS AND LITERATURE

Since Freud regarded literary and clinical analysis as the working out of a single interpretive purpose, it is no surprise that the study of literature has been an important part of psychoanalysis from its inception. Aside from Freud's own attempts upon literature, already mentioned, the early years of psychoanalysis brought forth a number of important studies, including Otto Rank's "The Myth of the Birth of the Hero" (1914), which was constructed around the text of Freud's 1908 paper "Family Romances." Rank continued to contribute to theory of art throughout his career, though his later work betrays an unpsychoanalytic penchant for metaphysics. See Otto Rank, *The Myth of the Birth of the Hero and Other Writings*, edited by Philip Freund (New York: Norton, 1959). Another famous elaboration of a hint by Freud is Ernest Jones, *Hamlet and Oedipus* (New York: Norton, 1949), which developed out of a footnote in *The Interpretation of Dreams*. Readers should also consult the less familiar Jones essay "The Death of Hamlet's Father," *International Journal of Psychoanalysis* 31 (1950).

Other significant psychoanalytic studies of art include: Hanns Sachs, *The Creative Unconscious* (Boston: Sci-Art, 1942); Marie Bonaparte, *The Life and Works of Edgar Allan Poe* (London: Imago, 1949); Phyllis Greenacre, *Swift and Carroll: A Psychoanalytic Study of Two Lives* (New York: International Universities Press, 1955); Martin Grotjahn, *Beyond Laughter: Humor and the Subconscious* (New York: McGraw-Hill, 1957); and most especially Ernst Kris's excellent *Psychoanalytic Explorations in Art* (New York: International Universities Press, 1952; reprinted, New York: Schocken, 1964).

These are all instances of psychoanalysis coming to the library from the clinic. In the 1960s, however, spurred on by the recent completion of the *Standard Edition* and by external, largely political demands, criticism began to seek out analysis. A number of good books emerged from this renewed interest in the deep-psychic processes of artists and readers and of critics themselves. See Simon O. Lesser, *Fiction and the Unconscious* (New York: Random House, 1962), Daniel Weiss, *Oedipus in Nottingham* (Seattle: University of Washington Press, 1962), Norman Holland, *Psychoanalysis and Shakespeare* (New York: McGraw-Hill, 1966), *The Dynamics of Literary Response* (New York: Oxford, 1968), and Frederick C. Crews, *The Sins of the Fathers: Hawthorne's Psychological Themes* (New York: Oxford, 1966).

Against this background of rising interest in psychoanalysis by critics recent attempts at criticism or literary biography by professional analysts tend to sound naïve or complacently diagnostic. Thus, for example, books like K. R. Eissler, *Goethe: A Psychoanalytic Study, 1775–1786* 2 vols. (Detroit: Wayne State University Press, 1963), or his later *Discourse on Hamlet and "Hamlet"* (New York: International Universities Press, 1972), and Bernard Meyer, *Joseph Conrad: A Psychoanalytic Biography* (Princeton: Princeton University Press, 1968).

Similar studies coming out of England, however, where psychology is not institutionally subordinated to medicine, are generally more sensitive to aesthetic questions. See Marion Milner's self-exploratory *On Not Being Able to Paint* (New York: International Universities Press, 1957) and her later account of a sixteen-year-long analysis of a schizophrenic girl, *The Hands of the Living God* (New York: International Universities Press, 1969). See also Charles Rycroft, *Imagination and Reality* (New York: Basic Books, 1968), and D. W. Winnicott's posthumous volume *Playing and Reality* (London: Tavistock, 1971). The latter contains Winnicott's famous essay on the transitional object, as well as some of his extrapolations from transitional childhood phenomena to the entire realm of human culture.

Existing anthologies of psychoanalytic criticism are of rather uneven value. The best of them is *Art and Psychoanalysis*, edited by William Phillips (New York: Meridian, 1963). But look also at *Psychoanalysis and American Fiction*, edited by Irving Malin (New York: Dutton, 1964), and *Psychoanalysis and Literary Process*, edited by Frederick C. Crews (Cambridge, Mass.: Winthrop, 1970).

Several periodical publications are devoted wholly or in part to psychoanalytic criticism, though none is consistently reliable. *Literature and Psychology*, which comes out of the English department at Fairleigh Dickenson University, is to be mentioned because it exists, but its level of intellectual energy is distressingly low and the studies it prints rarely get beyond rudimentary symptom-hunting. *American Imago* and *The Psychoanalytic Review* are somewhat more hopeful journals, though of very uneven quality. The student will be on surer ground in the area of psychoanalysis in general, for the ranking journals, the *International Journal of Psychoanalysis* and *Journal of the American Psychoanalytic Association*, are consistently useful, and one can stay current with developments in theory by keeping up with them.

There are no definitive bibliographical guides to literature and psychology—nothing, at least, that approaches Grinstein in completeness. See, however, these partial bibliographies: Norman Kiell, *Psychoanalysis, Psychology and Literature: A Bibliography* (Madison: University of Wisconsin Press, 1963); the previously mentioned Ernst Kris, *Psychoanalytic Explorations in Art*, pp. 319–341; and Frederick C. Crews, "Literature and Psychology," in *Relations of Literary Study: Essays on Interdisciplinary Contributions*, edited by James Thorpe (New York: Modern Language Association, 1967).

I would further mention the following articles on literature and psychology.

Marshall Bush, "The Problem of Form in the Psychoanalytic Theory of Art," *The Psychoanalytic Review* 54, 1 (Spring 1967).

Frederick C. Crews, "Anaesthetic Criticism" in *Psychoanalysis and Literary Process*, edited by Crews (Cambridge, Mass.: Winthrop, 1970).

George Devereux, "Art and Mythology" in *Studying Per-*

sonality Cross-Culturally, edited by Bert Kaplan (New York: Harper & Row, 1961).

K. R. Eissler, "Psychopathology and Creativity," *American Imago* 24, 1 and 2 (Spring–Summer 1967).

W. R. D. Fairbairn, "Prolegomena to a Psychology of Art," *British Journal of Psychology* 28 (January 1938).

———, "The Ultimate Basis of Aesthetic Experience," *British Journal of Psychology* 29 (October 1938).

E. H. Gombrich, "Psychoanalysis and the History of Art," *Meditations on a Hobby Horse and Other Essays on the Theory of Art* (London: Phaidon, 1963).

Phyllis Greenacre, "Play in Relation to Creative Imagination" in *The Psychoanalytic Study of the Child* vol. 14 (New York: International Universities Press, 1959). Reprinted in the two-volume collected papers of Phyllis Greenacre, *Emotional Growth* (New York: International Universities Press, 1972).

———, "The Family Romance of the Artist" in *The Psychoanalytic Study of the Child* vol. 13 (1958). Collected in *Emotional Growth*.

Norman Holland, "H. D. and the 'Blameless Physician,'" *Contemporary Literature* 10 (1969).

———, "Fantasy and Defense in Faulkner's 'A Rose for Emily,'" *Hartford Studies in Literature* 4, 1 (1972).

Melanie Klein, "The Importance of Symbol-Formation in the Development of the Ego" in *Contributions to Psychoanalysis: 1921–1945* (New York: McGraw-Hill, 1964).

Marion Milner, "The Role of Illusion in Symbol-Formation" in *New Directions in Psychoanalysis*, edited by Melanie Klein, Paula Heimann, and R. Money-Kyrle.

William Niederland, "Clinical Aspects of Creativity," *American Imago* 24, 1 and 2 (Spring–Summer 1967).

Hanna Segal, "A Psychoanalytical Approach to Aesthetics," *International Journal of Psychoanalysis* 33 (1952). Reprinted in *New Directions*, edited by Klein, et al.

Lionel Trilling, "Freud and Literature" in *The Liberal Imagination* (New York: Doubleday, Anchor, 1957).

———, "Art and Neurosis" in *The Liberal Imagination*.

Leslie A. White, "The Symbol: The Origin and Basis of Human Behavior" in his *The Science of Culture, A Study of Man and Civilization* (New York: Farrar, Straus and Cudahy, 1949).

D. W. Winnicott, "Transitional Objects and Transitional Phenomena," *International Journal of Psychoanalysis* 34 (1953). Collected in his *Playing and Reality* (London: Tavistock, 1971).

——, "The Location of Cultural Experience," in *Playing and Reality*.

PSYCHOANALYSIS AND JAMES JOYCE

When we consider the nature of Joyce's books and consider, too, the effect psychoanalysis has had on the way we read literature, we have to be astounded that his life and work have not yet been subject to full-scale psychoanalytic study. Partial analyses have been undertaken, but most of them are either narrowly focused or subject to mistaken notions about the nature of psychoanalytic psychology. The most serious psychoanalytic gesture in Joyce's direction thus far has been Sheldon Brivic's "James Joyce: From Stephen to Bloom," in the Crews anthology, *Psychoanalysis and Literary Process*. Brivic's theory tends to be limited and archaic—his proclivity for the oedipal patterns in Joyce's fantasy life confines his analysis to a rather narrow, if scrupulously orthodox, corner of Freudian psychology. Still, this minimal theory is rigorously applied, and it taps a rich vein of psychic ore in Joyce's books. After Brivic, the ranks thin out quickly. Alan Dundes' "Re: Joyce—No In at the Womb," *Modern Fiction Studies* 8 (1962), is a brief foray into the transsexual fantasy life of Leopold Bloom, and Dundes' analysis of Bloom as a bisexual figure is echoed by Richard Wasson's similar conclusions about Stephen Dedalus in "Stephen Dedalus and the Imagery of Sight: A Psychological Approach," *Literature and Psychology* 15 (Fall 1965). See also the surprisingly acute account of one writer's obsession with another in Rebecca West's *The Strange Necessity* (Garden City, N. Y. Doubleday, 1928).

Less important for the student of literature and psychology, because they are less serious about psychoanalysis, are: Robert Fenichel, "A Portrait of the Artist as a Young Orphan," *Literature and Psychology* 9 (1959); Darcy O'Brien, "Some Determinants of Molly Bloom," in *Approaches to Ulysses,* edited by Bernard Benstock and Thomas F. Staley (Pittsburgh: University of Pittsburgh Press, 1970); Darcy O'Brien, "Some Psychological Determinants of Joyce's View of Love and Sex," in *Papers from the Second International Joyce Symposium, Dublin, 1969,* edited by Fritz Senn (Blooming-ton: Indiana University Press, 1972), and Edward Brandabur, *A Scrupulous Meanness: A Study of Joyce's Early Work* (Chicago: University of Illinois Press, 1971). Fenichel's ar-ticle merely belabors much that is obvious, while O'Brien and Brandabur, otherwise serious and intelligent critics, are dilettantes at psychoanalysis. See my review of Brandabur and Brivic, "Freud on Joyce," *James Joyce Quarterly* 9, 2 (Winter 1971).

The matter of the "influence" of psychoanalysis upon Joyce has been discussed at some length. See especially Frederick Hoffmann, "Infroyce" in his *Freudianism and the Literary Mind* (Baton Rouge: Louisiana State University Press, 1945), reprinted in *James Joyce: Two Decades of Criticism,* edited by Seon Givens (New York: Vanguard, 1948). See also Hanns Schiefele, "Freuds Bedeutung für die Kunst Betrachtung: Marcel Proust, James Joyce, Thomas Mann" in *Lebendige Psychanalys: Die Bedeutung Sigmund Freud für das Verstehen des Menschen,* edited by Fritz Rieman (Munich: Beck, 1956). Neither study strays from the highway of scholarship into the forest of interpretation, and neither is properly a critical essay.

The history of applied psychoanalysis has been burdened by the movement's own schismatic tendencies, and the break be-tween Freud and Jung has been especially confusing for stu-dents of literature. Lacking any personal acquaintance with the clinical evidence for psychoanalytic theories of mind and therefore lacking a basis for personal validation, some critics approach Jung and Freud even-handedly, ready to turn toward whoever "feels" closer to their subjects. Thus, Jung is pre-ferred to explain the "archetypal" Hesse, while Freud is called upon to interpret the "neurotic" Kafka. Other critics have re-solved the dilemma by plundering these two psychologies indiscriminately for interpretations, as though the crucial dif-ferences between them were of no consequence to criticism. That seems to be the case in Joyce studies. Typical of this is William York Tindall, *James Joyce: His Way of Interpreting the Modern World* (New York: Grove, 1950), an indifferently Freudo-Jungian translation of Joyce's work into the appropri-ate "symbols" of psychoanalytic interpretation. Like Branda-bur's *A Scrupulous Meanness*, Tindall's book is chock full of "insights" that seem randomly appropriated from handy di-gests of psychology, but it lacks a theory of mind to give them order and meaning. Another study perched ambivalently be-tween psychology and mythology is Ruth von Phul, "Circling the Square: A Study of Structure," in *A James Joyce Miscel-lany: Third Series*, edited by Marvin Magalaner (Carbondale: Southern Illinois University Press, 1962). Finally, see Jung's own attempt upon *Ulysses*, "Ulysses: A Monologue," trans-lated and most recently published in *Hidden Patterns: Studies in Psychoanalytic Literary Criticism*, edited by Leonard and Eleanor Manheim (New York: Macmillan, 1966). Jung's essay is enlightening and honest criticism (he admitted that *Ulys-ses* put him to sleep), but it should not be confused with psychoanalysis.

Index